active java

Other titles on Java available from Addison-Wesley

Hooked on Java
Creating Hot Web Sites with Java Applets
Arthur van Hoff, Sami Shaio and Orca Starbuck, Sun
Microsystems Inc.
208 pp with CD ROM. $29.95 US
ISBN: 0 201 48837 X
Available now

Java for C and C++ Programmers
Barry Boone
336 pp
ISBN: 0 201 47946 X
Due for publication: May 1996 (US)

active java

Object-Oriented Programming for *the World Wide Web*

Adam Freeman

Knowledge Media Institute
The Open University

& Darrel Ince

Department of Computing
The Open University

Addison-Wesley Publishing Company

Harlow, England • Reading, Massachusetts • Menlo Park, California
New York • Don Mills, Ontario • Amsterdam • Bonn • Sydney • Singapore
Tokyo • Madrid • San Juan • Milan • Mexico City • Seoul • Taipei

Addison Wesley Longman Limited
Edinburgh Gate
Harlow
Essex
CM20 2JE

Cover designed by op den Brouw, Design and Illustration, Reading
Text typeset by the author
Printed and bound in the United States of America

First printed 1996

ISBN 0 201 40370 6

British Library Cataloguing-in-Publication Data
A catalogue record for this book is available from the British Library.

Library of Congress Cataloging-in-Publication Data is available

Adam Freeman would like to dedicate his part of the book to Jacqui for tolerating his moods and generally being wonderful, to Phil for being a bright light, and to his mother who is finding out that the oncoming light is not a train.

Darrel Ince would like to dedicate his part of the book to Stephanie for being as patient as ever.

PREFACE

The authors of this book met while they were working on two separate projects at the Open University. Adam Freeman was working as a consultant on the KMI/Stadium project at the Knowledge Media Institute of the Open University. This project has the aim of delivering real-time audio and video to 100 000 simultaneous users while providing a high level of tele-presence. Darrel Ince was a principal author on a major Internet-based distance learning course which will be studied by over three thousand students from 1997 as part of their degree studies. Previously both of us were mightily impressed by the power of the Internet, but were somewhat frustrated by the limited facilities that Internet application technology provided. For example, we found that standard Web facilities provided an excellent information resource, but imposed quite a passive role on the user. Time and time again we kept looking for a technology which would provide us with the ability to deliver interactive applications over the Internet relatively easily and without the painstaking programming that we had encountered previously.

The announcement of the Java system in mid-1995 brought the potential of this technology to our notice and our subsequent use has convinced us that it represents the next major step for Internet providers.

This book has two aims. First it is a gentle introduction to the Java system which can be read with profit by any reader with programming experience. Second it is a distillation of the experience that we have gained in using Java over the past year. The next two years should see a large number of reference material and advanced texts produced on the Java system. Many of the potential readers of these texts will be unable to access them cold initially, but will require an introduction to the main concepts of Java and how to develop Java applications which can be hosted on the Internet. We hope this book will provide it.

The book is partitioned into two sections: the first section comprises six chapters and describes the main programming concepts associated with Java; the final six chapters concentrate on the development of Java applications. In particular the final chapters describe how the Java class libraries can be accessed in order to carry out functions such as interfacing with the Internet and developing windows-based interfaces.

Over the next two years we shall be maintaining a set of Web pages which will contain useful information connected with the book, details on how to access and run the various Java programs presented within the book and any updates made necessary by changes to the base Java technology. These pages can be accessed at the URL

HTTP://WWW.AW.COM/CSENG/AUTHORS/FREEMAN.A/ACTJAVA/ACTJAVA.HTML

Adam Freeman
Darrel Ince

January 1996

CONTENTS

CHAPTER ONE

Java and the Internet

AIMS

- To outline a brief history of the Java project.

- To describe the main principles underlying the Java programming language.

- To briefly outline the history of Java and Java–compatible browsers.

- To describe how the various categories of reader of this book can efficiently access it.

- To describe what we hope you will have learnt after completing the book.

1.1 Introduction

The past four years have seen a phenomenal rise in interest in the Internet. Tens of millions of users regularly access this network to carry out operations such as browsing through electronic newspapers, downloading bibliographies, participating in news groups and emailing friends and colleagues. The number of applications that are hosted within the Internet has also grown; however, there are major problems in developing such applications:

- The first problem is security. There are still many problems concerned with ensuring that unauthorized access is prevented. This is becoming one of the major drag factors why commercial applications, particularly those involving the direct transfer of funds across communication lines, have been relatively slow in developing as compared with academic applications.

- The lack of a specific programming language for Internet applications. Currently applications are written in a wide variety of languages including C, Pascal and TCL/TK which have to access fairly low-level facilities such as protocol handlers.

- It is very difficult to build interaction into an Internet application. Most of the applications that have been developed tend to give the impression of being interactive. However, what they usually involve is just the user moving through a series of text and visual images following pointers to other sections of text and visual images. The most one often gets with the vast majority of Internet applications is some small amount of interactivity, for example an application asking the user for an identity and a password and checking what has been typed against some stored data which describes the user.

- The majority of interactive applications are non-portable: they tend to be firmly anchored within one computer architecture and operating system by virtue of the fact, for example, that they tend to use run-time facilities provided by one specific operating system.

1.2 The Java programming language

1.2.1 The language

The Java programming language originated at Sun Microsystems. It was developed initially as a programming language for consumer-electronics products; however, its later versions address the problems that have been outlined in the previous section. The designers of the language had a number of design goals:

- *The language should be familiar.* It should have no strange syntax and, as much as possible, it should look like an existing language. However, this principle was not taken to the point where problems with other languages would be carried through to Java. The control structures and data types in Java look like some of those provided in the C programming language, while those facilities which make it object-oriented resemble those in the programming language C++. The developers of the Java language felt that on both commercial and technical grounds Java would have the greatest success if the learning curve was not too steep. Its similarity to the C family of programming languages means that a wide variety of users are able to program in it: ranging from professionals at the cutting edge of Internet technology to the home computer user.

- *The language should be object-oriented.* A programming language is object-oriented if it offers facilities to define and manipulate objects: self-contained entities which have a state and to which messages can be sent. At this stage of the book do not worry too much about the meaning of the term *object-oriented*. In Chapter 2 we provide a tutorial on the concept and, in Chapter 5, we show in detail how object-orientation is provided within the Java programming language.

An object-oriented programming language has two major advantages. First, by adhering to a small set of programming principles it is possible to write systems which are relatively easy to modify. This is massively important in today's world. Customer requirements for systems can change quite quickly, even during the development of an application; for example, a company that contracts for a financial reporting system might be affected by changes in tax laws which require major changes to the system. All the surveys that have been carried out on the amount of resource expended on software development have come up with figures which suggest that companies who have a significant software development capability spend somewhere between 60 and 80% of their development resources in changing existing software – the changes being due to a variety of factors ranging from errors to changes in requirements – with the latter predominating.

As you will see in this book Java, being an object-oriented language, provides facilities whereby systems developed using the Java technology are relatively easy to modify as compared to systems which have been developed using other languages.

The other feature of an object-oriented programming language is that it allows a high degree of reuse; in such a language programmers can develop objects which represent HCI items such as buttons, menus and scroll bars and application items such as accounts, invoices and air traffic radars which can be reused time and time again with little extra effort. One of the features of the Java system is a large library which can be used to instantiate objects that can be used for Internet applications.

- *The language should be robust.* One of the problems with some of the more popular programming languages is the fact that it is quite easy to produce applications which collapse. Sometimes this collapse can manifest itself immediately; however, it can also occur outside the application because, for example, the application has corrupted some memory which is not used by another application until a few days later. Probably the most notorious programming language which is guilty of having features which lead to non-robust performance is C. One example of a facility within C which can give rise to problems is the fact that it provides a pointer type which can be employed by programmers. Pointers enable variables to contain the address of a location. Such addresses can be manipulated as if they are arithmetic entities: they can be added to, subtracted from, multiplied and even divided. Once a programming error has been committed with a pointer a number of events could happen depending on the nature of the error. Some common events include memory being unusable and memory becoming corrupt leading to a crash of the application or even the host operating system. One of the design aims of the developers of Java has been to eliminate features of programming languages such as C which lead to such problems. For example, there is no notion of a pointer in Java.

- *The language should have a high performance.* One of the features of the Java programming language is that of **threads**. These are multiple concurrent executions of code which provide a high-level implementation of concurrent processing. This allows a Java program to switch between each of its threads when the processing in one thread reaches a point where it cannot progress. This leads to a highly efficient utilization of processor cycles and a fast response time.

- *The language should be portable.* A major aim of the designers of Java was that a program developed in Java code for, say, a Sun workstation running the Solaris operating system, should be capable of being ported across to a PC running another operating system, for example Windows NT or Windows 95.

- *The language should be as simple as possible.* Many languages – Ada is probably the best example – have become overburdened with features. This has a number of effects: first, such languages are often expensive to compile and their run-time support is so large that even a small program occupies a large amount of memory; second, the learning curve for such languages is long and hard; and third, compiling programs in such languages can take quite a long time. The designers of Java have tried to keep the base facilities of the language to a minimum and have provided many extras within a number of libraries.

1.2.2 A simple Java program

In order to give you a flavour of what Java looks like we have reproduced a simple Java program below. You will find this program in Chapter 10 which describes how you develop applets: programs which can be embedded in Web pages. If you want to run the program and modify it, you will find information on how to do this at

HTTP://WWW.AW.COM/CSENG/AUTHORS/FREEMAN.A/ACTJAVA/ACTJAVA.HTML

This is the URL of the Web pages that we will be maintaining in connection with this book. These pages will contain all the applets which we describe and other information such as new items of documentation which we think would be of interest to you.

```
import java.awt.Graphics;
public class HelloWorld extends java.applet.Applet {
  public void init() {
    resize(100,100);
  }

  public void paint(Graphics g) {
    g.drawString("Hello World!",5,20);
  }
}
```

The first line informs the Java system that the graphics library associated with the system is to be used. The next line introduces a class. A **class** is an object-oriented concept which will be described in Chapters 2 and 3. For the time being just assume that a class implements a series of chunks of code each of which implements some function. The class in the example is known as `HelloWorld`. The keyword `extends` is part of the object-oriented baggage connected with Java. This concept will be discussed at length in Chapter 5; for the time being assume that `extends` implements a facility whereby program code identified by `java.applet.Applet` is made available to the code within `HelloWorld`. `java.applet.Applet` is another example of a class which contains chunks of code useful for developing applets.

The two chunks of code within the class `HelloWorld` are `init` and `paint`. The header line which describes `init` states that it can be used by any other code in the system (`public`) and the code does not return any value (`void`), it just carries out some processing. `init` is called initially when a Java-compatible browser loads the applet. The processing that it carries out is to call a chunk of code called `resize` which forms part of `java.applet.Applet`; all this code does is to increase the amount of space that the browser page occupies to 100×100 pixels. The second chunk of code `paint` writes the string `"Hello World!"` at the coordinates 5, 20 on the browser page space; this chunk of code is invoked when the applet is first asked to display itself.

Do not be too worried about whether you fully understand the code presented above. You will find that a lot will become clearer during the reading of the first five chapters of this book.

1.2.3 The system

The Java code distribution currently includes the following important components:

- *The Java interpreter.* This is the language processor which has been ported to a number of systems. It works by reading and interpreting Java code rather than compiling it to object code.

- *The Java compiler.* This is the language processor which translates Java code to some object code format. Normally it is used for the development of high-performance code.

- *The Java disassembler.* This displays files created using the Java compiler.

- *The document generator.* This processes files which contain Java code and displays useful bureaucratic information similar to some of the information provided by conventional cross-reference generators.

- *The profiling tool.* This is a tool which displays the output of the interpreter when the `prof` option is invoked. This produces a listing of where the execution of Java code has occurred.

- *The applet viewer.* This is a utility which enables the developer to look at the displays and output from an applet without the overhead of a browser.

- *The Java debugger.* This is a hybrid debugger which debugs interpreted code.

1.2.4 The current state of the system

The Java system currently exists as version 1.0 beta at 12 November 1995. It has been ported to the Solaris 2.3, 2.4, 2.5 operating system for Sun workstations, Windows NT, Windows 95 and there is a version expected for the Macintosh System 7.5 in very early 1996. Our experience with the beta release for the Solaris and NT implementations is that it seems very stable – much more than for a beta release – and that the libraries that are part of the Java system are a great improvement over the alpha libraries.

1.3 The evolution of browsers

1.3.1 Browsing and the Internet

Almost certainly the main area of the Internet which has expanded well beyond the wildest hopes of its inventors has been the World Wide Web. The Web was the brainchild of Tim Berners-Lee, a researcher at the European Laboratory for Particle Physics in Geneva (CERN), who proposed a system of interlocking documents within CERN, where references or links to other documents could be embedded in another document with the facility for a user of the CERN system to navigate via these links.

Originally Berners-Lee's system was meant only to be a relatively local system for CERN and its early development took place on CERN local area networks and central computers. Initially the growth of the Web was quite small. However, in 1993 an application was developed which transformed it. This was *Mosaic*, developed by an undergraduate named Marc Andreessen who was then at the University of Illinois at Urbana-Champaign. *Mosaic* was the first usable graphical interface to the Web: it allowed users to navigate through the links in the Web with relative ease. The development of *Mosaic* provided a huge impetus and other tools were developed of which *Netscape* is probably the most used and well known.

The state of the World Wide Web at the beginning of 1995 was that it was immensely popular, with the main medium used to develop Web pages being the language HTML (Hypertext Markup Language). The browsers which enabled users to traverse links within documents in the Web implemented in HTML were moderately sophisticated. However, such browsers did not really support very much interaction. Certainly the users of such browsers were able, with little effort, to traverse links which spanned continents but, apart from simple functions such as checking a user's password, the browsers extant at the beginning of 1995 implemented little more than the traversal of links.

This changed in mid-1995 with the release of a browser known as *HotJava* which was the first browser to provide interactive access to Web documents. The history of Java and HotJava started around 1991 and was preceded by the development of a programming language known as Oak at Sun Microsystems. The driving principle behind Oak was the development of consumer-electronics products that would be simple and bug free. The direct parent of Oak was C++. However, the process of refining Oak to the point that it became Java involved the simplification and deletion of some of the facilities within C++.

In 1994 a browser known as *WebRunner* was written using Java and released at the end of 1994. In May of 1995 Sun announced their full support for Java and the successor of *WebRunner* known as *HotJava*.

Almost at the same time the developers of Netscape announced that future releases of this very popular browser would incorporate facilities whereby it could interpret Java code.

Java programmers can produce two types of software, **applets** and **applications**. The latter are standalone applications which can run independently. The former are programs which can be included in Web documents. Their inclusion of Java code in such documents marks a transition point in the development of the World Wide Web. From being a passive repository of data it becomes a store of interactive applications – albeit applications embedded in the linking technology. Users of browsers which recognize Java code are now able to execute programs which have the functionality of programs written in any other programming language.

Two specific types of programs that can be written in Java are **protocol handlers** and **content handlers**. The former are programs that can be loaded into a Java–compatible browser and interpret an Internet protocol such as HTTP. The latter are again programs which can be loaded into a Java-compatible browser and which interpret differing file formats.

1.3.2 The current state of browsers

HotJava is now no longer bundled with the Java system. However, there are current rumours that it will be re-bundled with the final Java system. The Java-compatible Netscape browser (Netscape Navigator 2) is at beta test level and industry predictions are that a stable version of this browser will be available in the second quarter of 1996. Until this release users of Java will only have the applet viewer to view the output of Java code.

1.4 This book

1.4.1 Summary

The book is structured into 12 chapters. The first five chapters describe the main elements of Java and also introduce the idea of object-oriented programming. Chapter 2 is an introduction to the idea of objects: the fact that a computer system can be regarded as a network of objects which implement the functions of the system via the act of passing messages to each other. Chapter 3 describes the main object-oriented mechanism found in Java: the class. A class is a language facility which allows the programmer to define the data associated with objects and also its behaviour. Chapter 4 describes the main data types and control structures of the Java programming language. If you have programmed in C, then you should be very familiar with the detailed descriptions that are contained in this chapter. Chapter 5 is a description of how classes are implemented in Java and provides a number of examples of such classes. Chapter 6 describes how libraries are documented in Java and how the programmer can use facilities offered by a library.

One of the strong features of the Java system is that it provides a whole host of facilities which are useful for writing Internet applications; for example, one of the libraries, the Network Interface Library, offers facilities which enable the programmer to write applications which interface with the Internet; another library, the Window Toolkit Class library, offers facilities which enable a programmer to define windows-based interfaces. Chapter 6 is an introduction to the use of libraries through the utility class library `util` which offers facilities for developing complex data structures.

The next two chapters discuss the two most important libraries within the Java system: the AWT library which contains facilities for developing windows-based applications, and the net library which contains facilities which allow seamless interconnection to network resources such as Web pages, audio files and images.

Chapter 9 describes the Java development kit. Chapters 10 and 11 bring together the first nine chapters of the book. Chapter 10 shows how you can develop applets; Chapter 11 is structured in the same way as Chapter 10 but discusses how you develop standalone applications.

Finally Chapter 12 looks at the portability issues of using Java (both as a stand-alone and hostable language) and introduces the concept of native classes and the associated costs/benefits that accrue. Additionally the chapter discusses the way that Java is compiled and interpreted and concludes with the future of Java and likely innovations.

1.4.2 Prerequisites and entry points

This book has been written as an introduction to developing applets in Java. We have had to assume some background in programming from the reader. In general we are expect that readers of this book will have programmed before in a third-generation programming language such as Pascal, C, Fortran, Ada or even COBOL.

Readers of this book will come from a number of backgrounds. In a sense we are less interested in where they come from – the book can be read with profit by someone who is on the cutting edge of Internet technology as well as the home computer user – but are more interested in their programming background since there are a number of entry points into the book depending on what programming languages readers are familiar with and the degree of familiarity with object-oriented programming and object-oriented technology.

In the following list we have enumerated a number of types of readers of this book, together with the route which they might like to take through it. Obviously you can read the whole book, but you may have had your appetite whetted by the prospect of being able to write fully interactive Internet applications and want a fast track through to the point where we discuss how to write these applications.

- *The programmer who has used a simple programming language which is not C*. If you have used a simple procedural language such as Pascal or Fortran then we would advise you to read every chapter of the book.

- *The programmer who has used C*. We would advise you to read Chapters 1 to 3, to skim-read Chapter 4 and continue reading the book from Chapter 5.

- *The programmer who has used C++.* We would advise you to read Chapter 1; you could then skip to Chapter 5, skim-read this chapter and then continue with Chapter 6.

- *The programmer who has a background knowledge of object-oriented technology but has usually programmed in a non-object-oriented language such as Pascal.* We would advise you to read Chapter 1, skip to Chapter 4 and continue reading the book.

1.5 What you will learn from this book

There are a number of overall aims we have set ourselves:

- To teach you the elements of the Java programming language. In an introductory book such as this we have not set out to teach 100% of the language. We estimate that we will have taught you 85% of the language; however, we would claim that in doing this we will have taught you *all* of the important parts of the language.

- To teach you how to develop both standalone applications and browser-compatible applications known as applets.

- To teach you how you can write Java programs which can interface seamlessly with entities that can be found on the Internet, for example World Wide Web pages.

- To teach you what an object-oriented approach to software development is and how you can use the object-oriented paradigm to develop Internet programs.

- To teach you how to access the extensive library of software that comes bundled with the Java system.

CHAPTER
TWO

Objects

AIMS

- To show how computing applications can be regarded as consisting of objects.
- To introduce the vocabulary terms: object, message and state.
- To describe how communication occurs in an object-oriented application via messages.
- To show some very simple examples of Java code.
- To show that objects can also, in turn, consist of objects.

2.1 Introduction

The past five years have seen a huge increase in the use of object-oriented technology. Programming languages such as C++ and Objective C are now becoming relatively commonplace, object-oriented databases are starting to become efficient enough to use on commercial projects and every degree course in computing contains at least one course which focuses on object technology. Unfortunately most of the teaching literature on object-orientation tends to be quite difficult to access; since Java is an object-oriented programming language we have decided not to dive straight into a full description of the language, but briefly introduce you to some of the main concepts of object-orientation.

In order to do this a number of examples of computer-based systems will be described and an object view taken of their architecture. In describing these systems we will introduce some very small fragments of Java code.

2.2 Some examples of object-based systems

This section will describe a number of computer applications and show how each can be regarded as consisting of a collection of objects and an outside world where the system executes via the process of message passing.

2.2.1 A simple air traffic control system

The first example which we shall describe is a simple system for keeping track of the planes in the air space surrounding an airport. The system is simple as we do not intend that any detail should come between you and the teaching of object concepts that will be carried out in this section. An example of such a system is shown in Figure 2.1.

This is a very simple view of an air traffic control system. Figure 2.1 is just a snapshot taken at a particular time during its execution and shows that five planes are currently under the control of the human air traffic controllers who supervise the traffic to and from the airport. Each plane is an example of an **object**: some entity which is represented in the store of the computer on which the application runs.

Each object will consist of a unique **identifier** and some stored data which is associated with it; the unique identifiers in this case are the flight numbers attached to each plane in Figure 2.1.

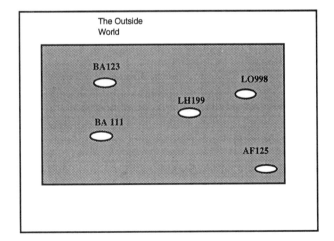

Figure 2.1 A very simple air traffic control system.

The stored data will be necessary for the functioning of the system in which the objects are embedded. In the example of the air traffic control system there is potentially a large amount of data that can be associated with a flight. Since we are only considering a very simple system we shall assume that only four items of data are associated with each object: the plane's x coordinate position, y coordinate position, z coordinate position and the type of plane. These four items of data are important for the functioning of an air traffic control system; indeed the first three items are mandatory as it would be impossible to do very much in such a system without knowing where the planes are. The final piece of data is required in order to assign a runway on which the plane is to land as the airport may have a number of runways suited to different types of plane. The collection of data associated with an object is known as its **state**.

Figure 2.1 is split into two parts. The shaded part represents the air traffic control system, while the unshaded part represents the outside world: the world of real aircraft, human controllers and concrete airports. Events occur in this outside world which affect the object world. A typical event might be a radar informing the system that a particular plane has moved its position or a particular plane has disappeared because it has removed itself from the area of the skies administered by the air traffic control system. These events will access or affect the object world within the computer – normally this is manifested in the destruction of existing objects, the construction of a new object, the updating of an object's state or the retrieval of data from the object world. Let us look at some of these events and how they affect the simple air traffic control system:

- A plane appears in the air space controlled by the system. This results in a new plane object being created and given values for its state.

- A plane disappears from the air space. This can occur for a number of reasons: the plane may have left the air space during its onward journey, it could have landed or, very rarely, it could have crashed. This results in the disappearance of the plane object.

- The plane moves its position in the sky. This is normally monitored by radar equipment and it results in the x, y and z coordinates of the plane being updated.

- Data about a plane's position is sent to a controller on the ground. The object world remains the same; the only thing that happens is that the x, y and z coordinates of a plane are sent to the outside world.

The way in which the object world within the shaded area is altered and accessed is achieved via a mechanism known as a **message**. An example best explains what a message looks like. The line below shows a Java message being set to the aeroplane AF565; the effect of the message is to update the position of the plane to which the message is sent. At this stage don't worry about how such messages are programmed in Java; the important thing you should be concentrating on at this stage in the book is the format of messages:

This indicates the position of the plane in x, y, z axis.

```
AF565.newPos(12, 444, 22);
```

receiver object   *selector*   *arguments*

Message

The line consist of two components. The first component is an object known as the **receiver object**. In the line above, this is the plane identified by AF565. The second component is the message. The message above consists of four components. The first component is known as the **selector**, which identifies the message that is to be sent. The remaining three components are known as the **arguments** of the message. Thus, in the example above, the receiver object AF565 receives a message identified by the selector newPos and arguments 12, 444, 22 which are associated with the x position, y position and z position of the plane. Do not worry about the semicolon that is at the end of each statement. In Chapter 4 in which we outline some Java programming constructs we describe the use of semicolons.

As we have implied above, messages are generated by events which occur in the outside world. The message example above might correspond to the event of a plane moving and its new position being detected by a radar. Messages either update objects, update objects and return with some value or just return with some value without updating any objects. Another example of a message associated with the air traffic control system is:

```
LH123.getxPos();
```

This message is sent to the receiver object LH123 and returns with the x position of the plane. Here the selector is not associated with any parameters so the brackets following it are empty.

This message is differentiated from the previous one that we examined in one way: it does not have any arguments. A message in Java can consist of an arbitrary number of arguments ranging from zero up to some arbitrary number imposed by the Java interpreter you use.

Another example of a message is:

```
AF555.getyPos();
```

This sends the message getyPos to the receiver object AF555 and returns with the y position of the plane. Another example of a message associated with the simple air traffic control system is:

```
BA126.removePlane();
```

This removes a plane from the air space. This message would normally be sent when a plane flies outside the air space covered by the system. A final example of a message is:

```
BA133.landPlane();
```

This would result in the receiver object (BA133) landing and disappearing from the world of plane objects. It is worth pointing out that the messages which we have discussed are all associated with some Java programming code which carries out the processing associated with the message. However, at this point you should not worry too much about how this code is defined. You will find full details in Chapter 5.

2.2.2 A more complicated air traffic control system

The previous example was used to describe some of the core concepts of object-oriented technology. This example provides some reinforcement of these concepts and also introduces some new properties of messages.

The example involves an air traffic control system in which the planes are held in a number of queues. Each queue will have a collection of planes awaiting landing. Normally a plane lands by being transferred from the front of one queue to the end of another queue below it. The system also keeps track of the planes that have landed. A snapshot of the system is shown in Figure 2.2.

This shows that the air space has been divided into three queues with the topmost queue containing planes which have the longest time to wait before landing. The instance also shows a collection of planes which have landed. The important point to make about this application is that not only does it contain simple objects such as planes, but it also contains objects which themselves contain objects. For example, the collection of landed planes is a set of plane objects and the queues of planes awaiting landing are also objects which in turn contain other objects (planes).

Since this is a more complicated system than that described in the previous subsection it will have more messages associated with it. An example of a message is shown below:

```
queues.moveDown(1);
```

This takes the first plane in queue 1 and places it at the end of the queue below it (queue 2). The receiver object in this case is queues. This illustrates another important point about objects. The receiver object for this message is not a simple object such as a plane but a collection of objects.

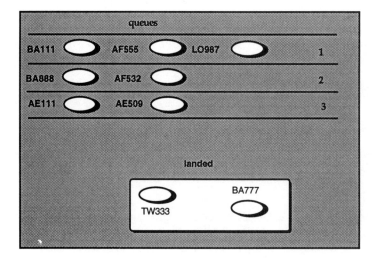

Figure 2.2 An instance of the air traffic control system.

Some more examples of the typical messages associated with this application are shown below:

```
queues.moveUp(2);
queues.land();
queues.movePlane(AF555,2,3);
queues.emergencyLand(BA7630);
```

The first message consists of a selector and one argument. Its function is to take the first plane in the second queue and place it at the end of the queue above it; this message might be generated when an air traffic controller is attempting to find some space in a queue – perhaps for a plane that wants to land in a hurry.

The second message lands the plane which is nearest the ground. This message is a frequent one since it corresponds to the normal operation of the air traffic control system and might be generated when a controller lands a plane normally.

The third message, which consists of a selector and three arguments, moves a plane from its current position to a new position within a queue. The example shown above moves the plane AF555 to the third position in queue 2.

The final message, which just consists of a selector and a single argument, lands a plane in an emergency: no matter where the plane is in the queues, it joins the planes which have already landed on the ground. Clearly this corresponds to a major incident at the airport. Some further examples of messages are shown below:

```
queues.moveUp(3);
queues.movePlane(TU878,1,3);
queues.adjustPlane(TU878,3,1);
queues.land();
```

With the first message the plane which is at the head of queue 3 is moved up so that it is at the end of queue 2. Next, the plane TU878 is sent to the third position in queue 1. Then, the same plane is sent to the first position in queue 3. The next line of code results in the plane at the head of the lowermost queue (queue 3) being landed. This is plane TU878.

Again it is important to point out that each of the messages shown above is associated with program code which is executed when the message is sent to the receiver object.

2.2.3 A print spooler

The final example that I will discuss is a print spooler. This is a piece of system software that forms part of a multi-user operating system. During the operation of such an operating system computer users will ask for files to be printed. The computer normally has limited printing resources and so the print requests are queued up for each printer in the system, with the print spooler controlling the addition of print requests to the queues and the selection of those print requests that are to be satisfied. A snapshot of a print spooler is shown in Figure 2.3.

This shows a number of objects. The first is a table which lists all the printers in the system together with their upper and lower print limits. For example, one entry in the table states that printer TH44 will only be available to print files between 5000 to 10 000 lines of text; obviously the technology used in this printer is best for

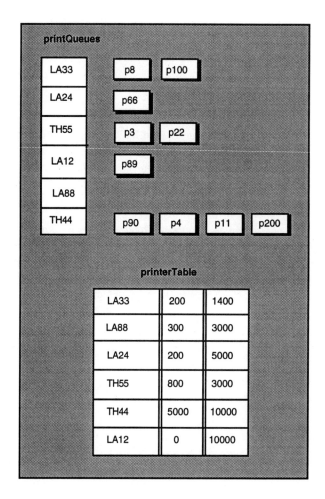

Figure 2.3 An instance of a print spooler.

large print runs. Each item in the table is itself an object, so in Figure 2.3 the printer table currently holds six objects which describe the printing limits of individual printers. One thing which is worth noticing in Figure 2.3 is that we give objects names which start with lower case letters.

The other objects shown in this figure are the print requests (the shadowed boxes) which are identified by an initial letter *p*, and a collection which contains the names of the available printers together with a pointer to their queues of print requests – some of which could be empty. Each item in the collection is itself an object, the queues are objects and the print requests in the queues are objects. So it is quite a rich model.

A whole variety of messages might be generated during the execution of such a print spooler. For example:

```
printQueues.addRequest(LA245,p107);
```

would add a print request identified as p107 to the end of the queue for the printer LA245. The message addRequest(LA245, p107) would be sent to the object printQueues containing the queue information for the spooler.

Another example of Java code containing a message for the spooler would be:

```
printQueues.removeRequest();
```

This shows the receiver object printQueues being sent the message removeRequest() which results in the first item in the queue associated with this object being removed from the queue.

As well as the queues being associated with messages, the table holding print details would also be associated with messages. For example, the Java code:

```
printTable.adjustPrinterLimits(LA24,100,3000);
```

contains a message sent to the receiver object printTable which adjusts the lower and upper limits of print requests which the printer LA24 can handle, with the lower limit being 100 lines and the upper limit being 3000 lines. The code:

```
printTable.newPrinter(LA777,100,7000);
```

would add a new printer to the table with a lower print limit of 100 lines and an upper limit of 7000 lines of code. This message would also give rise to a new message:

```
printQueues.setNewPrinter(LA777);
```

generated by the code associated with the newPrinter message which would establish a new object corresponding to LA777 within the print request queues. This message would be generated by the print table object rather than emanating from outside the system. This is an important point: up till now I have described the fact that messages are generated from the outside world by events that happen in that world. While this is true of many messages you will also find, throughout this book, that messages can be generated by objects and sent to other objects.

A line of code which contains a receiver object and a message will be referred to in the remainder of this book as a **Java expression**.

2.3 Summary

A number of points have emerged from this chapter:

- A system can be regarded as a collection of objects.
- Such collections of objects carry out the functions of the system by sending messages to each other.
- The objects in a system can be simple or can be collections of other objects.

- During execution of a system messages are sent to objects. The object to which a message is sent is known as a receiver object.

- A message can be sent to a receiver object from the outside world or can be sent from another object.

- Messages are normally associated, directly or indirectly, with an event that occurs in the outside world.

- A message consists of a selector and a number of arguments – anything from zero up to a predefined limit.

CHAPTER THREE

Classes

AIMS

- To show how objects can be described by classes.

- To introduce the vocabulary terms: instance method, class method, instance variable, class variable and inheritance.

- To describe how the mechanisms of inheritance can be used to develop reusable software.

3.1 Introduction

The previous chapter described the fact that computing systems can be viewed as consisting of objects which cooperate with each other in order to carry out a task by means of the mechanism of message sending. Events in the outside world such as a user requesting some information from an applet or application will give rise to a series of messages interchanged between objects within that applet or application until one or more objects send some data to the outside world.

The previous chapter was, of necessity, brief and introductory. The aim of this chapter is to look at objects in more detail and, in particular, show how they are implemented in the Java programming language. In order to understand this it is worth examining what happens when a message is sent to an object. For example, let us assume that an object `obj` has been sent a message `mess`:

```
obj.mess;
```

What happens is that the object receives the message and decodes it. The decoding consists of looking at a list of all the messages that it can receive and then executing the code corresponding to the message mess. The question that this poses is how does the object access this information? The answer is that objects in Java are defined by means of a mechanism known as a **class**. A class is very much like a template which defines the stored data associated with an object and the program code which is executed when particular messages are received.

The outline architecture of a class is as shown below:

```
Class Name {
State
    Method1
    Method2
    Method3
    . . .
    Methodn
}
```

or changed entries

State — individual items of an object.

Codes that are executed when the message is sent.

The first line contains the Java language statements which define the name of the class. The state contains statements which define the individual data items that make up an object and the lines labelled method1, method2 and so on contain the code corresponding to each particular message that is sent. We use the term **method** to describe the chunk of code that is executed when a message is sent. For example, if an object can receive a message *x* then there will normally be code identified by *x* within the class definition; this code is executed when the message is received by the object.

The state part of a class will contain data items which are important to the object defined by that class. For example, assume that we have written an applet which allows password access to some stored data. In such a system there will be an object defined by a class User. In order for users to be processed correctly by this applet there will need to be some means whereby such users can be identified and their passwords stored. The state for each user is hence defined by two items of data: a password and some unique identification such as that given to users when they are registered at their home computer. In this example where there are two items of data associated with each object, such items will be held in variables known as **instance variables**. Each user object within the applet will contain these two items of data.

It is worth lingering a little longer with this example. In the applet user objects will be sent messages such as:

```
user1.getPassword();
daveUser.newPassword("klxxx");
daveUser.newId("Dave33");
rolandUser.changeId("Roland66");
rolandUser.changePassword("zlxxghj");
robUser.checkPassword("xxkoil99");
```

The first expression involves the object identified by user1 being sent the message getPassword(). The result of this communication is that the password for the user is returned and could then be used within the applet. The second expression involves the object identified by daveUser being sent the message newPassword("klxxx"). This communication involves the instance variable corresponding to the password being given a value ("klxxx"). The third expression involves the object identified by daveUser being sent the message newId("Dave33"). This results in the instance variable corresponding to the identity of the user being updated to the string value "Dave33". The fourth expression involves the sending of the message changeId("Roland66") to rolandUser. This would result in the instance variable which holds the user's identity being changed. Similarly the fifth expression would involve the instance variables representing the password of the user rolandUser being changed to a new value ("zlxxghj"). The final Java expression involves the message checkPassword("xxkoil99") being sent to the user identified by robUser. This results in a check being made that robUser has the password value "xxkoil99" in the instance variable which holds the current password of the user.

An important point to make about the messages above is that two pairs of messages look very similar; for example, newPassword and changePassword seem to do the same things. What we have assumed here is that they correspond to slightly different processing. For example, the message corresponding to newPassword might access another instance variable which contains data that describes the date on which the user was first allowed access. This instance variable would not be accessed by changePassword. If the processing required by these two methods and the methods changeId and newId were the same, then they could, of course, be replaced by just one message.

A class template for users that also have associated with them the date of last access would look something like this:

```
Class User{
// Declarations of variables for the password of a user,
// the identity and the date of first access
// Code defining the method getPassword
// Code defining the method newPassword
// Code defining the method newId
// Code defining the method changeId
// Code defining the method changePassword
// Code defining the method checkPassword
...

// Code for other methods
...
}
```

The symbols // introduce a comment on a single line. Once you have defined such a class within a Java applet or application new users can be defined and space allocated for them. The code:

```
User rolandUser, daveUser, janeUser;
```

defines three user variables which will identify User objects. Each of these users will eventually contain the variables which hold their password, their user identity and the date they first accessed the applet.

The statement above just informs the Java system that the variables rolandUser, daveUser and janeUser will be User variables. To allocate space requires a facility known as the new facility. For example, to allocate memory space for the object identified by rolandUser you will need to write:

```
rolandUser = new User();
```

In order to reinforce the ideas just presented let us take another example from a Java application. Let us assume that we have written an applet which allows users to interrogate the prices of shares on a stock exchange. We shall assume that the user of such an applet carries out functions such as finding the current price of a share and also examining the price of the shares as far back in the past as 365 days. This means that we will need an object which we shall call ShareHistory. This contains the last 365 days of prices for each share taken at the end of the dealing day.

The template for this object will look like:

```
Class ShareHistory {
// Instance variable holding the last 365 prices for
// each of the shares listed on the stock exchange

// Method code for findCurrentPrice

// Method code for findAnyPrice

// Method code for updatePrice
}
```

The first method, findCurrentPrice, will find the price of a particular share which is the last one posted – normally the price for the previous day's close of business. The second method, findAnyPrice, given a day within 365 days of the current day, will deliver the price of a particular share on that day. The third method will update the price of a share at the end of a day's trading.

Such an applet can deal with a number of stock exchanges which in Java can be declared as:

```
ShareHistory tokyo, london, newYork;
```

with typical Java expressions being:

```
tokyo.findCurrentPrice("Daiwa");
london.findCurrentPrice("UNISYS");
newYork.findAnyPrice("IBM", "22/09/95");
newYork.updatePrice("General Motors", 333);
```

The first message to the receiver object tokyo results in the current stock price of the Daiwa company being returned, the second message sent to the object london results in the current price of the computer company UNISYS being returned, the third message sent to the New York exchange results in the price of the stock for IBM on 22 September being returned. Finally, the fourth line updates the price of General Motors on the New York stock exchange.

The two examples above are structurally similar. As you proceed through the book you will find that all classes will follow this pattern of class definition, definition of variables and definition of methods.

What are the reasons for defining data in such a way? Later in this chapter you will see how some of the more advanced facilities related to objects lead to a high degree of reuse. Apart from reuse there is also the advantage of maintainability.

Software systems are subject to major changes in their lifetime. Recent surveys have suggested that as much as 80% of the development effort expended by a software company is devoted to modifying existing systems. When you define objects using classes one of the things that you can do is to ensure that no user can use the instance variables of an object: that all access to the information stored in an object is via methods. This principle is known as **information hiding**: the user of an object does not happen to know the details of how that object is implemented. This means that when a developer wants to change the implementation of an object, for example to speed up access to the object, then the instance variables and code of all the methods change but the interface to the object – the method names and arguments themselves – do not change. For example, after using the stock exchange system detailed above for a number of months the developer may discover that there is a particular pattern of access to objects, for example he or she may discover that most of the access is to recent data, and that a new way of storing the stock prices which takes advantage of this access leads to an enhanced run-time performance. This new way of storing the price data would inevitably lead to large changes in the code of the methods that the stock exchange object recognized. However, it would not lead to any changes in the format of the messages. For example, users could still send messages such as:

```
tokyo.findCurrentPrice("Daiwa");
london.findCurrentPrice("UNISYS");
newYork.findAnyPrice("IBM", "22/09/95");
newYork.updatePrice("General Motors", 333);
```

as before, without any changes being made to the applet. This means that any applet or Java application which uses the stock exchange class does not need to be changed.

3.2 Some concepts

Almost certainly the next question that you are asking yourself is: what is the detailed syntax of a class in Java? This question will be answered fully in Chapter 5. At this stage in the book we would like to give you an idea of how you write such classes. An example of a simple Java class is shown below. It is simple, and hence unrealistic; however, we have included it for teaching reasons: we do not want to get the detail of classes in the way of understanding what, for many, is regarded as a difficult concept.

3.2.1 A robot

The class below is taken from a screen robot applet. Here the user can direct a robot to move on a two-dimensional board, where the coordinates of the board are expressed as x and y coordinates. When the robot is moved the screen updates itself by showing the next position. The lowest x and y positions are 1 and the highest x and y positions are 8. An example of this board and the current position of a robot is shown in Figure 3.1.

Let us assume that we need a number of messages to be sent to the robot which can send the robot vertically upwards (to the north), vertically downwards (to the south), horizontally leftwards (to the west) and horizontally rightwards (to the east). We also want to be able to send messages to the robot to send it upwards and to the right, upwards and to the left, downwards and to the left and downwards and to the right.

Examples of these messages are shown below:

```
newRobot.up();
oldRobot.down();
newRobotleft();
oldRobot.right();
oddRobot.leftUp();
oddRobot.rightUp();
smallRobot.leftDown();
smallRobot.rightDown();
```

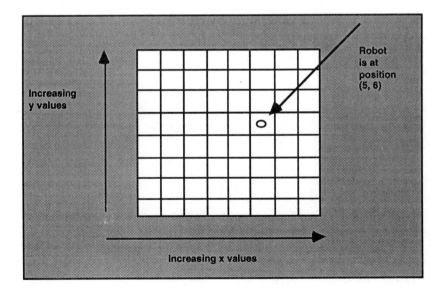

Figure 3.1 A robot board.

where the robots are defined as:

```
Robot newRobot, oldRobot, oddRobot, smallRobot;
```

In the discussion that follows we shall assume that there is no possibility that the robot will travel beyond the confines of the square grid. This would normally be achieved by means of messages which would be sent to a robot to check that it is not on the edge of the grid.

The first part of the Java class definition for a robot is shown below:

```
Class Robot {
int x, y;
```

This states that the class is known as `Robot` and that there will be two instance variables x and y which define where the robot is on the grid; these variables will hold integer values. The definition of the up, down, `right` and `left` messages is shown below:

```
public void up() {
y++;
}

public void down() {
y--;
}

public void right() {
x++;
}

public void left() {
x--;
}
```

Each of the method definitions starts with the keyword `public`. This specifies that the method can be used by other objects and by code written outside the class. The keyword `void` states that no value is to be returned by the method; this keyword is followed by the name of the method and a list of its arguments; in the case of the four methods above there are no arguments. The first method up moves the robot one grid upwards and the code following the first curly bracket does this. For those of you who have programmed in C or C++ you will recognize the statement y++ as the code which increments the value of the instance variable y by one. This is equivalent to a statement such as y:= y + 1 in a programming language such as Pascal.

The code for the down message is similar except that it decrements the instance variable y by one, hence moving the robot downwards. The code for `right` and `left` is similar apart from the fact that it accesses the x instance variable.

The code for the other methods is shown below:

```
public void upRight() {
y++;
x++;
}

public void downRight() {
y--;
x++;
}

public void upLeft() {
y++;
x--;
}

public void downLeft() {
x--;
y--;
}
```

The code for these methods is self-explanatory.

Let us assume that as well as methods which move the robot we require methods which find out the position of the robot, for example to discover whether the robot is in a position where it is possible to move. Assume that the two methods we need will be called findxPos and findyPos. When a message corresponding to findxPos is sent to a receiver object what is returned is the x position of the object and when a findyPos message is sent to a receiver object what is returned is the y position of the object. The code for these two methods is shown below:

```
public int findxPos() {
return (x);
}

public int findyPos() {
return (y);
}
```

There are a number of things to notice about this code. First, the two methods are declared as public; this means that they can be accessed by other methods and by code outside the class which defines robots. The second thing to notice is that the keyword int is used instead of the previously used void. This means that the method will return with an integer value. The final thing to notice about the code is that in the body of the method, between the curly brackets, the keyword return is used. This means that the value specified by the return is the one that is returned by the method. In the case of the findxPos method this is the value of the x instance variable.

So far we have described methods without arguments. The next collection of methods show how arguments can be used. The first method checkAtPoint checks whether a robot is at a specific point on the grid. The second method moveToPoint moves a robot from its current point to a new point specified by two arguments. The code for these two methods is shown below:

```
public boolean checkAtPoint(int xPos, yPos) {
return (x==xPos && y==yPos);
}

public void moveToPoint(int xPos, yPos) {
x = xPos;
y = yPos;
}
```

The first method is headed with the boolean keyword. This means that it will return a value which is either true or false. The two arguments to the method are xPos and yPos which represent a possible position of the robot. The body of the method returns true if the x instance variable contains the same integer as the xPos argument and the y instance variable contains the same value as the yPos argument. Again those of you who have programmed in C and C++ will realize that Java has similar facilities to those found in these languages. The == symbol stands for arithmetic equality while the operator && stands for Boolean *and*.

Thus, when the Java interpreter executes the code shown below:

```
strangeRobot.checkAtPoint(3,4);
```

it checks whether the receiver object strangeRobot is at the point (3, 4).

What happens is that the interpreter first recognizes strangeRobot as of class Robot. This will be because it will have been defined previously in the Java program which uses the code as, say:

```
Robot strangeRobot;
```

The interpreter will look for a method corresponding to the name checkAtPoint. It will find the method and execute the code. However, before executing the code it will copy the values 3 and 4 to the arguments xPos and yPos. It will thus evaluate the expression:

```
x==3 && y==4
```

and will return either true or false depending on whether the receiver object is at the position which is defined by the contents of its instance variables.

The code for the method movePoint returns no value since it is headed by the keyword void. It has two arguments xPos and yPos which are the new points to which it is to be sent. The code within the body of the method updates the two instance variables with the values given by the arguments.

So far in this section we have described methods which access the state (instance variables) of an object and which update those variables. There is, however, one class of method which we have omitted: methods which create an object. There are a number of ways of creating an object. We have said very little about how objects are created apart from the fact that the new facility is used, for example the declaration:

```
Robot fredRobot = new Robot();
```

declares a variable `fredRobot`, allocates space for a `Robot` object and identifies this space as `fredRobot`.

The one problem with this form of declaration and allocation of space is that the instance variables of the objects declared in such a way are uninitialized. Java contains a facility whereby an object can be given a value when it is declared as above. In order to do this all that is required is to declare a new method within the class template which has the same name as the class. So, for example, in our `Robot` class we would need to define `Robot` as:

```
Robot() {
x = 1;
y = 1;
}
```

The effect of this is that whenever you declare a `Robot` object, for example in:

```
Robot slowRobot = new Robot();
```

the Java interpreter will first examine the methods defined in `Robot` looking for a method which has the same name as the class name. If it does not find such a method, then it will just create an object which has uninitialized instance variables. However, if it discovers a method with the same name, then the code for the method is executed. In the case of the code shown above this will create a robot which is initially positioned on the bottom left square of the grid. The method, known as `Robot`, is called a constructor. Constructors can have specified defaults such as `Robot` shown above where the default is that a newly created robot object is placed on the square (1,1). However, constructors can also be associated with arguments which represent a user's specified initial value. An example of a `Robot` constructor which sets the *x* position and *y* position of a robot taken from values supplied by the programmer is shown below:

```
Robot(int xPos, yPos) {
x = xPos;
y = yPos;
}
```

An example of its use with the new facility is shown below:

```
Robot denseRobot = new Robot(6, 5);
```

This line of code declares an object `denseRobot` which is created by applying new to the `Robot` method. This method requires two arguments (in the example above these are 6 and 5) which are used to update the `x` and `y` instance variables within `denseRobot`.

3.2.2 Messages and classes

It is worth recapping the mechanisms used within Java for sending messages and what happens to these messages. When the Java interpreter encounters an expression such as:

```
receiverObject.message(arguments);
```

it will first determine which class the destination object is defined by. To do this it will scan all the declarations within the code of the applet or Java application. If it finds the name of the object within a declaration then it recovers the name of the class which describes it. It will then scan the code of the methods associated with this class. If it finds a method with the same name as the message string then the code is executed; if not an error is flagged. If the message is associated with any arguments these are copied through as the arguments of the method and the code associated with the method is executed. This is a slight simplification as you will see later in this chapter. However, in essence, it represents the processing cycle that occurs.

3.3 Inheritance

So far we have outlined a number of powerful facilities contained in the Java programming language which are used to construct objects and define the methods which correspond to the messages that Java objects receive. This section introduces what is certainly the most powerful facility within Java: that of inheritance. In order to introduce the idea we will first describe three increasingly complex examples of where inheritance is useful. The first example will introduce the idea of inheritance in an abstract way. Later chapters of the book show how inheritance is used within more realistic applets and applications.

3.3.1 The augmented set

The first example concerns a set where we need methods which find out the size of the set and add integers to the set, together with an operation which finds the sum of the elements in the set. One very efficient way of implementing such a set in such a way that summation is not too inefficient an operation is to have a class which has two instance variables: `intSet`, the set of integers, and an integer `sum` which contains the current sum of the integers. This is an efficient implementation because any method which needs to find the sum only needs to look it up in the variable `sum` rather than iterating through `intSet`.

An example of an object described by this class is shown in Figure 3.2. Here the instance variable `sum` contains the current sum of the integers in the instance variable `intSet`. Let us assume that we have already implemented a set of integers described by the class `intSet` shown below, where the code for each of the classes is not shown and where we have just listed the instance variables without defining their types. The class does not require a summation method and hence does not require an instance variable to contain a sum.

```
Class IntSet {
int intSetvar[];

   public boolean includes(int no) {
   ...
   }
```

```
public int size(int no) {
   ...
}

public void add (int no) {
   ...
}

public void remove(int no) {
   ...
}

}
```

Let us assume that this set has been implemented for another project and is associated with the four methods shown above which check that a particular number is in the set, find the size of the set, add an element to the set and removes an element from the set.

Now let us assume that we need a set to which we wish to send messages that calculate its sum. We are faced with one choice immediately: we can program a new class from scratch. However, another choice is to use a facility known as inheritance which takes advantage of the set class we have just written. Before seeing it in action it is worth providing some definitions.

Inheritance is a relationship between two classes: if a class *A* inherits from a class *B*, then class *A*, as well as being able to use all of its own instance variables and methods, can use all the methods that *B* can use and can also use any instance variables that *B* can use. As an example of this consider the two classes X and Y below without the code for their methods.

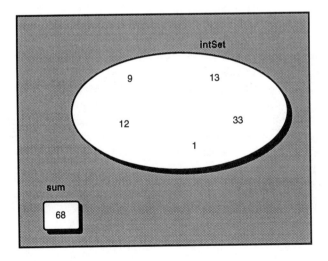

Figure 3.2 An implementation of a set of integers.

```
Class X {
// Declarations for u v and w

    // Code for method A

    // Code for method B

    // Code for method C

}
```

```
Class Y {
// Declarations for l and m

    // Code for method R

    // Code for method S

    // Code for method T
}
```

If class Y inherits from class X, then, firstly, all the methods in class Y can refer to not only the instance variables in class Y but also the instance variables in class X; and secondly an object described by class Y can have messages corresponding not only to the methods R, S and T but also the methods A, B and C.

Classes can inherit from classes which inherit from other classes. As an example consider the three classes shown below:

```
Class X {
// Declarations for u v and w

    // Code for method A

    // Code for method B

    // Code for method C
}
```

```
Class Y {
// Declarations of l and m

    // Code for method R

    // Code for method S

    // Code for method T
}
```

```
Class Z {
// Declarations of n and o

    // Code for method G

    // Code for method H

    // Code for method I
}
```

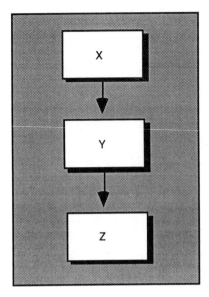

Figure 3.3 A diagrammatic representation of hierarchy.

Here if class Z inherits from class Y which, in turn, inherits from class X, then objects described by class Z can be sent messages which correspond to the methods which class Y can use; these not only include the methods R, S and T but also the methods inherited from class X, namely methods A, B and C. This means that objects described by class Z can be sent messages corresponding to the methods G, H, I, R, S, T, A, B and C.

The same holds for the instance variables: methods in class Z can refer to not only the instance variables n and o defined in Z, but also the instance variables l and m which it inherits from Y and also the instance variables u, v and w which Y inherits. We can represent this relationship graphically as shown in Figure 3.3.

This diagram, which shows that class Z inherits from class Y which, in turn, inherits from class X, is known as a **class hierarchy diagram**. Class hierarchies are a very powerful way of describing the relationship between classes. This relationship lies at the heart of the use of an object-oriented programming language as a medium for software reuse.

Consider the classes described below where B inherits from A:

```
Class A {
// Declarations of a b and c

   // Code for method J

   // Code for method K

   // Code for method L

}
```

```
Class B {
// Declarations of e f g and h

   // Code for method X

   // Code for method Y

   // Code for method Z
}
```

Also consider the statements:

- An object of class B can be sent a message associated with method K.

- An object of class A can be sent a message associated with method B.

- Method Z in class B can refer to the instance variable a.

- Method Y in class B can refer to the instance variable e.

- Method K in class A can refer to the instance variable g.

Which of these statements are true?

The first is true since A contains a method K which B inherits. The second is false since there is no method called B, only a class called B. The third is true since there is an instance variable a in A which is inherited by B. The fourth is true since the instance variable e is defined in the class B. The final statement is false; class A does not inherit from class B, but vice versa.

There is only one further rule that needs to be explained about inheritance before we return to the example that started this section. This concerns classes which contain methods that have the same name as methods in the class which they inherit. Consider the classes shown below, where class B inherits from class A.

```
Class A {
// Declarations a b and c

   // Code for method J

   // Code for method K

   // Code for method L
}

Class B {
// Declarations e f g and h

   // Code for method X

   // Code for method K

   // Code for method Z
}
```

If a message with the name K was sent to an object of class B which method would be executed?

The answer is that it would be the method in class B. The general rule is that whenever a class inherits from another class and there is duplication of method names between the class and the one it inherits from, then the method from the class that inherits is the one invoked.

Consider the classes shown below:

```
Class D {
// Declarations of a b and c

    // Code for method J

    // Code for method K

    // Code for method L
}

Class E {
// Declarations of e f g h i and j

    // Code for method J

    // Code for method K

    // Code for method Z
}
```

The following statements are true:

- When a message is sent to an object described by class E and the message uses the selector J, then the method J defined in E is invoked.

- When a message is sent to an object described by class E and the message uses the selector Z, then the method Z defined in E is invoked.

- When a message is sent to an object defined by class E and the message uses the selector L, then the method L defined in class D is invoked.

However, the following statement is not true:

- When a message is sent to an object defined by class D and the message uses the selector K, then the method K defined in E is invoked.

Because D does not inherit from E, the method corresponding to K defined in D is invoked.

This rule about similar names for methods holds whatever the level of the inheritance hierarchy. For example, consider the three classes shown below:

```
Class A {
// Declaration of r and s

    // Code for method J

    // Code for method K

    // Code for method L
}


Class B {
// Declarations of e f and g
```

```
    // Code for method J

    // Code for method U

    // Code for method V
}

Class C {
// Declarations of l m n and o

    // Code for method U

    // Code for method R

    // Code for method S
}
```

If class C inherits from class B which, in turn, inherits from class A, then when a message involving the selector U is sent to an object defined by C, the method U defined in C is invoked; when a message using the selector J is sent to the same type of object, the method J defined in class B is invoked.

Before returning to the summable set example it is worth defining a concept that you will meet a number of times later in the book. The **protocol** of a class is the list of messages that can be sent to an object defined by that class. The protocol will contain those method names defined within the class, together with the methods from those classes it inherits from. For example, the protocol of the class C defined above contains the messages corresponding to the methods U, R, S, J, V, K, L.

It is now worth continuing with the summable set example. You will remember that we had already defined a set of integers as:

```
Class IntSet {
int intSetvar[];

    public boolean includes(int no) {
    ...
    }

    public int size(int no) {
    ...
    }

    public void add(int no) {
    ...
    }

    public void remove(int no) {
    ...
    }
}
```

and that we wanted to define a new class which provided all the facilities of IntSet but also provided a method which summed the integers within the set.

You will remember that the way to do this is to somehow define a new class which has an instance variable which holds the current sum of the values and an inherited instance variable which holds the members of the set. We can easily define this new set by writing down its name, specifying the names of the instance variables and then writing code for the five methods. However, inheritance allows us to save some time, since by using inheritance we can reuse some of the elements of `IntSet`.

We shall assume that the new class which describes summable sets is called `SummableSet`. The code skeleton describing its structure is shown below:

```
Class SummableSet {

int sum;

  public int totalSum() {
  ...
  }
}
```

Here a new method `totalSum` is defined which returns with the sum of the set; also defined is an instance variable `sum` which holds the current sum of the set.

In Java if we wish to specify that a set inherits from another set then we write this using the keyword `extends`. The full definition of `SummableSet` is then:

```
Class SummableSet extends IntSet {

int sum;

  public int totalSum() {
  ...
  }
}
```

This states that we have defined a new class called `SummableSet` which inherits the instance variables and the methods from the existing class `IntSet`. If this class inherits from `IntSet`, then an object described by `SummableSet` can be sent messages corresponding to the methods `includes`, `size`, `add` and `remove`. There seems to be no reason why we cannot now write code such as:

```
SummableSet sms;

sms = new SummableSet();
sms.add(23);
```

where the semicolon is used as with most C-like programming languages to terminate individual Java statements.

Unfortunately, there is a problem: the code for the methods `add` and `remove` is incorrect. The code for `add` and `remove` would correctly alter the set of integers by adding and removing items from it; however, they do not affect the current sum. For example, there may be three integers in the summable set which are 45, 3, 10 with the instance variable `sum` holding 58 which is the sum. If `add` is invoked with the argument 20, then 20 would be deposited in the set but the sum would remain at 58. What we need are new versions of `add` and `remove`.

These need to be embedded in the class SummableSet, making its code skeleton look like:

```
Class SummableSet extends IntSet {
int sum;

  public int totalSum() {
  . . .
  }
  public void add(int no) {
  . . .
  }
  public void remove (int no) {
  . . .
  }

}
```

The code for the method add would add no to the set and also add the value of no to the instance variable sum. The code for the method remove would remove no from the set and subtract its value from the instance variable sum. Perhaps we could then expect the code for add to look something like:

```
public void add(int no) {
add(no);
sum = sum + no;
. . .
}
```

where the first line introduces the method, the second line uses the method add declared in the class IntSet to carry out the insertion of no into SummableSet and the third line adjusts the instance variable sum so that it is up to date and contains the current sum. We might also expect the code for remove within SummableSet to look like:

```
public void remove(int no) {
remove(no);
sum = sum - no;
. . .
}
```

There is one problem, however. Which version of add does the first extract refer to: the one defined in IntSet or the one defined in SummableSet? Similarly which version of remove does the second extract refer to: the one defined in IntSet or the one defined in SummableSet? Well, the rule that we have given previously states that when a method *M* is invoked associated with a class *C*, then method *M* is searched for in *C*, and if it is there then it is invoked; if it isn't there then the search continues in the next class that it inherits from, namely the class in the next level in the inheritance hierarchy. This means that, for example, inside the method add defined in SummableSet there is a call to itself. When this is invoked there would be another call to itself, and so on. This means that the method could be in a continuous loop and never exit. The same would, of course, be true of `remove`.

The way to get over this is to use a device which slightly overrides the way in which methods are searched for when they are invoked. This involves the use of a dot notation. In order to refer to the method in the class that `SummableSet` inherits we refer to it as `super.add`.

In order to see how this works, examine the code shown below for the correct version of `add` within `SummableSet`:

```
public void add(int no) {
intSetvar.super.add(no);
sum = sum + no;
...
}
```

This instructs the Java interpreter to start its search for a method to execute not within the class which describes the object `SummableSet`, but within the class `IntSet` (the keyword `super` instructs the Java system to look at the class above). The code for `remove` would be similar:

```
public void remove(int no) {
intSetvar.super.remove(no);
sum = sum - no;
...
}
```

It is worth recapping the points that the example and supporting text has illustrated. First, it has shown how inheritance works. Second, it has illustrated reuse to a certain extent: the reuse of `IntSet` was not massive since we had to redefine the methods `add` and `remove` within `SummableSet`, but nevertheless some reuse was employed. Finally, the text described the way in which the Java system looked for methods to execute: by traversing the inheritance hierarchy, normally starting with the class that was defined by the object which is being sent a message, but with the use of the dot notation facility overriding this starting point.

3.3.2 Invoices

A common document used by many companies is the invoice. This is used to bill another company or individual for goods or services. A typical invoice is shown in Figure 3.4.

If you look at a number of invoices, you will see many common items of information. These include the items or services that are being invoiced, the address of the company being invoiced and the address of the company doing the invoicing. These are shown in Figure 3.4 and can be found on invoices from a wide variety of sources: electrical companies, catering companies, individual consultants and educational establishments.

A general invoice class might look like:

```
Class Invoice {
// Definition of instance variables which hold the name
```

```
// of the invoiced company and the individual items
```

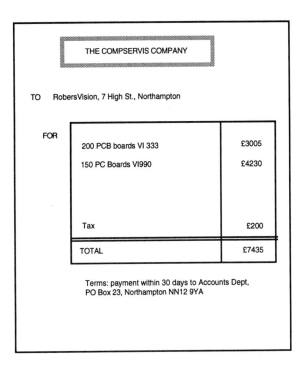

Figure 3.4 A typical invoice.

```
public string invoicedCompanyName ( ) {
...
}

public void setInvoicedCompanyName (String name) {
...
}

public void addItem (String itemName) {
...
}

public void addCost (String itemName, int itemCost) {
...
}

public void addNumber (String itemName, int no) {
...
}

public int calculateTotalCost () {
...
```

```
    }

}
```

where a selection of the possible methods are shown. `invoicedCompanyName`
is a method which returns the name of the company that is to be invoiced,
`setInvoicedCompanyName` adds the name of the company to be invoiced to
the instance variable `invoicedCompany`, `addItem` adds an item which is to be
invoiced, `addCost` sets the cost of an item, `addNumber` sets the number ordered
of an item and, finally, `calculateTotalCost` calculates the total cost of an
invoice. These are just a sample of the methods which might be available for
sending messages to invoices.

Sometimes, however, a company might require something which is only specific
to them or to the type of company they are. For example, many companies often
experience trouble getting customers to pay within the time that it allows them. In
order to provide some incentive they will often quote two prices for an invoice: the
normal price and a price which holds if the invoice is paid within a particular
period; for example, they might apply a five percent discount if the invoice is paid
within 15 days.

Someone who wishes to send invoices which contain discount information
would, quite naturally, develop a new class called, say, `DiscountedInvoice`
which inherited the instance variables and methods from `Invoice` and which
added new methods. For example, such a new class might contain a method which
calculated the discount for an early delivery.

This is just one example of a new invoice class being derived by inheritance
from a general invoice class – there are many other examples. For example, a class
could be developed for companies which have rules for determining discounts
based on a complicated formula which gives discounts for quantities ordered for
particular items. If this class does not require any facilities for handling early
payment, then it could inherit from the class `Invoice` direct; however, if it does
require these facilities, then it would inherit from the class `EarlyPayInvoice`
which contains these facilities and which was formed by inheritance from the
discounted class. This latter case is shown in Figure 3.5.

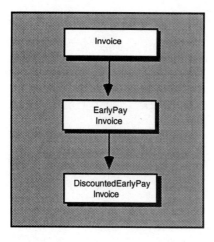

Figure 3.5 A two-level inheritance hierarchy.

What such diagrams represent is a hierarchy showing different levels of generality. As you proceed down the hierarchy the objects defined by the class at a lower level are much more specialized than those that are defined at an upper level, thus `DiscountedEarlyPayInvoice` is a much more specialized version of an `EarlyPayInvoice` which, in turn, is a much more specialised version of `Invoice`.

3.3.3 Employee records

One of the most common systems found in commercial companies is a personnel system. Such a system keeps track of the employees in a company: what their names are, their current salary, where they work, and so on. Such systems are used in a number of ways: normally they are used for providing data which is used in the calculation of the monthly or weekly pay of staff; sometimes they are used to keep track of the training received by staff and sometimes they are used for keeping track of benefits such as a company car.

Such a class would normally have as its instance variables the name of the member of staff, their department, their sex, their annual pay and some indication of a tax coding which determined how much income tax would be deducted from their pay.

In order to see how a hierarchy of employee records might be built up using inheritance we shall first assume that the company that wishes to use this general employee record has two types of employee: weekly paid employees and monthly paid employees. The former are paid on the basis of the number of hours worked: normally a weekly paid employee would work 40 hours per week, but the company we are considering sometimes asks its hourly paid staff to work evenings and pays them at an increased rate. If the company just had this simple division of staff the inheritance hierarchy for its personnel system would look like the hierarchy shown in Figure 3.6.

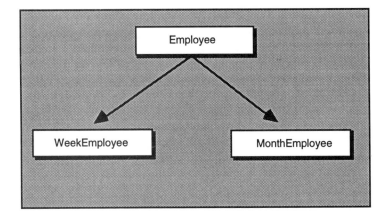

Figure 3.6 The initial hierarchy for the personnel system.

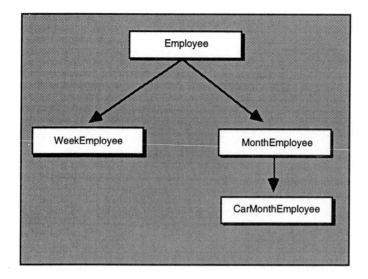

Figure 3.7 The hierarchy from Figure 3.6 modified to show members of staff who drive company cars.

Now let us assume a further complication: that some monthly staff are allowed to drive company cars. Personnel systems often have information about the car that a current member of staff drives. This information is used for a wide variety of purposes, from finding out who has misparked the car in the company car park to determining whether a new car is needed for a member of staff.

Given this further complication we need another class which will contain instance variables connected with the car an employee runs, for example the make of the car and the date when the car was assigned to the member of staff.

The hierarchy showing this new situation is given in Figure 3.7. The new class will inherit from MonthEmployee since only monthly employees are allowed to drive company cars.

Let us examine a further complication: the company employs sales staff whose job is to sell the items that the company manufactures. These sales staff are monthly employees and need a company car since they travel long distances visiting customers' premises. They differ from other monthly employees in that their pay is made up of two elements: a basic monthly pay and a commission based on the amount of sales they make in their current pay month. The company wishes to keep data on sales in their staff's payment record; typically this data will include the monetary value of the current month's sales and the sales that have been made this year to date. This means that a new class would need to be developed. Figure 3.8 shows one attempt at including this new class, called SalesEmployee, in the hierarchy.

This is not the correct version of the hierarchy since it ignores the fact that a SalesEmployee is allowed to drive a car. The position of SalesEmployee in the hierarchy means that it will not inherit all the facilities available for processing car data that are available in the class CarMonthEmployee. The correct version of the hierarchy is shown in Figure 3.9.

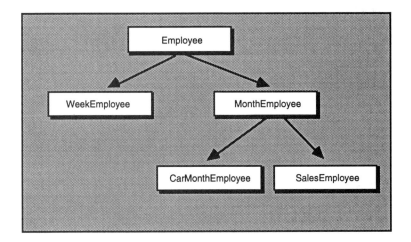

Figure 3.8 A new hierarchy showing sales staff.

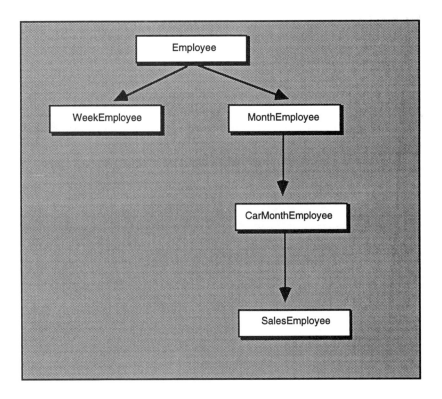

Figure 3.9 The correct version of the inheritance hierarchy showing the correct position of SalesEmployee.

Again with this hierarchy you can see that as we proceed downwards the classes become more specific and hence less generally useful: at the top of the hierarchy is a class which contains common information that almost every personnel system could use, at the second level are classes which only companies that employ both weekly and monthly staff could use, at the third level is a class which only companies that provide company cars could use and at the bottom of the hierarchy is a class which only companies that have a sales force could use.

As you proceed down the hierarchy more and more methods and instance variables will be included in classes. For example, the class `CarMonthEmployee` shown in Figure 3.9 would probably contain an instance variable which provides details of the type of car that the member of staff described by this class is currently driving and would also contain an instance variable which details the date on which this employee was given this car so that the company can replace it within a specified time period. This class would also contain methods which access, update and use these instance variables, for example a method `carType` which returns the type of the car that is currently driven by an object described by this class. The class `SalesEmployee`, further down the hierarchy, might contain an instance variable which details the current sales for the month for a sales person and the current sales for the year for the same sales person. There would also be methods associated with these instance variables, for example methods which add a new sale to these variables and which retrieve the values stored in them.

3.4 Class libraries

At this stage in the book it is worth providing some vocabulary. When a class A inherits methods and variables from a class B, then A is known as the **subclass** of B and B is known as the **superclass** of A. Modern object-oriented programming languages such as C++, Smalltalk and, of course, Java provide extensive class libraries which contain a large number of facilities useful to the programmer.

One concept that is useful to know about when using a class library is that of an **abstract class**. Such an abstract class will contain methods known as **abstract methods**. These methods carry out no actions at all but are just place holders which are filled when a subclass is formed by means of inheritance from the abstract class. In order to explain what you might think is a weird idea it is worth looking at an example of an abstract class.

```
Class A {
// Instance variables for the class

   // Code for method 1

   // Code for method 2

   // Code for method 3

   abstract AbsMethod { }

   // Code for method n

}
```

Class A is regarded as abstract because one of its methods (AbsMethod) contains no code at all and is headed by the keyword abstract.

You will not be able to use AbsMethod direct; however, you will be able to use AbsMethod in a subclass by employing inheritance. For example, if we want a class B which inherits the methods and variables of A and provides code to implement AbsMethod then we would write:

```
Class B extends A {

// Any new instance variables

// Code for method AbsMethod
}
```

Using the rules for inheritance, B would become a class from which objects can be created since the new code for AbsMethod would be used whenever a message involving AbsMethod is sent.

You may think that this is a somewhat strange way to proceed. However, class libraries get much of their power from abstract classes. For example, a class library may contain an abstract class which represents window objects on a screen. It could be that such a class would contain abstract methods which define the way that the border is displayed: that whenever you wish to develop a new screen object which has a different border all you need to do is to extend the abstract window class with a new method which carries out the drawing of the border.

The Java system contains a very large class library in which some of the classes are linked via inheritance. There are five main class libraries:

- *The language foundation classes*. These classes implement low-level data types such as integer and contain the code for the methods which operate on these basic data types.

- *The I/O class library*. This contains classes which provide facilities for low-level input/output, for example for the reading of data from files.

- *Another window toolkit class library*. This contains all the classes needed for the interaction between an applet and the user. It contains classes for basic HCI components such as fonts, colours, events, buttons and scroll bars. This library is used in Chapter 7.

- *The utility class library*. This library contains useful facilities such as a data class, tables, vectors and stacks. This library is introduced in Chapter 6.

- *The network interface class library*. This vitally important library contains classes which are used to communicate within a network. They extend the facilities that are available in the I/O class library and provide ways of, for example, connecting to other interfaces such as Telnet.

This has been a very brief introduction to the extensive library of classes that are provided with the Java system. Chapters 6 to 9 will provide much more detail and give you plenty of examples of the use of these libraries in developing applets and Java applications.

3.5 Summary

This is probably the key chapter in the book. It describes a deceptively simple idea:
that Java contains a mechanism known as inheritance which enables a class to use
methods and instance variables from other classes. This is the main mechanism for
reuse in an object-oriented programming language like Java. The chapter also
describes an importance graphical device known as an inheritance hierarchy, often
called a **class hierarchy**. Such a device describes the relationship between classes.
It shows how classes are related to each other in terms of the methods and instance
variables they inherit from each other. An important point made in this chapter
about the inheritance hierarchy is that as you proceed down it, the classes at the
bottom become more and more specialized. There is still much more to learn about
classes. However, this detail will be presented later in Chapter 5. Before doing this
it is necessary to provide a tour of the programming facilities within Java. This is
the subject of the next chapter.

CHAPTER
FOUR

Data types and control structures

AIMS

- To describe the main data types within the Java language.
- To describe the main control structures within the Java language.
- To present some examples of Java code.

4.1 Introduction

The first thing to say is that, with some small exceptions, the data typing within the Java language is very similar to that found in the C programming language and its later, object-oriented derivatives C++ and Objective C. Apart from the primitive data types in the Java programming language everything else is treated as an object. Those of you who are C programmers will be able to read this chapter very quickly, while those coming from other languages such as Fortran and Pascal will need to approach this chapter in the same way as any other chapter on a new programming language.

The same remarks hold for the control structures in Java. Apart from a small number of exceptions the flow of control in a Java program is specified in much the same way as in a C, C++ or Objective C program.

4.2 Data types

4.2.1 Primitive data types

Java contains all the primitive data types you would expect in a modern programming language. There are four integer numeric data types. These are `byte`, `short`, `int` and `long`. These correspond to stored integers of a maximum length 8 bits, 16 bits, 32 bits and 64 bits respectively. Data type lengths in Java are fixed to ensure portability across implementations of the language. Variables are given types by writing the name of their type before them, so, for example, the code:

```
int newSocket, oldSocket;
```

declares two variables which will hold 32 bit integers and:

```
long userCodeId, userSwitchId;
```

declares two variables which will hold 64 bit integers. When a variable is declared it can be given a value by means of the = symbol, so, for example:

```
byte lastByte, controlByte = 12;
```

will declare two 8 bit variables `lastByte` and `controlByte` and will assign the value 12 to the second of these, leaving the first variable uninitialized. Integer values can be denoted by writing them as shown above or by writing them in octal or hexadecimal. If you wish to specify an integer in octal, the integer needs to be preceded with a zero; if you wish to write an integer in hexadecimal, you precede the integer with a 0 followed by an x. Thus:

```
int    streamId = 017, streamControlId = 0xF,
       switchId = 0xBB;
```

declares three 32 bit integer variables. The first declaration sets `streamId` to be octal 17 (decimal 15), the second declaration sets the 32 bit integer variable `streamControlId` to be hexadecimal F (decimal 15) and the third declaration sets the 32 bit integer variable `switchId` to be hexadecimal BB (decimal 187).

There are two real number types in Java. The first is `float` which represents 32 bit floating point numbers and the second is `double` which represents 64 bit floating point numbers. Thus the statement:

```
float cashValue = 23.8, newCashValue, oldCashValue;
```

declares three variables `cashValue`, `newCashValue` and `oldCashValue` with the first variable being set to 23.8. Floating point numbers are denoted either by writing them as *integerpart.fractionalpart*, or by using scientific notation where the character e or E denotes the fact that the number is to be raised to the power of the integer following the e or E. Thus:

```
float newTotal = 1.56e2, oldTotal = 2.34E4;
```

declares two floating point variables `newTotal` and `oldTotal` with the first variable holding the value 156 and the second variable holding the value 23 400.

There is a char data type called `char` in the Java language. This uses the 16 bit Unicode character set with characters being denoted by the value enclosed within single quotes. Thus:

```
char senseChar, ringChar = 'e';
```

declares two character variables `senseChar` and `ringChar`, with the second of these variables being initialized to contain the character e.

There is a Boolean data type known as `boolean`. Variables of this type can hold either the value `true` or the value `false`. Thus,

```
boolean loopSensor, pollSensor = true;
```

declares the Boolean variables `loopSensor` and `pollSensor` and sets the second of these to the value true.

All the primitive data types that are provided in Java are associated with operators which are used to build up expressions. Binary arithmetic operators can be used both with floats and with the various integer types. A list of these is shown in Table 4.1.

The only operator which needs a little explanation is the `%` operator which is applied to data that is of an integer type. It returns the value which is the remainder when its left operand is divided by its right operand. For example, the value of:

```
34 % 5
```

is 4 since this is the remainder when 34 is divided by 5. This is similar to modulo arithmetic.

There is also a class of operators known as arithmetic assignment operators. These mainly carry out some arithmetic operation such as addition and then assign the result to one of the variables used in the expression containing the operator. These are shown in Table 4.2.

Table 4.1 Arithmetic operators.

Operator	Symbol	Written as	Meaning
Multiplication	*	a * b	a times b
Division	/	a / b	a divided by b
Remainder	%	a % b	The remainder of a divided by b
Addition	+	a + b	b added to a
Subtraction	–	a – b	b subtracted from a

Table 4.2 Assignment operators.

Symbol	Operator	Written as	Meaning
=	Assign	a = b	Put the value of *b* into *a*
+=	Add and assign	a += b	Put the value of *a+b* into *a*
-=	Subtract and assign	a -= b	Put the value of *a–b* into *a*
*=	Multiply and assign	a*= b	Put the value of *a*b* into *a*
/=	Divide and assign	a /= b	Put the value of *a/b* into *a*
%=	Remainder and assign	a %= b	Put the value of *a%b* into *a*

As an example of the use of this operator consider the section of code shown below:

```
int a = 12, b = 22;
a+=b;
```

This results in the sum of a and b being formed (34) and the result being deposited into a. The code shown below:

```
int   div = 12, newDiv 22;
      newDiv %= intDiv;
```

results in the remainder when 22 is divided by 12 (10) being placed in the variable newDiv.

Two operators which you have seen in the previous chapter are the increment and decrement operators ++ and -- . These exist in two forms: postfix form and prefix. The postfix variant returns the old value while the prefix form returns the new value. Thus the expression which uses the postfix ++:

```
newInc++;
```

increments the value of the variable newInc and places this value back into newInc. It returns the old value of newInc. So, for example, if the value of newInc was 44 the result of this expression would be to modify the variable newInc to contain 45 and then return the value 44. The processing associated with the prefix version of the ++ operator can be shown by explaining the processing that occurs within the expression:

```
++newInc;
```

Table 4.3 Increment and decrement operators.

Symbol	Operator	Written as	Meaning
Postfix increment	++	x++	Add 1 to x and return the old value
Prefix increment	++	++x	Add 1 to x and return the new value
Postfix decrement	--	x--	Take 1 from x and return the old value
Prefix decrement	--	--x	Take 1 from x and return the new value

if newInc has the current value 79. First 79 is incremented by 1 and this value is placed back in the variable newInc. This new value is then returned.

Since the increment and decrement operators deliver results, they can be used in any context where the value can be used, for example in assignments:

```
int j=0, k;
k = j++;
```

first increments the variable j by 1 to give it a value of 1 and then sets k to be the value 0 which was the old value of j. The action of the -- operators is the same, except that subtraction rather than addition occurs. The properties of the ++ and -- operators are shown in Table 4.3.

Java also contains a number of relational operators which give rise to Boolean values. These operators can be applied to both integer and floating point numbers. They are summarized in Table 4.4.

Table 4.4 Relational operators.

Symbol	Operator	Written as	Meaning
==	Equal to	x == y	True if x equals y, otherwise false
>	Greater than	x > y	True if x is greater than y, otherwise false
<	Less than	x < y	True if x is less than y, otherwise false
>=	Greater than or equal to	x >= y	True if x is greater than or equals y, otherwise false
<=	Less than or equal to	x <= y	True if x is less than or equals y, otherwise false
!=	Not equal to	x != y	True if x is not equal to y, otherwise false

Table 4.5 Logical operators.

Symbol	Operator	Written as	Meaning
&&	Logical and	a && b	Returns true if both *a* and *b* are true, false otherwise
||	Logical or	a || b	Returns false if both *a* and *b* are false, true otherwise
!	Logical negation	!a	Returns false if *a* is true, returns true if *a* is false

These operators deliver Boolean values and hence can be used in assigning values to Boolean variables. For example, the code:

```
int a = 12, b = 23;
boolean checkList, newList;
checkList = (a < 12);
newList = (b >= 23);
```

first sets checkList to be false since the value of a is 12 and then sets the value of newList to be true since b has the value 23.

There are a number of logical operators in Java. These are similar to logical operators in most other languages. Table 4.5 provides a summary of these operators. Such operators can be used in expressions involving relational operators and variables having numeric types. For example, the code shown below:

```
int a, b, c = 44;
boolean newVal, oldVal;
a = 22;
b = 33;
newVal = (a < 10) && (b == 33);
oldVal = !newVal && !(b < 22 && a < 23);
```

first assigns values to the integer variables in the Java program. It then assigns Boolean values to the variables newVal and oldVal. The value false is placed in the variable newVal because a is not less than 10 and hence the whole expression to the right of the = operator evaluates to false. The second assignment results in the value true being placed in the Boolean variable oldVal. This is because the expression on the right hand side of the = symbol evaluates to true (the value of the expression is actually true && true).

An important point to make about Java is that it does not tolerate the rather free and easy type conversions found in languages such as C, where variables can be implicitly converted from one type to another. In Java if you want to do this, you have to use a device known as a **cast**. Casting involves the enclosure of a data type within round brackets. An example of this is shown below:

```
int cVal = (int) realVar;
```

Here the integer variable cVal is given the value of the integer part of the real variable realVar.

4.2.2 First class objects

Java treats some data types as objects and hence the message passing mechanism shown in the previous chapter can be used with these data types. The two important examples of data types treated as objects are arrays and strings. An example of an array declaration is shown below:

```
int newBuffer[] = new int[10];
```

This declares the variable newBuffer to be an array of integers which will have space for ten integers. The declaration:

```
char streamChars[] = new char[20];
```

declares an array called streamChars which will contain 20 characters.

One of the important ideas of this section is that some data types, which in other languages would be treated as basic or primitive data types, are regarded as objects in Java and hence can be sent messages. For example, in order to get the number of items in an array a message length can be sent to an array. For example, the expression:

```
buffArray.length();
```

consists of a receiver object (buffArray) and a message (length()); the result of this message is an integer which represents the number of items in the array. The concluding parts of this chapter will look at this idea in more detail; all that you should really know at this stage is that arrays are objects and, hence, messages can be sent to them.

Another important object is the string. Strings can be defined in the same way that primitive data types such as int and char can be defined. For example, the code:

```
String nodeName, nodeDestination;
```

declares two variables which will contain strings, both of which will be uninitialized.

Strings are denoted by enclosing their characters in double quotation marks. Thus, the statement:

```
String lpLocation, user = "David Jones";
```

declares two string variables: lpLocation which will be uninitialized and user which will contain the string "David Jones". In the same way that arrays are regarded in Java as objects, so are strings. There is, for example, a method associated with strings called length which can be used when sending a message to a string in order to ascertain its length. For example, the expression:

```
telnetId.length();
```

delivers the number of characters in the string `telnetId`.

All the primitive data types within Java can be given values by means of assignment statements. For example, the code shown below:

```
int a, b, c;
a = 10;
b = 23;
c = 45;
```

declares three variables a, b and c and then uses assignment statements to give them the values 10, 23 and 45. The code:

```
char newStopChar;
float total;
int buffSize = 23, newTelLocation;
newStopChar = 'u';
newTelLocation = 017;
total = 1.2e2;
```

declares a character variable, a floating point variable and two integer variables. The third declaration sets the variable `buffSize` to 23 with the remaining assignment statements setting `newStopChar` to the character u, the variable `newTelLocation` to octal 17 and the floating point variable `total` to 120.

Normally in Java if you wish to give an object a value you will need to send a message to it. However, an exception is made for strings and arrays. If you wish to give a string object a value then an assignment can be made just as with primitive data types. So, for example, the code shown below:

```
String userId;
userId = "Thom Gunn";
```

would initialize the value of `userId` to the string `"Thom Gunn"`. Arrays can be initialized in the same way. For example, the code shown below:

```
int commsSteps[] = new int[5];
commsSteps = (1, 3, 5, 6, 9);
```

initializes the integer array `commsSteps` declared in the first line to contain the five integers 1, 3, 5, 6 and 9, starting with 1 in the first position of the array.

4.3 Control structures

As befits a modern procedural programming language Java contains the main programming constructs usually found in other languages such as C and Pascal. The control constructs look very much like those that are provided as part of the C programming language.

First, statements in the Java programming language are terminated by a semicolon. This is in antithesis to the use of semicolons in languages such as Pascal

where they are used as a separator. A sequence of statements in Java would be
written as:

```
statement1;
statement2;
statment3;
```

while in a language such as Pascal you will need to write this sequence as:

```
statement1;
statement2;
statement3
```

Groups of statements in Java can be treated as a compound statement by enclosing
them in curly brackets. For example, the statement:

```
{int i, j= 24;
String newName = "Ince", oldString;
i = j++;
oldString = newString;}
```

is an example of a compound statement consisting of four statements, two of which
declare variables.

4.3.1 Conditional processing

Java contains conditional processing facilities which allow whole sections of code
to be executed if a certain condition is true or if that condition is false. This has the
form:

```
if (condition)
   true statements;
else
   false statements;
```

where true statements are executed if the condition is true and false statements are
executed if the condition is false. The statements that are executed can be a single
statement or a compound statement which is enclosed in curly brackets. For
example, the code:

```
if (newString.equals("telNetId"))
   found = true;
else
   i++;
```

has two single statements. The first found := true is executed if the identifier
newString is equal to the string "telNetId", the second i++ is executed if
the string is not equal to "telNetId". The code:

```
if (userCount > 1) {
   userCount++;
   nextId = "first";
}
```

```
else{
  sourceSwing++;
  networkSwitchId++;
}
```

consists of two compound statements. The first:

```
{
  userCount++;
  nextId = "first";
}
```

is executed if the variable userCount is greater than 1, while the second is executed if the variable is less than or equal to 1.

As well as providing a true/false switch via the if-else statement, Java contains a conditional facility which executes statements if a condition is true and drops through to the next statement if the condition is false. The form of this statement is:

```
if (condition)
  statements;
```

Two examples of this statement are shown below. The first involves a compound statement:

```
if (ipLink.equals("special") && htmlSwitch) {
  linkCount++;
  forkCount--;
}
```

the second a single statement:

```
if (forkCount < 0)
  forkCount = 0;
```

The first example executes the statement:

```
  linkCount++;
  forkCount--;
```

if the string variable ipLink contains the string "special" and also the Boolean variable htmlSwitch is true (remember that the symbol && stands for logical and). The second example involves the execution of the statement:

```
forkCount = 0;
```

if the value of the integer variable forkCount is less than zero.

If statements tend to be used very frequently in any program, irrespective of what programming language is being used. However, sometimes there are occasions when the use of an if statement can be somewhat clumsy and verbose. The main occasion is where a number of outcomes are required to occur based on the value of a variable or an expression. For example, assume that we have a variable `ipBreak` which is going to have values ranging from 1 to 5, and that, at a particular point in the code, some statements need to be executed if the value of this variable is 1, some other statements need to be executed if the value of the variable is 2, and so on. This can be implemented using `if` statements but the result is usually quite verbose and rather unreadable. Java contains a switch facility which enables this form of multiconditional processing to take place. The general format of the switch facility is:

```
switch (argument){
    case firstcase   : statements;
    case secondcase  : statements;
    case thirdcase   : statements;
    case fourthcase  : statements;
    case fifthcase   : statements;
    case sixthcase   : statements;
...
    case nthcase     : statements;
}
```

Each of the cases `firstcase`, `secondcase`, `thirdcase` and so on can be integers or characters. The statements that are associated with each case can be a single statement or a compound statement. Each set of statements is executed when the case corresponding to the set of statements is delivered by the argument following the `switch` keyword.

Once a statement, or set of statements, associated with a `case` keyword are executed, transfer of control is made to the set of statements associated with the next case unless a statement known as a `break` statement is encountered. If such a statement is encountered, then control passes to the end of the `switch` statement. As an example of this consider the `switch` statements shown below:

```
switch (bufferId) {
    case 1: statements1;
    case 2: statements2;
    case 3: statements3;
    case 4: statements4;
}
```

where `bufferId` is an integer variable. If `bufferId` has a value 1, then the statements labelled `statements1` are executed, if the variable has a value 2 then the statements labelled `statements2` are executed and so on. If the value of `bufferId` is 1 and `statements1` does not contain a `break` statement, then execution carries on with the statements in `statements2`; if these statements still do not contain a break statement, then execution proceeds to those statements labelled `statements3` and so on.

It is normally quite unusual for this form of processing to occur where a set of statements associated with a `case` keyword drops though to the next set of statements. Normally the `break` statement is used to take the processing to the end of the `switch` statement. An example of this is shown below:

```
switch (telControlChar) {
```

```
    case 'a':       videoId = 3;
                    break;

    case 'b':       videoId = 19;
                    soundId = 12;
                    break;

    case 'c':       videoId = 11;
                    link++;
                    break;
}
```

Here the character variable `telControlChar` determines which chunk of code is to be executed. If the value of this variable is the character `'a'` then the integer variable `videoId` is set to 3 and the `break` statement transfers control to the end of the `switch` statement, effectively transferring control to the statement following. If the value of the `telControlChar` variable is the character `'b'`, control is then passed to the three statements:

```
videoId = 19;
soundId = 12;
break;
```

After the first two statements have been executed the `break` statement is invoked and, again, control is passed to the statement following the `switch` statement. The final part of the `switch` statement:

```
videoId = 11;
link++;
break;
```

is executed when the variable `telControlChar` contains the value `'c'`. The final statement is the `break` statement; this again transfers control to the end of the `switch` statement. This statement is strictly not necessary since, if it was omitted, the processing would pass to the end of the `switch` statement anyway. However, we regard it as good programming practice: you will often find that you will need to modify a program after it has been tested, and one common set of modifications involves adding new cases to a `switch` statement. If you needed to make a change to the code above which required a new case following the last case, and had not inserted a final break, then you would need to remember to add this break to the case corresponding to character `'c'`; often you will forget and this would mean that your code would look like:

```
switch (telControlChar) {
    case 'a':       videoId = 3;
                    break;

    case 'b':       videoId = 19;
                    soundId = 12;
                    break;

    case 'c':       videoId = 11;
                    link++;
```

```
    newcase:      code for new case
}
```

When the processing for the case corresponding to the character 'c' has completed, the processing will fall through to the new case that you have added, which is not what you intended. This sort of error is really difficult to detect. Thus, even though the final break is vestigial, it is good practice to include it: it may waste a small amount of memory, but you could find yourself being saved a very large amount of development time.

One more important facility associated with switch statements needs to be mentioned. This is a facility which enables you to specify what processing is required when none of the conditions you expected occurs. One of the disadvantages of the code that you have seen above is that the variable telControlChar could take on other values, apart from those specified following the case keyword; for example, the variable could have a value 'z'. What happens here is that none of the statements in the switch statement are executed. This may not be the processing that we require; for example, if the variable telControlChar contained another character rather than 'a', 'b' or 'c', then this might be a serious error that we might want to pick up and carry out some processing for.

The switch statement contains a facility which enables this type of processing to occur: this uses the keyword default to indicate a section of code that is to be executed when none of the other cases in a switch statement conforms to the value of the variable in the switch part of the statement. So, if in the example above, we wish some error processing to take place, then all that we need to do is to label a set of statements which carry out the error processing with the word default. This is shown below:

```
switch (telControlChar){
   case 'a': videoId = 3;
             break;

   case 'b': videoId = 19;
             soundId = 12;
             break;

   case 'c': videoId = 11;
             link++;

   default:
             // Code for carrying out some error
             // processing
             break;
}
```

4.3.2 Repetitive processing

All programming languages contain facilities which enable sections of code to be executed repeatedly, either while, or until, some condition is satisfied for a fixed number of times. Java provides similar facilities. However, before describing these facilities it is worth saying a few things about a facility which the language does not contain. Many of the readers of this book will come from a background of programming in languages such as C and Fortran where repetitive processing often involves the use of a statement known as the `goto` statement. This statement is usually written in the form:

```
goto label;
```

where `label` is either an integer or some string which identifies a chunk of code later in the program. An example of this is shown below:

```
...
goto 123;
...
123: statement1;
statement2
statement3;
...
```

When the statement `goto 123` is encountered control is passed to the chunk of code which is labelled 123. Java does not contain a `goto` statement, although `goto` is a reserved word in the language. We suspect that for those readers who are C programmers this will prove a major hurdle which they will need to overcome. Throughout the book we will try to present examples of good practice which show how cleaner and more easily maintainable code can be developed without the `goto`. Our only advice to the reader is to persevere: one of the authors (DCI) learned programming with a language where `goto`s were unavoidable and found the switch to another language, where their use was violently discouraged, something of a difficulty; however, what he found was that after a comparatively short period of pain (about three days) a programming style which did not rely on `goto` statements came quite naturally. If this does not totally satisfy C programmers who are reading this book there is a piece of good news in that Java does contain some facilities for a disciplined transfer of control and we will be describing them later in the book; indeed you have met one of the facilities (the `break` statement) in connection with the `switch` statement described in the previous section.

The first repetitive facility that we will introduce is the `while` statement. This has the form:

```
while(Boolean expression)
    statements;
```

where `statements` can be either a single statement or a compound statement. The semantics of the `while` statement are:

> While the Boolean expression is true the statements are executed.

A very simple example of the use of the `while` statement which uses a compound statement is shown below:

```
int i = 0, sum = 0;
while (i < 5) {
```

```
    sum+=vals[i];
    i++;
}
```

This simple piece of code first carries out an initialization and then repeatedly adds the `ith` element of the array `vals` into the variable `sum`; after this it increments the variable `i` which is used to index the array by one. The effect of the code is to find the sum of the first five elements of the array `vals`.

Another example of a `while` statement in action is shown below. It examines the array `remoteNodes` which contains strings and finds the count of the number of times that the string `"nodeId"` occurs in the array. The code assumes that there are `noOfIds` strings in the array:

```
int i = 0, count = 0;
String searchedForString = "nodeId";
while (i < noOfIds ) {
   if (remoteNodes[i].equals(searchedForString)){
     count++;
   }
   i++;
}
```

The only point worth making about this code is that whenever you write nested control statements, always carry out some indenting of the code in order to increase readability and make sure that all the opening curly brackets are associated with a closing curly bracket.

It is worth showing at this point how a disciplined form of unconditional transfer of control can be used within Java, a form of control which is similar to the `goto` statement, but which is of a more limited form that enhances readability. In the text which described the `switch` statement we described the use of the `break` statement. The effect of this statement, within the context of the `switch` statement, was to transfer control to the end of the statement, that is, to the statement which followed the `switch` statement. This use of the `break` statement can be generalized to any statement which implements repetitive processing. If you write `break` within a repetitive statement, then when the Java interpreter encounters this statement it will transfer control to the statement following the repetitive statement in which it is embedded. For example, the code fragment below shows a code skeleton in which a `break` statement is embedded:

```
statement;
while(expression) {
   statement1;
   statement2;
   statement3;
   statement4;
   if (some expression)
     break;
   statement5;
   ...
```

```
    statementn;
}
nextstatement;
```

If, when the loop starting at statement is executed, and some expression is true, then the Java interpreter will transfer control to the statement following the loop. This is statement nextstatement.

A more concrete example of this in action is shown below. It is a fragment of code which looks for a user "Jones" within an array of strings identified by userTable. The code assumes that the array contains totUsers strings and will return with the Boolean variable in set to be true if the name is found and false otherwise. If the name is found, then the integer variable index is set to contain the position of the name within userTable.

```
boolean in = false;
String nameToBeSearchedFor = "Jones";
int counter = 0, index;
while(counter < totUsers ) {
   if (userTable[counter].equals(nameToBeSearchedFor)) {
      in = true;
      index = counter;
      break;
   }
   counter++;
}
```

The break statement here transfers control to the statement following the while statement.

Java contains a second repetitive statement which is similar to the while statement which we have described above. This is the do-while statement. It is similar to the while statement in that it implements repetitive processing *while* a certain condition is true. However, the test as to whether a loop needs to be terminated occurs at the end of the statement as compared with the while statement where the test is made at the beginning. The general form of the do-while statement is:

```
do
   statements;
while (expression);
```

The semantics of this statement are: execute the statements identified by statements while the expression on the third line is true. However, the check whether it is true or false occurs after statements is executed. This means that statements will be executed at least once; this is in contrast to the while statement where it is possible for the statements within the loop to be just skipped over, for example where the while statement is processing an array and there are no elements currently stored in the array.

An example of some code involving the do-while statement is shown below:

```
int i = -1;
do
   i++;
while (!names[i].equals(lastNodeName));
```

This code searches for the string contained in the string variable `lastNodeName` in the string array `names`. It repeatedly increments the integer variable `i` until the name is found. It is important to point out that this code assumes that the name is contained in the array; if it wasn't, the loop would eventually index over the bounds of the array and the Java interpreter would flag a run-time error.

Another example of the use of the `do-while` statement is shown below:

```
int firstIndex, lastIndex, i;
String nameArray[100];
...
i = firstIndex - 1;
do{
   i++;
   nameArray[i] = "";
}
while (i<>lastindex);
```

This sets a section of the string array identified by `nameArray` to contain null or empty strings. The section is identified by `firstIndex` and `lastIndex` which delimit the first item in the array and the last item respectively.

These are statements which carry out repetitive processing *while* some condition is true. We find that we use the `while` statement much more than the `do-while` statement, as the latter involves carrying out some subtraction on a variable before the loop is entered, and while subtraction is not too inefficient an operation in Java it is easy to forget it and cause a programming error which is quite difficult to spot.

The final repetitive statement which implements repetitive processing in Java is the `for` statement. The general form of this statement is:

```
for (expression1; expression2; expression3)
   statements;
```

The semantics of the `for` statement is as follows:

> The statements are executed continually with a variable, which we shall call a **control variable**, being given a value in `expression1`; each time the statement(s) are executed `expression3` defines the new value of the variable as it progresses through each iteration of the statements; the loop terminates when the condition expressed in `expression2` becomes false.

An example of the use of the `for` statement is shown below:

```
for(int i = 0; i < 10; i++)
   a[i] = 0;
```

Here the statement `a[i] = 0;` is continually executed. On the first pass through the statements the value of i is 0 (i = 0 corresponds to `expression1`). The next time that the statement a[i] = 0 is executed i will be incremented by 1 (i++ corresponds to expression3). When the statements are finally executed i will be equal to 10.

This was a very simple example of a loop which started at 1, was incremented by 1 and stopped after a single integer value was encountered. For statements can be more complex. For example:

```
for(int i = start+newList; i <= followBitSum; i += 2)
    statements;
```

executes statements repeatedly, starting with the control variable having the value start+newList with it being incremented by two each time that it traverses the statements, finishing when i is greater than the contents of the integer variable followBitSum.

The for statement:

```
for (expression1; expression2; expression3)
    statements;
```

is equivalent to the code:

```
expression1;
while(expression2){
    statements;
    expression3;
}
```

The for statement exists in a number of forms, each of which represents the original form specified above, but with one or two of the expressions missing; usually these are either expression1 or expression3 but not both. If expression1 is missing the control variable will have been assigned a value in a section of code which has been executed previous to the execution of the for statement. If expression3 is omitted then, within the statements of the for statement, there is some updating of the control variable. Thus all the following are equivalent:

```
for(int i = 0; i < 10; i++)
    a[i] = 0;
```

and

```
int i = 0;
...
for(; i < 10; i++)
    a[i] = 0;
```

and

```
for(int i = 0; i < 10;) {
    a[i] = 0;
    i++;
};
```

The main thing to notice is that whenever an expression is omitted between the round brackets of the `for` statement the semicolon associated with it is not omitted. It is also worth saying that very rarely do you find Java code with both `expression1` and `expression3` omitted since writing a `for` statement in this way is equivalent to a `while` statement; also it is very rare to find `expression2` missing since there is almost always a need to have a terminating condition for the loop and it would be unwieldy to write the terminating condition within the loop using an `if` statement and a `break` statement.

Before leaving the topic of repetitive processing it is worth mentioning another device similar to `break` which allows a limited form of flow of control. This is the `continue` statement. You will remember that the `break` statement, when executed, results in the current loop that is being executed being exited. The `continue` statement interrupts the processing in a loop, but in a less drastic manner. When the `continue` statement is encountered in a loop the Java interpreter will terminate the current execution of the loop and will return the thread of processing to the beginning of the loop. For example, consider the code shown below:

```
for(int i = 1; i < newVal; i++) {
    statement1;
    statement2;
    statement3;
    if (condition)
        continue;
    statement4;
...
    statementn;
}
```

If, during the execution of the set of statements, the condition within the `if` statement is true, then the execution of the loop will be interrupted and resumed at `statement1`. This assumes that the condition `i < newVal` is true; if it wasn't then the loop would terminate.

An example of Java code which shows this facility being used is displayed below.

```
for(int i=0; i < arrayNumber; i++) {
    if ((signalSensor[i] >= 10) && (signalSensor[i]
        <= 20))
        continue;
    signalSensor[i]++;
    modifyFlag = true;
}
```

Here the loop traverses through the integer array `signalSensor`. If the value at each element lies outside the limits 10 and 20 inclusively, then it is incremented and a Boolean variable called `modifyFlag` is set to become true. This is achieved by means of the `continue` statement within the `if` statement. Once this is executed it transfers control to the end of the loop, thus missing the final two statements which carry out the processing.

You have now seen a number of examples of break and continue being used. It is worth providing you with a warning about them. The frequent use of these facilities often leads to making your code as unreadable as if you had used goto statements. In many cases there is a much better solution to the problems that you intended solving using break and continue. For example, the code above could have eliminated the continue by rewriting the for statement as:

```
for(int i = 0; i < arrayNumber; i++) {
   if ((signalSensor[i] < 10)&&(signalSensor[i] > 20)){
      signalSensor[i]++;
      modifyFlag = true;
   }
}
```

4.3.3 Strings as objects

The previous two sections of this chapter have concentrated on the basic data types and control structures of Java. To conclude the chapter we are returning to strings. There are a number of reasons behind this. First, strings in Java are regarded as objects and we feel that before reading the next chapter it would be useful for you to see more messages being sent to objects and, also, since many of you will be familiar with strings within other programming languages it would be easy for you to understand the main object concepts that you need to program in Java. Second, strings, while being regarded as objects in Java, have some properties of basic data types; these properties have been designed to appeal to C programmers who may have used strings in their programs in a non-object-oriented way.

Before proceeding it is worth reminding you of an item of vocabulary which will be used within this section. A **message** is something that is sent to an object. A message consists of a name and some arguments with the possibility of there being zero arguments. When a message is sent to an object a variety of things could occur: first, the state of the object could be changed; second, the state of the object could be changed and a value returned from the message; third, the state of the object could remain unchanged and a value be returned.

Messages will correspond to the methods which are associated with the class which describes the receiver object. When a message is sent to a destination object its class is discovered and the code corresponding to the message executed.

In Java there are two types of sequences of characters. These are String and StringBuffer. Objects described by the former are constants which cannot be changed, while objects described by the latter can be modified. Normally Java code involves strings being converted into StringBuffers, modified and then reconverted into strings.

There are a number of ways of creating Strings and StringBuffers. The first is to declare them using the normal declaration facility that you have seen previously. For example, the declaration:

```
String filename, rootDirectory;
StringBuffer userName;
```

declares two strings called `filename` and `rootDirectory` and a `StringBuffer` called `userName`. These can be initialized by means of an assignment. For example:

```
userName = "James Davis";
```

sets the contents of `userName` to be the string `"James Davis"`. This is very straightforward but hides a subtle point that we made in the first paragraph: in Java strings are regarded as objects, but there are facilities within Java for strings which are not object-oriented, but which have been included to smooth the path of programmers who are used to other languages (most notably C) when they program in Java. If strings were pure objects in Java, then assignments such as the above would be disallowed. The only way to communicate properly with a real object is via a message, so if strings were pure objects the way of setting the value of a string would be to write an expression such as:

```
newUser.setStringValue("James Davis");
```

which sets a string value within the object `newUser`. There are other examples of this compromise within Java. For example, when you want to join together (concatenate) two strings and set a `StringBuffer` variable equal to the result of this operation, you would use the + operator. For example, the code:

```
StringBuffer pcFile = userId + "." + extension;
```

concatenates the string in `userId` with the single character string `"."` and the string in `extension`. The + operator carries out this concatenation and returns with the string which has been so formed. If strings were pure objects in Java the concatenation process would have to be achieved by sending a series of concatenation messages to `pcFile`.

Since strings are objects – albeit slightly impure objects – there are still a large number of messages that can be sent to them. A list of the five most frequently used methods is shown in Table 4.6. These methods give rise to the messages which we shall describe later in this section.

The `length` method is an example of one of those messages that do not affect the receiver object but which return a value. For example, the code below declares two string objects `str1` and `str2` and then sends a `length` message to them; each of these messages will return a value and the sum of these values is placed in the integer variable `sumUp`.

```
int sumUp;
String str1, str2;
...
// Code in which the strings are given values
...
sumUp = str1.length() + str2.length();
```

In object terms the receiver objects (`str1, str2`) have been sent `length` messages. These messages have no arguments, but result in a value being returned which is the length of the strings in terms of the number of characters found.

Table 4.6 Some string messages.

Method	Meaning	Returns
length()	Finds the length of a string and returns it.	An integer
charAt(ch)	Finds the character ch at a specified place within a string.	A character
indexOf(str)	Searches for a particular string str within the destination object and returns the position of the string. The search starts at the front of the string.	An integer
lastIndexOf(str)	Searches for a particular string str within the destination object and returns the position of the string. The search starts at the back of the string.	An integer
substring(int1, int2)	Returns with a specified substring of a string which starts at int1 and finishes at int2.	A string

The charAt() method has one argument which represents the position within a string of a particular character. When a string object is sent a charAt() message the string is not modified (it wouldn't be a string if it was) but the character at the position given by the argument is returned. So, for example, if the string fileName has the value "dataPlex.txt" then the result of:

```
fileName.charAt(2);
```

would be for the message charAt(2) to be sent to the receiver object fileName with the character in the third position of the file name ('t') being returned.

Since messages such as the one above return values, they can be placed in any part of a Java program which expects the type of data which is to be delivered. For example, the code below finds out how many times the vowels 'a', 'e' or 'i' occur within a string:

```
int count = 0;
String nameOfId;
...
// Code which gives a string value to nameOfId
...
int i = 0;
while (i < nameOfId.length()) {
  char value = nameOfId.charAt(i);
  if (value = 'a' || value = 'e' || value = 'i')
    count++;
  i++;
}
```

This code involves two messages. First, the message `length()` is sent to the receiver object `nameOfId`. This results in the value of the length of the string being returned and then compared with `i` during the execution of the body of the `while` statement. The second example of a message being sent is within the body of the `while` statement where the message `charAt(i)` is sent to the receiver object `nameOfId`. This results in the character at the `i`th position in the string being returned.

The method `indexOf()` searches a string for a substring within the receiver object. When it finds the string it returns with the index within the receiver object of the substring that has been found. The search for the substring starts at the beginning of the receiver object. For example, if the receiver string object `receiver` that is being searched is `"newLinknearNext"` and the substring is `"ne"`, then the processing that takes place when:

```
receiver.indexOf("ne");
```

is executed is that the message `indexOf("ne")` is sent to the receiver object (`receiver`). The method `indexOf` associated with the string class is located and the code executed: this results in the search for the string `"ne"` from the beginning of the string; this is found at the leftmost part of the string and the result is that the value 0 is returned since it represents the first index within the string object where the `"ne"` string was found (remember that strings and arrays within Java start at 0). If a different message was sent, for example:

```
receiver.indexOf("near");
```

then the result would be different; the result of the message being sent to `receiver` would be 7 which represents the starting index of the substring `"near"` within the destination object `"newLinknearNext"`.

The method `lastIndexOf()` is similar to `indexOf()` in that it searches for a string within a particular string which is the receiver object. However, it differs in that the search for the substring within the destination object starts at the end of the destination object. For example, the code:

```
receiver.lastIndexOf("ne");
```

would return with 7 which is the first occurrence of the substring `"ne"` when the search starts from the end of the receiver object.

At this stage it is worth reiterating the statement that the programming examples that we are presenting are all well-behaved. In the case of the demonstration of `lastIndexOf()` and `indexOf()` above we have assumed that the receiver object contains the substring that is being searched for. Real life is very rarely like that and frequently we will carry out actions where there is scope for some error to occur or some action to fail. Java contains a facility known as the **exception** facility which provides facilities for monitoring such events and carrying out some processing corresponding to them. For the time being we will ignore what might be called this deviant processing and assume a perfect world. However, the next chapter will discuss exceptions in more detail.

The final string method that we need to discuss here is substring(). What this method does is to extract out the substring of the string which is the destination object. It has two arguments which delimit the substring. For example, assume that the string variable name contains the string "Darrel Ince". When:

```
name.substring(2,5);
```

is executed the substring message is sent to name. This results in a string being returned which is the substring of the destination object that is indexed by 2 and 5. Therefore the string "rrel" is returned. Java contains an extensive set of facilities for handling strings; however, we have found that the five discussed here are the ones that we have most frequently used.

The other type of string object is the StringBuffer object. This differs in two ways from String objects in that objects which are StringBuffers can be changed and also they are treated as pure objects. For example, it is incorrect to write:

```
StringBuffer lanLocation = "Node12";
```

in a similar way to that found when initializing strings. You will need to declare StringBuffer identifiers and then use new to create the string. To achieve the effect of the incorrect statement above we would have to write:

```
StringBuffer lanLocation = new StringBuffer("Node12");
```

StringBuffer objects also recognize the five methods outlined above. However, since such objects can be changed they can also respond to methods which alter their state. The three popular methods for changing a string buffer are append(), insert() and setCharAt().

The append() method adds a character to the end of a string buffer. An example of its use is shown below:

```
newName.append('c');
```

This results in the message append('c') being sent to the receiver object newName. The message adds the character 'c' to the end of newName. If newName is empty, then the string so formed would just consist of the single character 'c'.

The method insert() takes two arguments. The first is an index and the second is a string. The result of a message corresponding to this method being sent to a receiver object is that the string which is the second argument is added to the receiver object at the position specified by the index. For example, the code:

```
StringBuffer fileName = new StringBuffer ("DataFilter");
...
fileName.insert(4,"1.txt");
```

results in the message insert(4,"1.txt") being sent to the object fileName. The result of this message is that the string "1.txt" is added to the string stored in fileName at the position indexed by the first argument of the message (4). This results in `fileName` being changed to `"Data1.txt Filter"`.

The final method useful for StringBuffers is `setCharAt()`. This has two parameters. The first is a character and the second is the position within a string. When a message involving `setCharAt` is processed by the Java interpreter the receiver object, which is a string, is modified by overwriting the character at the position indicated by the first argument by the character which is the second argument.

For example, the code:

```
StringBuffer ipName = new StringBuffer("NewLog");
...
ipName.setCharAt(4,'h');
```

results in the message `setCharAt(4,'h')` being sent to the receiver object `ipName` with the character at the 4th indexed position (`'o'`) in the object being replaced by the character `'h'`; this ensures that the value of the receiver object is now `"NewLhg"`.

As one example of the use of Strings and StringBuffers, consider an application which processes email addresses. British addresses have the general form:

```
UserName@Location.Type.UK
```

where `UserName` is the name of the sender of the email (usually some convenient abbreviation), `Location` is their location – often the name of a company or an educational institution – and `Type` is the type of institution that the sender of the email currently works in, for example `ac` stands for an academic institution while `co` stands for a company. UK email addresses are always terminated by the final string "UK". First let us assume that we have an applet which has managed to store a series of addresses in an array of strings called `addressList`. The first example of string processing that we will show is the construction of a new array `ukAddressList` which will contain all the email addresses from the United Kingdom. The code for this is shown below; in the code the identifier `maxListSize` contains the limit of the number of email addresses that can be found in the lists and the variable `noOfAddresses` contains the current number of addresses that are found in `addressList`.

```
...
String    ukAddressList[] = new String[maxListSize],
          addressList[] = new String[maxListSize];
int       noOfAddresses, noOfUkAddresses,
          lastDotPosition, ukCount;
...
// Code which sets up the list addressList
...
ukCount = 0;
for (int i = 0; i < noOfAddresses; i++) {
   lastDotPosition = addressList[i].lastindexOf(".");
   If (addressList[i].substring(lastDotPosition + 1,
```

```
        addressList[i].length() - 1).equals("uk")) {
            ukAddressList[ukCount] = addressList[i];
            ukCount++;
        }
}
```

This item of code contains a number of `String` and `StringBuffer` messages. The `for` statement has the effect of moving through the addresses contained in the string array `addressList` examining each item in the array to see whether it represents a United Kingdom address. The first statement in the body of the `for` statement:

```
lastDotPosition = addressList[i].lastindexOf(".");
```

finds the index of the substring consisting of the dot character in the destination object. The destination object is the `i`th item in the array containing email addresses. The message uses the `lastIndex` method since we want to search from the end of the address as the country designator is found at the end. The `if` statement then extracts the substring delineated by the index after the dot and the end of the string and compares it with the string `"uk"` (we have made the artificial assumption that all the email addresses stored in `addressList` have the country in lower case). Once an email address has been found that satisfies this condition, it is written to the array containing United Kingdom email addresses.

Let us now assume that we wish to process the list of email addresses from the United Kingdom in order to discover how many times users who have the address `"open"` are in the array.

The code for this is shown below; we have again made another artificial assumption that user names do not contain a full stop character.

```
...
int atPosition, dotPosition, openCount = 0;
for(int i = 0; i < ukCount; i++) {
    atPosition = ukAddressList[i].indexOf("@");
    dotPosition = ukAddressList[i].indexOf(".");
    if(ukAddressList[i].substring(atPosition+1,
        dotPosition-1).equals("open"))
            openCount++;
}
```

Three variables are declared: `atPosition` will contain the position of the @ character within the email string, `dotPosition` will contain the position of the first dot character within the email string (remember that we are assuming that user names do not contain dots) and `openCount` will contain the count of the number of email addresses which have `"open"` as their location.

The `for` statement will iterate over the email addresses within the string array `ukAddressList`. Each element of this array will be a string object and two messages are sent to these objects; the first extracts the position of the @ character within the email string, the second extracts the position of the first dot character.

The search for these characters starts at the leftmost part of the string since the method indexOf is used. Once these positions are found a further message:

```
substring(atPosition+1,dotPosition-1)
```

is sent to each email address in the string array ukAddressList. This selects the substring starting after the @ character and before the first . character. This results in the location of the email address being returned; this is then compared with the string "open" and the count openCount is incremented if equality is found.

4.3.4 Comments

Comments can be written in two ways in Java. For comments written after programming statements the characters // start a comment and the end of the line concludes the comment. For example:

```
newTelId = 0;      // Initialization of TelNet variables
fileType = vaxFile;
interfaceId = "NewSocket"
```

The second type of comment is used where the comment text spans a number of lines or occupies a single line: the characters /* start the comment, while the characters */ conclude the comment. For example:

```
/*
Initialization of the TelNet variables
These are only accessed by the methods which form part
of the classes NewInterface and TelInterface
*/
newTelId = 0;
fileType = vaxFile;
interfaceId = "NewSocket"
```

There is a third type of comment which starts with the characters /**. This comment is used to produce class documentation. Its use is discussed in more detail in Chapter 9.

4.4 Summary

Much of the material in this chapter will have been familiar to you if you have used a modern programming language; it should certainly be very familiar if you are a C programmer and certainly familiar in concept if you are a programmer in another language. What we have tried to do in this chapter is to introduce you to the main data types and control structures that are used within Java and display some small fragments of code. Towards the end of the chapter we have tried in a very gentle way to orient you towards the major change that will occur in the next chapter. This chapter will describe the main key ideas of an object-oriented programming language and their implementation in Java. We have tried to prepare the ground by devoting some time to the string data type in Java. The Java language is a little schizophrenic in its treatment of strings: in some respects it treats them like any other data type in a non-object-oriented programming language, at the same time as providing facilities for sending messages to string objects. It is this latter facet that we have concentrated on. We would hope that by explaining that the main processing mechanism in Java involves messages being sent to receiver objects, and by continually using sentences which usually contain the words *message* and *receiver object*, we have prepared you for the conceptual change that will occur in the next chapter.

This conceptual change means that those of you who have programmed in languages such as Pascal and C will need to move your focus away from functional descriptions to descriptions of the behaviour of objects. In many books this change in emphasis can be a rude awakening for the programmer who has used conventional languages; however, we hope that it will not be too large for the readers of this book since we have taken great pains to prepare you for it in this chapter and in Chapter 3.

CHAPTER
FIVE

Classes in Java

AIMS

- To show how Java defines objects using the class facility.

- To describe the concepts of instance variable, static variable, instance method and static method.

- To show how inheritance can be used within Java.

- To briefly introduce the Java class library.

5.1 Introduction

The previous chapter has described the processing facilities and data types that are available within Java. A casual reader who has just read that chapter without reading the rest of the book would be forgiven for assuming that Java was not substantially different from other programming languages; in particular the programming language C. You could say that it had a somewhat strange syntax for calling what looked like subroutines, but apart from that there is little that differentiates Java from other programming languages. The aim of this chapter is to dispel this notion. It is not difficult to write Java programs in a way resembling those of conventional procedural programming languages. However, to derive the most power from Java it is necessary to develop code which is object-oriented. By the end of this chapter you should be able to do this.

5.2 Objects

It is worth carrying out a little revision before looking at how Java implements objects. An object is something which has a state: it is associated with some stored data value or data values. Everything can be regarded as an object. The user of an email system is an object whose state may contain data that describes his or her location and name. A bank account is an object whose state may be the name of the account holder, the current balance, the overdraft limit and a list of recent transactions. A plane in an air traffic control system is an object; its state might consist of data which identifies the plane, its position and its eventual destination. A pull-down menu in the user interface of an applet can be regarded as an object; its state might consist of a list of the commands that make up the pull-down menu, the type of box that encloses the menu when it is instantiated on a screen and the colour of the pull-down menu. Thus, the first thing that needs saying is that the object paradigm is universal.

Another important point is that objects can receive messages. By now you will have seen plenty of examples of messages in Java and should be totally familiar with the dot notation that is used to indicate that a message is being sent to an object. The expression:

```
obj.mess(arg1, arg2...argn);
```

has the interpretation that the message `mess` is sent to the object `obj`. The message consists of n arguments which are used when the code corresponding to the message is executed (n could be zero).

An applet or application can be regarded as a set or collection of objects which communicate with each other by means of messages in order to achieve some processing demanded by the world outside the applet. For example, assume that we have an application which is a simple word processor and a user wishes to count the number of words in the document. The user will pull down a menu which contains the word count command, instantiate this command and the count will be displayed on the screen. This seemingly simple piece of processing would contain quite a large amount of processing which involves messages being sent to receiver objects. First, the mouse object would send a message to the pull-down menu object; this would result in the display of the pull-down menu, and the mouse would then send a message to the pull-down menu when it has selected the word count command. This will then generate a message sent from the pull-down menu to the object which represents the document whose word count is to be found. This document will then send a series of messages to the words in the document with a count being incremented each time a word is found. When this processing has finished a message would be sent to a window asking it to display the word count on the user's computer monitor.

Java contains facilities for defining an object, naming an object and creating an object. Naming an object requires a simple declaration of the form:

```
ObjectType objectname;
```

Here `ObjectType` is the name of an object type and `objectname` is the identifier which is used to refer to the object. Thus, if the user had defined an object `emailUser` the code:

```
emailUser john, jim, angela, forbiddenUsers[];
```

would declare three objects `john, jim, angela` and an array of user objects identified by `forbiddenUsers`. It is important to point out that such a declaration does not create the objects, but just informs the Java system that the names will be used to designate the objects.

In order to create an object you will need to use a facility known as new. This creates an object and binds a name to the object. For example, the code:

```
emailUser john = new emailUser();
```

results in an `emailUser` object being created which is identified by the name `john`. As you will see later in this chapter there are a number of variants which can be used when constructing new objects. The one above is the simplest: it has no arguments and results in a new object being created with its instance variables uninitialized. As you will see in the next section of this chapter there are a number of ways of writing code which creates objects with a wide variety of initial values.

One keyword which you will sometimes encounter in a Java program is `null`. This represents an empty object. It is similar to zero in arithmetic. An example of the use of `null` is shown below:

```
User John = null;
```

This creates a `User` variable named `John` but does not put any data in it.

5.3 Classes

5.3.1 Defining classes in Java

The class is the key concept in Java. A class represents a description of an object. A table containing class details is consulted by the Java interpreter when it is asked to create a new object. A class has two functions. The first is to define the state of an object described by the class, that is, what items of data make up the state and what sort of data they are; for example, whether they are integers, strings or objects defined by other classes. The second function of a class is to define the behaviour of an object, where we use the word *behaviour* to mean the messages that a class can respond to. An example of the initial lines of a class are shown below. We shall use this class as an example in this section of the book:

```
class User {
    String userId, emailAddress;
    int noOfAccesses, dateRegistered;
```

```
  . . .
  // Methods
  . . .
}
```

The keyword `class` introduces the name of the class. The declarations following this first line describes the state of an object defined by this class. The class shown above describes the user of an applet. Such a user will have an identity and an email address, both of which are strings. We shall also assume that we are interested in the number of accesses that each user has made to the applet and the date on which they were registered. We shall assume that this date can be represented by an integer which represents some number of days from a base date such as 1 January 1900. This is a little artificial since Java contains a date class in one of its libraries which we could have used here; however, we have not yet taught it so just assume for the time being that an integer value is enough to represent the date on which a user was registered.

These initial lines define the contents of an object. The lines following are used to define the methods, or chunks of code, which correspond to the messages that can be sent to an object. Java distinguishes between two types of methods: accessor methods which access and modify the instance variables and constructor methods which create new instances of an object.

It is worth concentrating on accessor methods first. We shall assume that a number of methods are required which: update each of the instance variables (four methods in all, one for each instance variable), read and return the values of the instance variables (another four methods) and a method which indicates that the user has used the applet and updates the instance variable which holds the number of accesses.

The program code for these nine methods is shown below. The first four set the values of the four instance variables while the next four access and return the values:

```
public void setUserId(String usIdVal) {
   userId = usIdVal
}

public void setEmailAddress(String emailAddressVal) {
   emailAddress = emailAddressVal;
}

public void setNoOfAccesses(String NoOfAccessesVal) {
   noOfAccesses = NoOfAccessesVal;
}

public void setdateRegistered(String dateRegisteredVal){
   dateRegistered = dateRegisteredVal;
}

public String getUserId() {
   return(userId);
}
```

```java
public String getEmailAddress() {
  return(emailAddress);
}

public int getNoOfAccesses() {
  return(noOfAccesses);
}

public int getDateRegistered() {
  return(dateRegistered);
}

public void access() {
  noOfAccesses++;
}
```

The keyword `public` in front of a method indicates that the method can be used outside its class. Because we have not placed this keyword in front of the instance variables, any program that creates objects described by this class, for example:

```java
userJohn = new User();
```

is not allowed to access the instance variables directly; for example, you will not be allowed to write statements such as:

```java
userJohn.noOfAccesses = 23;
```

Later in this chapter we shall discuss ways in which this rule can be overridden. However, good programming practice dictates that we rarely do this. The reason why classes are written in such a way that the instance variables cannot be accessed directly, but are accessed via methods, is to do with a concept known as **information hiding**.

The core idea behind information hiding is that the programmer who employs a class is not allowed to know anything about the way in which instance variables are stored and the detailed coding within a method. If a user was allowed to access an instance variable directly within his or her programs, then, if the class that implemented the instance variables changed, large amounts of code within the program would need to be changed. Take the `User` class as an example. Let us assume that we implemented the class in the way shown above and that users were allowed to access the instance variables. But now assume that later in the life of the class we decided to replace the two instance variables which hold the user's identity and his or her email address with a single string which merged this information, the decision being made for space efficiency reasons. Every program which referred to these variables would need to be modified. However, if access to these instance variables was just via the methods defined in the class, the only rewriting needed would be to change the declaration of the instance variables and the code which accessed the two string variables whose format would have changed.

The code for the methods in the class is relatively straightforward, the only slightly complicated aspect being the use of the `return` statement. What this does is to return a value when the message corresponding to the method is terminated.

It is worth looking at some more methods. Assume that the application in which the `User` class is embedded requires a method which checks whether a user has made any accesses before: let us call this method `zeroAccesses`; it returns a true value if the user has made no accesses and a false value if he or she has made at least one access.

```
public boolean zeroAccesses() {
   return (noOfAccesses == 0);
}
```

Let us also assume that there is a need for a method which returns an integer which holds the number of days since the user accessed the applet. For this the method will need an argument which would be set to the day that the method was invoked. The code for this method, known as `daysFromRegistered`, is shown below:

```
public int daysFromRegistered (int today) {
   return (today - dateRegistered);
}
```

All this method does is to subtract `dateRegistered` from the date `today`, which we have assumed is in the same integer format as `dateRegistered`. It then returns this value for use by the application or applet which gave rise to the message.

5.3.2 Access mechanisms

The classes that you have seen in the book have so far all been constructed in such a way that the instance variables *have not* been allowed to be accessed outside their class and the methods *have* been able to be accessed. This corresponds to good programming practice. However, Java does recognize that there are circumstances when other levels of access should be allowed. There are four levels of access known as **public, protected, private** and an access state known as **friendly**. If you precede an instance variable or a method with the keyword `public`, then any class outside the class in which the declarations occur can access the instance variables and the methods directly. For example, the class skeleton:

```
Class newId {
   public int xCoord, yCoord;

   public int a() {
   ...
   }
   public void b() {
   ...
   }

}
```

defines two instance variables `xCoord` and `yCoord` which can be directly referred to in other classes and two methods a and b which again can be referred to in other classes.

By prefacing a method or instance variable with the keyword `protected` the programmer specifies that the methods and instance variables can only be referred to in any class which inherits from the class in which the `protected` keyword occurs and in the class itself.

By prefacing a method or instance variable with the keyword `private` the programmer specifies that the methods and instance variables which are prefaced can only be referenced within the class that they were defined in.

The last access level is *friendly*. This is specified by the programmer not prefacing the instance variables and methods with any of the three keywords described above. Friendly access means that any class which is declared in the same package as the friendly class can access it. A package, as you will see in Chapter 6, is a collection of related classes. The various accesses that have been described here can be mixed throughout a class definition. Most of the Java classes that you will encounter will have most, if not all, of their methods declared as public with their instance variables declared as private. Sometimes some of the methods are declared as private within a class. These methods usually carry out some housekeeeping task which is needed by other methods which might be public; usually such methods provide an internal facility which is not needed by the user of the class and, indeed, they often provide internal information which destroys the principle of information hiding.

If you have defined a class in such a way that the instance variables are allowed to be accessed outside the class, then you would use a dot notation to carry out this access. For example, you may have defined a class `Point` which represents the *x*, *y* point on a screen. This class might be defined by:

```
class Point {
    public int xCoord, yCoord;
...
    methods
...
}
```

Then in order to access the `xCoord` instance variable of an object identified as `edgePoint`, all that is required is to write the name of the object followed by a full stop followed by the name of the instance variable as shown below:

```
edgePoint.xCoord;
```

5.3.3 Static variables and static methods

So far we have described instance variables and instance methods. The former are variables which hold data associated with each object. For example, if you defined a class as:

```
class newId {
    int a, b, c;

    // Definition of methods
}
```

then, whenever you created a new object described by class newId, and were able to look at the instance so created, you would find three memory locations corresponding to the instance variables a, b and c. There is another type of variable which is known as a **static variable**. This is often referred to as a **class variable**. When you declare a static variable in a class, what you are specifying is that the class itself will be associated with that variable, and that no objects defined by that class will contain data associated with that variable.

Static variables and methods are introduced by means of the keyword static. By prefacing a variable declaration with this keyword you are specifying that the identifiers following are to be variables associated with the class, *not* with each object. There are a limited number of uses of static (or class) variables. One common use is to declare a static variable to keep count of the number of objects described by the class that have been created. This class variable might be used when space is limited and the applet which uses the class would degrade badly in performance when an upper limit of objects described by the class is reached. Static (or class) methods are specified in the same way: by prefacing the definition of the method with the keyword static.

A static method differs from a normal method in that it is only allowed to access static variables: it is not allowed to read or write to instance variables. A typical use of a static method would occur with the scenario described in the previous paragraph where a static method would increment the class variable which describes the number of objects of the class which have been created.

Another use of class variables would be for identifying the version of a class. Classes undergo many revisions and it is useful to keep track of the current version of the class that is being used within a program. If the programmer uses a major version/minor version numbering scheme, where a major version number represents a big revision to an existing version and a minor version number represents some small tinkering, then this can be represented as two class variables, say majorVersion and minorVersion, declared in the class. Static methods can then be used to access this information but not change it. An example of this is shown below:

```
Class X {
    static int majorVersion, minorVersion;

    // Method to extract the major version number
    // and return it

    // Method to extract the minor version number
    // and return it
}
```

Some examples of static methods and variables will be presented in the remainder of this chapter. However, before doing so it is worth looking at two final concepts associated with the notion of a class.

The first is that of a **constructor** method. Such a method is used to create an object. In order to write a constructor method all you do is to name the method with the same name as the class within which it is embedded. An example of a constructor method is shown below:

```
Class Coordinate {
   int xPos, yPos, zPos;
   ...
   public Coordinate(int xVal, int yVal, int zVal) {
   xPos = xVal;
   yPos = yVal;
   zPos = zVal;
   }
   ...
   // Other methods
   ...
}
```

Here the constructor has three parameters which represent initial values of the three instance variables. Constructors are used in conjunction with the new facility which creates an object. For example, the code:

```
Coordinate newCoord = new Coordinate(0,0,0);
```

creates a new object described by the class `Coordinate` and sets its three instance variables to zero. Every class has associated with it an implicit constructor which creates an instance of an object described by the class, but which does not initialize any of the instance variables associated with the class. So, for example, even though we have defined a constructor above for the class `Coordinate` there is still a constructor method available for use which does no initialization, so that we could write code such as:

```
Coordinate newCoord = new Coordinate();
```

Often, when you are writing classes, you will provide a number of constructors which cater for a selection of initialization possibilities. For example, the code for the class `Coordinate` shown below contains three constructors as well as the implicit constructor. These initialize one, two or three instance variables respectively. It is good practice in constructors which only initialize some of the instance variables to set the other variables to some default. In the case of the example below this is 0.

```
Class Coordinate {
   int xPos, yPos, zPos;
   ...
   public Coordinate(int xVal, int yVal, int zVal) {
   xPos = xVal;
   yPos = yVal;
   zPos = zVal;
   }
   ...
   public Coordinate(int xVal) {
   xPos = xVal;
   yPos = 0;
   zPos = 0;
   }
```

```
    . . .
    public Coordinate(int xVal, int yVal) {
    xPos = xVal;
    yPos = yVal;
    zPos = 0;
    }

    // Other methods

}
```

The remaining chapters of the book will describe the Java class library and you will find it is the rule rather than the exception for a number of constructors to be provided for classes in the library.

The other important concept is the **finalizer**. A finalizer is a method which is written when an object disappears. Before looking at the way in which this type of method is written it is worth examining the concept of disappearance when applied to an object.

When an object is created, for example by means of the statement:

```
Classname identifier = new Classname();
```

the Java interpreter will create enough space for it to exist; in particular, it will allocate enough memory for its instance variables. When an object is no longer needed the Java interpreter will destroy the object and return the space allocated to the object back to a free reservoir of space used for new objects. For example, within a method a declaration:

```
Classname newObjIdentifier = new Classname();
```

would create space for an object newObjIdentifier described by Classname; however, when the method completes its processing the space allocated to newObjIdentifier will be marked as unused. Periodically the Java interpreter will examine all the unused space which is occupied by objects that have effectively disappeared and will return it to the reservoir of free space.

Programmers are allowed to write methods which are invoked when an object disappears within their classes. Such methods are given the name finalize and are made protected since they should not be accessed by classes outside the one in which they are declared.

In order to illustrate the use of constructors and finalizers consider the problem that we mentioned earlier: that we are developing an applet where space for objects is very limited and for some objects we want to establish an upper limit to the number that can be active in a program. In order to do this we need to keep a count of the number of objects created and destroyed. We shall make the assumption in this example that programmers are unable to use the implicit default constructor method to create objects.

Let us assume that the class whose objects we need to monitor is called IdPool and that it has two static variables which are both integers. The code for the methods which create and destroy IdPool objects is shown below:

```
class IdPool {
  int oldIdPool, newIdPool;
  static int classCount = 0; totIdPoolObjects = 200;

  public idPool(int firstVal, int secondVal) {
    if (classCount < totIdPoolObjects) {
      oldIdPool = firstVal;
      newIdPool = secondVal;
      classCount++;
    } else {
    // Code which handles the problem of too many
    // objects being created
    }

  protected void finalize {
    classCount--;
  }
  ...
  // Other methods
}
```

There are a number of things to notice about this code. First, two static variables are declared; as you will remember these are associated with the class rather than being created every time an object defined by the class is created. The first static variable classCount contains the count of the number of IdPool objects that have been created and the second static variable totIdPoolObjects contains the limit of the number of objects that can be created. Only one constructor method is defined. This takes two integer parameters and initializes the instance variables of an IdPool object with the values within the arguments. Before carrying out this initialization the method will check that the upper limit on the number of objects has not been breached. If it hasn't, then the initializations will take place; however, if it has, then some code which will cope with this problem will be executed. We have omitted details of this code which raises what is called an **exception**, since we have not yet taught exceptions. The finalize method is given the name finalize, it is made protected and returns no value. It carries out the simple processing of decrementing the count of objects by one so that when an object disappears the tally of active objects still remains the same.

An example of a static method which might be used in connection with the class IdPool might be a method which returns with the current number of IdPool objects which have been created. The code for this method is shown below:

```
public static int noOfIdPoolObjects() {
return (classCount);
}
```

This method is defined to be public so that other classes can use it and static which tells the Java interpreter that it is a static method. When a user of this method wishes to find out how many objects described by IdPool are currently active all that would be needed is to send the noOfIdPoolObjects message to the class name:

```
IdPool.noOfIdPoolObjects();
```

This expression will then deliver the total. The important point to make is that the message is sent to the class, *not* to an object described by the class.

5.3.4 Inheritance in Java

In Chapter 3 we described the concept of inheritance. In this chapter we will add a little more detail to the story that we told in that previous chapter. First it is useful to summarize what inheritance is all about. First and foremost it is a mechanism for exploiting the reuse of existing classes. When a class X is defined which inherits from another class Y, what happens is that all the methods and instance variables of the class apart from methods which are private in Y can be used by the class X.

To specify that a class inherits from another class you will need to write the keyword extends. An example of its use can be seen below:

```
class PrivilegedUser extends User {
    // Definition of any instance or static variables
    // Definition of any instance or static methods
}
```

Here the class PrivilegedUser is able to access the methods within the class User together with any instance or static variables which are defined.

The only exception to the rule concerning the use of methods and variables from the inherited class is that if we have two classes X and Y, Y inherits from X and contains methods which have the same name as methods in X, then when you invoke one of these methods from outside Y and if the methods are public, it is the methods which are defined in Y that are executed. For example, consider the code shown below which represents two classes A and B, where B inherits from A.

```
Class A {
    // Declaration of instance and static variables

    public method s {
        ...
    }

    public method t {
        ...
    }

    public method u {
        ...
    }
}

Class B extends A {
    // Declaration of instance and static variables

    public method q {
        ...
    }
```

```
    public method p {
      ...
    }
    public method u {
      ...
    }
}
```

If we encountered the code:

```
objA.u...
```

then, assuming that the object `objA` was described by class `A`, the method `u` embedded within the class definition of `A` would be executed. If we encountered the code:

```
objB.u...
```

then the method `u` associated with class `B` would be invoked. When a class has a method which has the same name as a method in one of its superclasses, this is termed **overloading**.

Inheritance is the key property of the Java programming language. The wise use of inheritance enables the programmer to reuse large chunks of software – not only software that he or she has written, but also software contained within the Java class library. As a simple example of using inheritance for reuse, consider a class which describes the users of an applet. This class would contain instance variables which contain data on each user: their name, their host computer, their email address and access data such as the number of times that they have accessed the applet. The class would also contain methods which access and update these instance variables.

Let us say that we have developed a number of applets using this class, but that we now want to write a new class where we want to differentiate between two types of users: normal users similar to the users of previous applets and privileged users. The former will be allowed to access some of the facilities of the applet; the latter will be able to access all the facilities of the applet but will need to pay for the privilege.

In order to cater for the privileged users we will need to keep track of the amount of use that they are making of the applet and also provide them with a password in order to prevent other users accessing the facilities they are allowed to use.

The important point to make at this juncture is that we can immediately use the class which described users for this applet, and since privileged users will still require the instance variables and methods associated with users we can develop a new class called `PrivilegedUser` which inherits from `User`. This is shown below:

```
Class User {
    // Instance and static variables defining users, for
```

```
   // example their email address

   //  Methods for accessing and updating users' instance
   //  variables
}

Class PrivilegedUser extends User {

   // Instance and static variables required in addition
   // to those in User. For example, a string instance
   // variable which contains the current password of a
   // privileged user.

   // Instance and static methods which access the
   // instance variables and static variables for a
   // privileged user. For example, a method which
   // changes a privileged user's password.
}
```

This reuse through inheritance extends throughout an applet. For example, the Java class library contains facilities for defining windows, menus and buttons which can be used directly and also inherited. For example, you may want to modify a window so that its borders are different or the colour of the window is different.

The only remaining concepts that we would want to remind you of is that of an abstract class and an interface. An abstract class is a class which you cannot directly use to create objects. An abstract class is distinguished from other classes by virtue of the fact that at least one of its methods contains no code at all. Consider the class skeleton shown below:

```
Class A {
   // Instance and static variables for class A
   ...
   // Normal methods
   ...
   abstract void first();
   abstract void second();
   ...
}
```

The keyword abstract in front of the name of a method indicates that the method will have no code attached to it. This means that any class which inherits from class A will have to provide two void methods called first and second.

A good example of the use of abstract methods might occur within an applet which has a wide variety of different types of users, each of which might be charged for their use in a different way. For example, one class of user might be allowed a certain access time free and then be charged at a particular rate; another type of user would not be allowed any free access time but charged at a specific rate from the moment when they start using the applet; and another user might have a highly graduated payment scale which splits their use of the applet into a number of bands which have increasing, or perhaps decreasing, cost. In order to implement this, an abstract class would be defined where the method which calculates charges would be prefaced with the keyword abstract, and a class would be defined for each of the categories of user with the charging method for that class defined within it.

Once this has been done objects described by this new class can be instantiated as before by using the new facility. You will only encounter abstract classes if you are an extensive user of the Java class library or your programs have a high level of reuse.

An **interface** is a similar idea to that of an abstract class. An interface is denoted by using the keywords public and interface. It specifies a number of classes whose body is empty. An example is shown below:

```
public interface NewHandler {
   public int newVal(int x);
   public boolean checkLimit(int x);
}
```

This provides a hook into which users can add their definitions of newVal and checkLimit. This is achieved by means of the keyword implements. An example of its use is shown below:

```
class NumBasher implements NewHandler {
   public int newVal(int x) {
   return (x+3);
   }

   public boolean checkLimit(int x) {
   return (x > 200);
   }
}
```

Here the bodies of the methods newVal and checkLimit are provided and both of these methods can be used to send messages to objects described by the class NumBasher.

You will encounter interfaces when we deal with the subject of multiprocessing later in this chapter.

5.3.5 Some examples of Java classes

The aim of this section is to present some simple examples of classes in order to reinforce some of the ideas that we have described in the chapter. In the following chapters you will discover how to use classes – particularly those associated with the Java class library – but the aim of this chapter is to show you how such classes are developed.

A line handler

The first class which we shall describe is comparatively simple. It defines a line in an applet which has a line drawing facility. A line defined by this class has four components: its starting x coordinate, its starting y coordinate, its finishing x coordinate and its finishing y coordinate. This is shown in Figure 5.1.

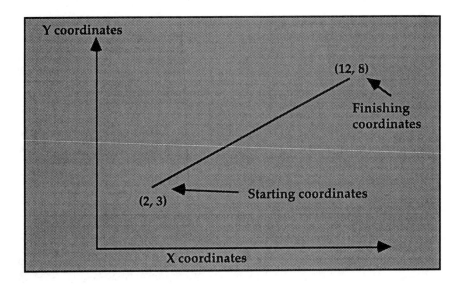

Figure 5.1 A coordinate system.

A number of methods are needed to implement such lines: a constructor method which creates a line given the four coordinate values, methods to access the four coordinate values, methods which alter the coordinate values, a method which returns with the length of a line and a method which checks whether a line is greater than a specified length. The code for this class is shown below:

```
class Line {
    int startX, startY, finishX, finishY;

    public Line (int startXValue, int startYValue, int
                 finishXValue, int finishYValue) {
    startX = startXValue;
    startY = startYValue;
    finishX = finishXValue;
    finishY = finishYValue;
    }

    public void changestartXValue(int newStartXValue) {
    startX = newStartXValue;
    }

    public void changestartYValue(int newStartYValue) {
    startY = newStartYValue;
    }

    public void changefinishXValue(int newFinishXValue) {
    finishX = newFinishXValue;
    }

    public void changefinishYValue(int newFinishYValue) {
```

```
finishY = newFinishYValue;
}

public int getStartXValue() {
return(startX);
}

public int getStartYValue() {
return(startY);
}

public int getFinishXValue() {
return(finishX);
}

public int finishYValue() {
return(finishY);
}

public double lengthLine() {
return Math.sqrt(Math.pow((double)finishX
            - startX,2.0) + Math.pow((double)finishY
            - startY,2.0));
}

public Boolean greaterThan(double lengthGiven) {
return (this.lengthLine() > lengthGiven);
}
```

By now you should be able to understand most of these methods. The only one which might give you some difficulty is the final method `greaterThan` which returns a Boolean value depending on whether the receiver object is greater in length than the argument of the method and which uses the method `lengthLine()` defined within the class. This method contains the keyword `this`. This is used whenever you want to refer to the destination object within a method. Thus, the semantics of:

```
return(this.lengthLine() > lengthGiven);
```

is that the message `lengthLine()` is first sent to the object which is the destination object of the `greaterThan` method. This results in the length of the receiver object being returned. This is compared with the argument of `greaterThan` and a Boolean true or false returned depending on whether the length was greater or less than or equal to the parameter. The `sqrt` operator in the Math library requires a double length numeric and the cast:

```
(double)finishY - startY;
```

is needed because the power operator which raises a number to its power requires a double length number.

A queue handler

The class which is described in this section is one which provides facilities for the processing of queues of users who are waiting to gain access to some of the facilities of a multi-user Java application. The queue will be organized in a first-in-first-out fashion, whereby whoever joins the queue at the earliest point will be the first to be removed from the queue and gain access to the applet. We shall assume that users are defined by the class User and that one of the methods within User, called userName, will retrieve the unique name of the user.

We shall also assume that a number of methods are required: a constructor method which creates an empty queue; a method addUser which adds a user to the queue; a method removeUser which removes the first user in the queue from the queue; a method isQueueFull which checks whether the queue is full; a method isQueueEmpty which checks whether the queue is empty; a method isUserInQueue which checks whether a user is contained in the queue; and noOfUsersInQueue which returns with the number of users currently being stored within the queue.

We shall organize the queue as what is known as a *circular list*. This means allocating an array to store the users with the front of the queue being indexed by the variable frontOfTheQueue (initially this variable would be set to zero). Users will be stored in the array sequentially, starting from the front of the queue, with a new user being placed in the first location after the last member of the queue. When the last member of the queue is at the final position in the array a new user is placed in the first location in the array. The insertion process is shown in Figure 5.2 for a queue implemented using an array with five locations. Initially the array contains three users (*u1*, *u2* and *u3*) starting with the first user at location 2.

Figure 5.2 shows what happens as a user is added, a user removed and two more users added. When user *u5* is added the queue is wrapped around to the next position in the array that can take an element.

The class for this queue can be described as:

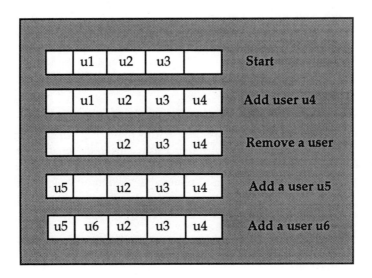

Figure 5.2 A circular queue.

```
Class UserQueue {
  int noOfItemsInQ, frontOfTheQueue, queueCapacity;
  String queue[];

  Queue(int capacity) {
  ...
  }

  public void addUser(User name) {
  ...
  }

  public User removeUser() {
  ...
  }

  public boolean isQueueFull() {
  ...
  }

  public boolean isQueueEmpty() {
  ....
  }

  public boolean isUserInQueue(User usName) {
  ...
  }

  public int noOfUsersInQueue() {
  ...
  }

}
```

The instance variable noOfItemsInQ contains the number of users in the queue, the instance variable frontOfTheQueue contains an integer which points at the first element in the queue and the instance variable queueCapacity contains the capacity of the queue in terms of the maximum number of users that can be stored in the queue. Let us now examine the detailed code for each of these methods. First the constructor:

```
Queue(int capacity) {
queueCapacity = capacity;
frontOfTheQueue = 0;
noOfItemsInQ = 0;
String queue[] = new String[capacity];
}
```

This just sets the queue to be empty with the first insertion position of a user being the first element of the array (don't forget that Java arrays start at index 0).

The code for the method addUser is shown below:

```
public void addUser(User name) {
noOfItemsInQ++;
```

```
If (noOfItemsInQ > queueCapacity) {
    // Code to handle the error condition of a user being
    // added to a queue which has reached its full
    // capacity;
}else
    this.addNthUser(noOfItemsInQ);
}
```

This code first increments the number of users in the queue by one and then places the user known as name into its position in the queue. This position is calculated by the method addNthUser which we shall define later. This adds an item to the queue at its nth position where the argument does not represent the index but the position in the queue. It is very tempting to specify that position will be 1 larger than the end of the queue; however, don't forget that the queue may wrap around and start again at the beginning of the array so when we come to write the code we must cater for this wrap-around. We have also omitted the code that would need to be written in order to cater for the error which would happen if someone used addUser to add a user to a queue which was already full.

The code for removeUser is shown below:

```
public User removeUser() {
if (noOfItemsInQ > 0){
    noOfItemsInQ--;
    if(frontOfTheQueue == capacity-1)
        frontOfTheQueue = 0;
    else
        frontOfTheQueue++;
}
else{
    // Code to cater for the error of a user being removed
    // from an empty queue
}
}
```

The code first checks whether there is a user in the queue to be removed. If the queue is empty, then code which responds to this error is specified; we have omitted it for the time being. The code which is executed if there is at least one user in the queue first decrements the number of users within the receiver object and then increments the pointer which points at the first item in the queue. Again you might have been tempted to increment the value of this instance variable by one. However, don't forget that this pointer may be at the end of the array which represents the queue and it will then need to be reset to 1. Instead of incrementing the pointer by one we have used an if statement to check if the queue needs to wrap around.

The code for the method isQueueFull is straightforward:

```
public boolean isQueueFull() {
return(noOfItemsInQ == queueCapacity);
}
```

It just returns a Boolean value which depends on whether the capacity of the array has been reached. Similarly the code for isQueueEmpty is straightforward:

```
public boolean isQueueEmpty() {
return(noOfItemsInQ == 0);
}
```

The code for noOfUsersInQueue is shown below. Again this is straightforward:

```
public int noOfUsersInQueue() {
return (noOfItemsInQ);
}
```

The final method that needs to be described is isUserInQueue. This checks whether there is a user in the queue who has a specified name. The code for this method is shown below:

```
public boolean isUserInQueue(User usName) {
int   count = 0;
while (count < noOfItemsInQ) {
   count++;
   if (this.getNthUser(count) == usname.userName()) {
     return (true);
   }
}
return(false);
}
```

This just loops around each user in the queue, starting at the first user, and returns true when the user has been found. It makes use of the method userName which we have assumed is defined for the class User and which returns the name of the user which is the destination object.

The code for the class now looks like:

```
ClassUserQueue {
   int noOfItemsInQ, frontOfTheQueue, queueCapacity;
   String queue[];

   Queue(int capacity) {
   queueCapacity = capacity;
   frontOfTheQueue = 0;
   noOfItemsInQ = 0;
     String queue[] = new String[capacity];
   }

   public void addUser(User name) {
   noOfItemsInQ++;
   If (noOfItemsInQ > queueCapacity) {
      // Code to handle the error condition of a user
      // being added to a queue which has reached its full
```

```
    // capacity;
  }
  else
    this.addNthUser(noOfItemsInQ);
  }

  public User removeUser() {
  if (noOfItemsInQ > 0) {
    noOfItemsInQ--;
    if(frontOfTheQueue == capacity-1)
      frontOfTheQueue = 0;
    else
      frontOfTheQueue++;
  } else{
      // Code to cater for the error of a user being
      // removed from an empty queue
  }
  }

  public boolean isQueueFull() {
  return(noOfItemsInQ == queueCapacity);
  }

  public boolean isQueueEmpty() {
  return(noOfItemsInQ == 0);
  }

  public int noOfUsersInQueue() {
  return (noOfItemsInQ);
  }

  public boolean isUserInQueue(User usName) {
  int  count = 0;
  while (count < noOfItemsInQ) {
    count++;
    if (this.getNthUser(count) == usname.userName()) {
      return (true);
    }
  }
  return(false);
  }
```

The only remaining part of the class which is not defined is the methods getNthUser and addNthUser. The former gets the *n*th user in the queue, where by the *n*th user we do not mean the user indexed by *n* in the string array but logically the *n*th user. The latter adds a user into the *n*th position in the queue where again we take the interpretation of *n* in the previous sentence. The first decision that needs to be made about these methods is what access status they should have. Since we have already stated that items are only added to the end of a queue we should not make the method addNthUser generally available, as an outside user of this method could, in theory, use it to write to the middle of the queue. We shall, hence, make this method private. Since there may be some applications which want to examine the *n*th item in a queue it is permissible to make getNthUser a public method. It will certainly do no harm since it does not alter the state of any destination object. The code for the method addNthUser is shown below; it is defined within the class UserQueue like all the other methods.

```
private void addNthUser(int n, User userToBeAdded) {
int index;
index = frontOfTheQueue + n - 1;
if (index >= capacity)
   index = index % capacity;
queue[index] = userToBeAdded;
}
```

The code uses the remainder operator to obtain the correct position within the array queue for insertion to take place.

The code for getNthUser is shown below:

```
public User getNthUser(int n) {
int index;
index = frontOfTheQueue + n - 1;
if (index >= capacity)
   index = index % capacity;
return(queue[index]);
}
```

An access table

This example forms part of the security system of an applet. One of the major concerns of the developers of software for the Internet is that of preventing illegal access to a system's resources and also identifying illegal access when it happens as quickly as possible. One of the most common ways of illegally accessing a system is via the password of a known user. There are a number of ways in which such passwords can be made available to a potential intruder. One way has been for the intruder to log in under a user's identity and try a number of passwords which the intruder has guessed. This can be a very successful strategy if the intruder knows anything about the personal circumstances of the user, as many employ their spouse's name, their own Christian name, the name of their dog or other related words as their password.

Another way of obtaining a password is via physical theft. Users often keep their passwords in diaries or in drawers in their offices; one of us has even visited a company where some of the employees seemed to keep their passwords on a white board in their office. A third way of appropriating a password is to tap a communication line and read the password letters as they are being typed in. These are just a few of the ways in which valid passwords can be obtained by an intruder. Given that there is a moderate risk that this would happen, how can a system determine that an intrusion has happened?

One way is to take advantage of the fact that the vast majority of users of computer systems are people of habit. For example, one of us tends to use a computer to access programs in the early morning and to log in three or four days a week. A sales clerk for a company may only access a system twice, stay logged on up until lunchtime, log off and then, after lunchtime, log on again. In order to determine whether a user is behaving in an unpredictable way, and hence may be being impersonated by an intruder, applications keep details of the accesses made by users. This data would include: the date of last logging on, the number of accesses since the beginning of the month, the average number of accesses per day and so on. A program known as a **security monitor** would scan through this data and display the identity of any users who were behaving in a different way to that in which they have behaved in the past. Normally applications keep large amounts of security data on users and it would be too ambitious to develop a class which stored all this data. For the sake of the aim of this chapter – that of learning about classes in Java – we shall assume that only two items of data are kept: the time of last access to the system and also the number of accesses made in the current day.

We shall assume that we require a class which will be known as SecurityRecord which holds security data. This class will require access to a class called User which will contain the time at which a user last accessed the system and the number of accesses that have occurred within the current day. This User class will look like:

```java
class User {
    int lastAccessTime, noOfAccessesToday;
    String userId;

    // Other instance variables such as the email address
    // of the user.

    public int getNoOfAccessesToday() {
    // Code for getNoOfAccessesToday
    }

    public int getLastAccessTime() {
    // Code for getLastAccessTime
    }

    public void setNoOfAccessesToday(int acceses) {
    // Code for setNoOfAccessesToday
    }

    public void setLastAccessTime(int time) {
    // Code for setLastAccessTime
    }

    public String getUserId() {
    // Code for getuserId
    }

    // Code for other methods which correspond to messages
    // that can be sent to a user.

}
```

The SecurityRecord class will contain an instance variable which is an array of UserRecords. Let us assume that a number of methods are required: a method logsOn which has two parameters, namely a userId and a time at which the user whose identity is userId has logged on; a series of methods which, given a userId, access the security information associated with that user; constructors which initialize the array containing the security information; and a method which adds a new user to the array.

The class description of this class will look like:

```
Class SecurityRecord {
  accessTable User[];
  int noOfUsers;

  public SecurityRecord() {
  // Code for this constructor method which initializes
  // the table containing security information. Assumes
  // that the default initialization will be 100.
  }

  public SecurityRecord(int arraySize) {
  // Code for this constructor method which initializes
  // the table containing security information. Assumes
  // that the default initialization will be given by
  // arraySize.
  }

  public int getNoAccessesForUser{String userIdentity) {
  // Code for getNoAccesses
  }

  public int getLastAccessforUser(String userIdentity) {
  // Code for getLastAccess
  }

  public void logsOn(userIdentity: String, time: int) {
  // Code for logsOn
  }

  public void addUser(User us) {
  // Code for addUser
  }

}
```

The main thing to notice about this class is that there are two constructors provided. The first allocates 100 elements to the array which holds user security details, the second allocates a number of elements specified by the user of the class.

The code for these two constructors is shown below:

```
public SecurityRecord() {
noOfUsers = 0;
accessTable = new User[100];
}
```

```
public SecurityRecord(int arraySize) {
noOfUsers = 0;
accessTable = new User[arraySize];
}
```

The code for the method which provides the number of accesses that a user has made, given the user's identity, is shown below. It uses a private method findIndex. This method finds the position within the array of the specified user and returns with the index of this position. For the time being do not worry about the operation of this method: its code will be shown later. The code is:

```
public int getNoAccessesForUser{String userIdentity) {
int index = accessTable.findIndex(userIdentity);
return (accessTable[index].getNofOfAccessesToday());
}
```

The code for the method which provides the time of last access is shown below. It is similar to getNoAccessesForUser.

```
public int getLastAccessforUser(String userIdentity) {
int index = accessTable.findIndex(userIdentity);
return (accessTable[index].getLastAccessTime());
}
```

The code for the method which updates the instance variables when a user logs on is shown below. Again it uses the private method findIndex to determine the position of the user within the security table.

```
public void logsOn(String userIdentity, int time) {
int index = accessTable.findIndex(userIdentity);
accessTable[index].setLastAccessTime(time);
accessTable[index].
  setNoOfAccessesToday(accessTable[index].
  getNoOfAccessesToday()+1);
}
```

Here the index of the user is found using findIndex, then the new time of access is set by sending the message setLastAccessTime and the number of accesses incremented by one by sending the message:

```
setNoOfAccessesToday(accessTable[index].
getNoOfAccessesToday()+1)
```

The final code, that for addUser, is shown below. All it does is to increment the total number of users and adds the new user to the end of the array holding users.

```
public voidaddUser(User us) {
noOfUsers++;
accessTable[noOfUsers] = us;
}
```

The final method is the private method findIndex which finds a specified user within the table containing security details. We shall make the rather simplistic assumption that a simple linear search is used. If the array contains a large number of users, then such a search would be inefficient. However, for the time being let us make this simplifying assumption; Chapter 6 describes some more efficient ways of organizing data. We shall also make the assumption that the user being searched for is contained in the array.

```java
private int findIndex(String usId) {
int i = 0;
while (i < noOfUsers){
  if (accessTable[i].getUserId.equals(usId)) {
    return (i)
  }
  i++;
}
```

Again this is defined as a private method since it has knowledge of how the security information is stored. This gives the full definition of the class as:

```java
Class SecurityRecord {
  accessTable User[];
  int noOfUsers;

  public SecurityRecord() {
    noOfUsers = 0;
    accessTable = new User[100];
  }

  public SecurityRecord(int arraySize) {
    noOfUsers = 0;
    accessTable = new User[arraySize];
  }

  public int getNoAccessesForUser(String userIdentity) {
    int index = accessTable.findIndex(userIdentity);
    return (accessTable[index].getNofOfAccessesToday());
  }

  public int getLastAccessforUser(String userIdentity) {
    int index = accessTable.findIndex(userIdentity);
    return (accessTable[index].getLastAccessTime());
  }

  public void logsOn(String userIdentity, int time) {
    int index = accessTable.findIndex(userIdentity);
    accessTable[index].setLastAccessTime(time);
    accessTable[index].
      setNoOfAccessesToday(accessTable[index].
      getNoOfAccessesToday()+1);
  }
```

```
public voidaddUser(User us) {
  noOfUsers++;
  accessTable[noOfUsers] = us;
}

private int findIndex(String usId) {
  int i = 0;
  while (i < noOfUsers) {
    if (accessTable[i].getUserId.equals(usId)) {
    return (i);
  }
  i++;
  }
}

}
```

5.3.6 General classes

So far the classes that we have described have dealt with specific data types. For example, the queue example that we used earlier processes queues of users. If we wish to take the reuse idea of object-oriented technology further, then we need to be able to develop more general classes. For example, queues are ubiquitous in computing: they are used in operating systems to contain the names of processes which are awaiting execution by a processor; they are also used in operating systems to hold print requests which are to be processed by a printer; in an air traffic control system they are used to hold the identity of planes awaiting landing; and in a communications system they are used to hold packets of messages awaiting processing by the computers in the system. Clearly, for queues there is some leverage in being able to write general-purpose packages which can process a wide variety of data. This holds not only for queues but also for many other classes.

Java contains facilities for developing general-purpose classes. In order to describe them we shall use a simple example of a look-up table which can contain a wide variety of data. The function of such a table is to hold items, for example integers or strings, where an important message which can be sent to a look-up table is one which checks that an item is stored in the table. We shall assume that a number of methods are required: two constructor methods which set up look-up tables, one of which has a default value for the maximum number of items in the table with the other setting up a specified number of entries provided by the user of the class. We shall also assume that the class describing such look-up tables requires a method which inserts an item in the table, removes an item, checks whether the table is full, finds the number of items in the table and checks whether an item is in the table.

Before looking at the code for such a general class it is worth looking at the way in which we can declare objects and allocate space for them. For example, let us assume that the class describing look-up tables is called LookUpTable. We can tell the Java system that certain variables are to hold look-up tables by the declaration:

```
LookUpTable variable list;
```

So, for example:

```
LookUpTable newTable, oldTable, midTable;
```

tells the Java system that three identifiers are to be used which will be look-up tables. This is just a declaration: it does not allocate any space. To allocate space the new facility is required. For example, the statement:

```
LookUpTable symbols = new LookupTable();
```

will allocate the space required for a look-up table `symbols`. If a constructor method corresponding to `LookUpTable()` has been defined, then the amount of space allocated would be found in the code associated with that method.

It is also worth looking at the use of the `this` keyword introduced in Section 5.3.5 and that of the keyword `super` which you have not met before. When `this` is used within an instance method it refers to the receiver object. When it is used within a constructor method the effect is subtly different. When `this` is encountered it is taken as a reference to the name of the class. So, for example, if the Java interpreter encounters the statement:

```
this(1000, 300);
```

within a constructor method for the class `ClassName` then it will assume that this is a reference to a constructor `ClassName` which has two arguments. It will then look for the constructor and carry out the code for it.

The action of `super` is similar. If the Java system encounters the word `super` either with no arguments, or with a series of arguments, then it will execute a constructor within the superclass of the class within which it is used. So, for example, if we have a class `Up` which has three constructors: one with no arguments, one with a single argument and one with two arguments, and a class `NewUp` which inherits from `Up`, then the code:

```
super();
```

within a constructor method of `NewUp` is taken to be a reference to the constructor within `Up` which requires no arguments and an object described by `Up` is constructed. However, if the code:

```
super(argument1);
```

is encountered then this is taken to be a reference to the constructor in `Up` which has one argument and the method for this constructor is executed. Finally if the code:

```
super(argument1, argument2);
```

is encountered then the two-argument constructor method of the superclass Up is executed and an object described by Up is created. Before looking at the use of both this and super within the constructors of a real class there is one more point to make concerning the use of super within a class which does not explicitly inherit from another class.

The discussion above must have seemed a little abstract so it is worth looking now at an example. Let us first look at the instance variables and the two constructor methods for look-up tables. These are shown below:

```
Class LookUpTable {
    int noOfItems, size;
    holder Object[];

    public LookUpTable(int sizeTable) {
        super();
        noOfItems = 0;
        size = sizeTable;
        holder = new Object [sizeTable];
    }

    public LookUpTable() {
        this(100);
    }

    // Code for the remaining methods within LookUpTable.

}
```

There are a number of important points to be made about this code. The first is that one of the instance variables is an array which is to hold objects. Also, remember that Object is a built-in type within the Java system and every object type that is declared within a Java program inherits from Object. Using Object effectively informs the Java system that we can add items of any type to a look-up table.

The code for the two constructor methods is also of note. The first statement super() within the constructor informs the Java system to look for methods within the body of the code which are contained in the class which is the superclass of LookUpTable. Once the LookUpTable has been constructed the remainder of the code initializes it. Remember that Object will know implicitly how to construct any object whose class you declare.

The second constructor method sets up a look-up table which will contain, as a default, 100 objects. First the number of items in the table is set to zero and then the method calls the constructor method defined previously to set up the look-up table. In this code the keyword this is used to denote the class LookUpTable, so the statement:

```
this(100);
```

is equivalent to :

```
LookUpTable(100);
```

It is worth asking why we use super in the code. You might say that the same effect can be achieved by the code shown below:

```
Class LookUpTable {
  int NoOfItems, size;
  holder Object[];

  public LookUpTable(int sizeTable) {
    this();
    noOfItems = 0;
    size = sizeTable;
    holder = new Object [sizeTable];
  }

  public LookUpTable() {
    this(100);
  }

  // Code for the remaining methods within LookUpTable.

}
```

The reason is that it creates an endless loop. In order to see this, consider what happens when the constructor with a single argument is invoked. The first statement in this constructor (this()) instructs the Java interpreter to invoke the zero argument constructor. The only statement in this constructor is:

```
this(100)
```

which means that the single argument constructor is invoked again. This, in turn, invokes the zero argument constructor and so on until the memory space of the Java interpreter is exhausted and it gives up with an error message.

The code for the remaining methods is shown below.

```
public void insertItem(Object item) {
  holder[NoOfItems] = item;
  NoOfItems++;
}

public void removeItem(Object item) {
  int i = this.findIndex(item);
  while (i < NofItems-1) {
    holder[i] = holder[i+1];
    i++;
  }
  NoOfItems--;
}

public boolean fullTable() {
  return (noOfItems == size);
}
```

```
public int noInTable() {
   return (noOfItems);
}

public boolean inTable(Object item) {
   int i = this.findIndex(item);
   return (i == noOfItems);
}
```

The code for these methods is fairly self-explanatory. Two of the methods, inTable and removeItem, require the use of the private method findIndex. The code for this method is shown below:

```
private int findIndex(object item) {
int i = 0;
while (i < noOfItems){
   if (this.holder[i].equals(item)) {
      return (i);
   }
   i++
}
return (i);
}
```

Again a simple sequential search is employed. The method looks for the object item within the array holder. If it encounters it then it returns with its index. However, if it does not encounter it, it returns with a value one greater than the number of items in holder. The one important thing to notice about this code is that in comparing equality we have not used ==. The reason for this is that we could be inserting objects into the table for which the == operator is not defined. We have assumed that in the class that defines the objects that can be inserted there is a method called equals which carries out some equality comparison between two objects. For example, if we were going to insert User objects into the look-up table and the User class defined these objects in terms of instance variables which contained a user's identity, email and so on, then we would need to define a method equals within this class which took two users and compared their identities. Only then could we start inserting users into the look-up table as, for example, in:

```
User newUser;
LookUpTable newCreatedUsers;
   ...
newCreatedUsers.insertItem(newUser);
```

When you encounter an object of type Object within a Java program you will often need to identify what type of object it is. The operator instanceOf does this. Its left hand operand is an object and its right hand operand is the name of a class. It returns true if the object is of the class and false otherwise. For example

```
stObj instanceOf StringBuffer
```

returns true if the object stObj is a StringBuffer and false otherwise.

5.3.7 Exceptions and other mechanisms

So far the examples which we have presented have had an air of unreality about them. For example, when we inserted items in a table we assumed that the table had enough room to contain each item, and when we removed an item from a table we assumed that the item was in the table. This is, of course, something of a simplification and it is now necessary to look at some of the techniques that can be used to cater for such error conditions.

The first technique is to use a method to check out a particular error condition before executing code which might encounter that condition. For example, assume that we are writing a method which inserts an item into some data structure such as a table. Before executing this method it would be wise to invoke another method which would check that the table had space for the item to be inserted. If it didn't then the method would not carry out the execution.

The second technique – really a variation on the second method – is to associate with a method some parameter which will indicate whether the error condition was met when performing the code within the method. For example, assume that we have defined a class which implements a queue and we wish to take the first element off the queue. If the queue is empty, an error will occur. Normally the method which takes an element from a queue will have no parameters and just return the element which has been removed. However, in order to cater for this error condition a Boolean parameter would be used. For example, the definition of such a method for a queue of strings might be:

```
public String removeFirst(boolean empty) {
If (noOfItems == 0) {
   empty = true;
   return ("");
}
else
{
// Code which is executed when the queue contains at
// least one entry
}
```

If the queue is empty, then the Boolean parameter is given the value true and the method returns the empty string.

This has been the style of coding that we have adopted for the Java code that we have written. However, there is a specific facility within Java which is often used to handle error conditions. It is known as the **exception** facility.

An exception is a piece of code which is executed when something untoward happens in some Java code. Exceptions can be used by the Java programmer to allow a program to die gracefully or recover from a potentially disastrous occurrence such as an array going out of bounds or a floating point overflow occurring. Within the Java class libraries there are a number of exceptions which are provided. For example, the Vector package described in Chapter 6 which implements tables is associated with a number of exceptions which are invoked when error conditions arise, such as an attempt being made to access a vector with an index which is a negative number. An example of the use of an exception is shown below.

Java contains an exception known as `ArithmeticException` which is invoked when, for example, an integer is divided by another integer and the second integer is zero. If the programmer wants to catch this exception, then Java provides a facility known as `try-catch`. An example of this facility is shown below:

```
try {
    result = old / new;
}
catch(ArithmeticException e) {
    System.out.println("You cannot divide by zero");
}
```

The statement(s) within the curly brackets following the keyword `try` are executed and if the exception specified (arithmetic overflow) within the `catch` occurs, then the code within the curly brackets part of the catch is executed. This results in a message "`You cannot divide by zero`" being displayed.

5.3.8 Threads

Java contains facilities for multiprocessing and concurrency implemented using a concept known as a **thread**. You may think that this discussion of multiprocessing is a little out of place within a chapter devoted to classes. However, the way that threads are implemented intimately involves the use of a class. A thread is a section of code which can be executed independently, with a Java applet or application consisting of a number of concurrent threads executing simultaneously. Threads are implemented by means of the built-in class `Thread`. One way to implement a thread is to subclass the `Thread` class and produce another class to which you can give any name; an example is shown below:

```
ClassMyThread extends Thread {
    public MyThread(String str) {
    super(str);
    }

    public void run () {
    // Code for thread
    }
}
```

What is happening here is that a new thread class (`MyThread`) has been created. The constructor method uses `super` to call the constructor within `Thread` which takes a string that uniquely identifies a thread. The method `run` overrides the method `run` within `Thread` and when used with `new` creates a new thread described by `MyThread`. For example, the code:

```
new MyThread("First thread").start()
```

constructs a new thread, gives it a string name ("`First thread`") and starts the execution of the thread. The method `start()` forms part of the `Thread` class.

The code that would be executed would be that contained in the body of the run method shown above. Similarly the code:

```
new MyThread("Second thread").start()
```

will create a second thread with another name ("Second thread") and start that. The code for this second thread is the same as the one in the first thread. Usually a thread's body is a loop, for example it may refresh a screen or implement some animation and the body of the thread will contain that loop.

A thread can be in a number of states:

- *New thread.* A thread can be created and not started. The system will not have allocated any resources to it.

- *Runnable.* The system has started the thread. It is important to point out that this does not mean that the thread is automatically running: the thread may have been implemented on a single processor system and another thread may have gained control of the processor.

- *Not runnable.* The thread cannot run. This can happen for a number of reasons. For example, some Java code has called the suspend() method – part of the Thread class which makes a thread unable to run.

- *Dead.* A thread could have died for two reasons: the code in its run body could have completed execution or a stop() message could be sent to it, where stop is a method implemented in the Thread class.

The description above indicates that there are a number of methods which Thread implements and which can be employed by the programmer. Some of the more important of these are shown below:

- Thread is a constructor which creates threads.

- start() is a method which makes a thread capable of being executed; if there are enough system resources available then the thread will be run.

- stop() kills a thread and makes it dead.

- isAlive() is a method which returns a Boolean. It returns true if the thread has been started and not stopped.

- setPriority() sets the priority of a thread so that within a series of concurrently executing threads those with a high priority will gain more use of the processor resources available.

It is possible to create threads using an interface known as Runnable. This forms part of the java.lang library. This interface consists of only one abstract method run which is defined as public abstract void. The code for the creation of a thread is defined in the example shown below:

```
class calcThread implements Runnable {
  public void run() {
  // Code for the thread here
```

```
        }
}
```

A class that has been developed using the `Runnable` interface can be executed by passing an instance of the class to a newly created `Thread` object. This is shown below:

```
calcThread name = new calcThread();
new Thread(name).start();
```

This, then, is a brief introduction to threads; in the last half of this book you will encounter them in action. They are a crucial facility when you develop applets.

5.3.9 Java programs

So far in the book we have described the elements of Java but have not fully described the structure of a Java program. You may remember from the first chapter that you can construct two types of entities using the Java programming language: applets, which are code fragments which can be embedded in any Java-compatible browser, and applications which are standalone programs. Chapters 10 and 11 describe how to develop each of these types of software in much more detail. However, it is worth describing the program structure of a Java application here for completeness' sake. The code below is that of a very simple Java application which can be executed:

```
public class HelloWorld {
        public static void main (String args[]) {
        System.out.println("Hello World");
        }
}
```

To construct a Java application all you need do is to declare a single class – the one above is called `HelloWorld` – and then declare a method within it called `main` which has a single argument that is an array of strings. The method will be static and will not return any values. The string arguments are used to pass data from the world outside to the application, although this is not done in the application above; however, you will always need to declare the arguments as part of the method `main`. Chapter 11 describes the use of these arguments in much more detail. The only processing that occurs within the `main` method is for the string `"Hello World"` to be displayed. This is achieved by means of the message `println("Hello World")` being sent to the object `System`. You will remember from the previous chapter that the Java system contains an extensive library used for stream-oriented input/output and that the statement `System.out.println ("Hello World")` is just an example of its use.

5.4 Summary

This chapter has now described all that you need to know about classes necessary for the development of applets and applications. We have described the fact that a class consists of a number of instance variables and instance methods, with the former implementing the state of an object. We have described the various access mechanisms that are available and also class variables and class methods which are associated with a class rather than with each object defined by a class. We have also shown how you can write general classes and how exceptions can be used to monitor error conditions.

CHAPTER
SIX

Libraries

AIMS

- To introduce the concept of a Java library.
- To introduce the concept of a Java package.
- To describe the main components of a Java library.
- To use the Java `util` package as an example of a package, concentrating specifically on the `Vector` class.

6.1 Introduction

The Java system contains a number of class libraries which enable the programmer to create a wide variety of objects which implement much of the functionality required for the type of network applications that Java is targeted at. The next three chapters describe the most important of these libraries and give you plenty of practice in their use. The aim of this chapter is to provide an introduction to the concept of a library. It is easy to write abstractly about libraries so we have decided to focus our introduction onto one of the more useful and easy-to-understand collections of classes: the Java utility package `util` and, in particular, one part of the library, the `Vector` class.

A package is the name given in Java to a collection of classes which have some connection with each other. The `util` package consists of a number of classes which are used to implement useful data structures and facilities. Briefly, the `util` package consists of:

- Data structure classes: these implement storage structures which programmers tend to use in most applications. These include bitset, hash table, dictionary stack and vector.

- The `Date` class: this implements dates in a variety of representations.

- The `StringTokenizer` class: this class provides the facility whereby a string can be converted into its constituents. For example, the class provides facilities which would convert the string `"Hello there I am a Java programmer"` to the seven strings `"Hello"` `"there"` `"I"` `"am"` `"a"` `"Java"` `"programmer"`.

- The `Properties` class implements data structures which implement system properties.

- The `Observer` and `Observable` classes implement objects which can 'watch' the state of other objects. For example, such objects can respond when another object has one of its instance variables changed.

- The `Random` class implements methods used for the generation of random numbers.

These, then, are the classes which form part of the Java utility package `java.util`. Each set of related classes is identified by a name which informs the reader that it forms part of the Java library and gives the name of the package and the name of the facility that the classes implement. For example, the `BitSet` facility within the `util` package is identified by the name:

```
java.util.BitSet
```

If you wish to use the facilities of a particular library you inform the Java system by means of the `import` directive. For example, the statement:

```
import java.util.Hashtable;
```

informs the Java interpreter that the `Hashtable` class within `util` is to be used by the program that follows. If you wish to import all the classes in a library then you can use the * character as a wild card. For example:

```
import java.util.*;
```

means import all classes in the package `java.util`.

6.2 Classes

The aim of this section is to examine a class which implements some very useful data structures that you will need time and time again. Using the `util` classes alone will considerably shorten the amount of code that you will need to write in a Java applet or application. Before looking at these classes in more detail it is worth describing what you will find in the documentation for a class library.

The current documentation for the packages provides standard bureaucratic details such as the version number, the date of the version and the developer who was responsible for it. After this comes the important documentation:

- *The constructor index*: a list of the constructors which can be used in Java programs. Most of the classes in the Java library have a number of constructors associated with them. There is usually a constructor which creates an uninitialized object described by the class and a series of constructors which initialize part or the whole of an object described by the class.

- *A list of instance variables*. Some of the classes within the Java library list the instance variables associated with the class. Almost invariably these are private and hence the user of the package is not allowed to access them directly. This is in accordance with the information hiding principle described in Chapter 5.

- *The method index*. This lists the methods which can be used by someone who employs the class within his or her applet or application. The current Java documentation gives the types of the parameters, the name of the method, its access status and a brief description of what it does.

It is important to point out that some of the classes found within the Java library are abstract classes: classes which have place holder methods which do not implement any code (for an explanation of such abstract methods see Chapter 5). A good example of such a method within the `util` package is the class `Dictionary`. This class is inherited by the class `Hashtable` to produce a class which is not abstract.

It is also important to point out that quite a large number of classes store objects which are described by the class `Object`. This means that they can store a wide variety of objects as described in Chapter 5.

Another important point to make is that the description of the methods within the Java class library often reference the exceptions which will be raised whenever an error condition occurs such as an attempt to store a value within a data structure when that data structure is full.

6.2.1 The `Vector` class

This is one of the most useful classes in the `util` package; one which we find ourselves using quite a lot within applets or applications. It describes objects which look like arrays in that they are indexable, but they differ from arrays in that they can extend themselves. This means that if a `Vector` object finds itself running out of space it can request more space from the Java run-time system to extend itself. It is important to point out that by describing the Vector class we are not elevating it in importance above other classes in the Java libraries, we are just using it as an example.

The Vector class is associated with three instance variables. The first is capacityIncrement which specifies the increase in storage which will be added to a vector when it runs out of space. If this instance variable is zero then the capacity of a Vector object is doubled when it runs out of space. The second is elementCount which contains the number of elements in the vector. The third is elementData which is an array where the items in the Vector object are stored.

There are three constructor methods associated with vectors. Vector with two int arguments sets up an empty vector with the first parameter holding the number of items that the vector is assumed to hold and the second parameter specifying the increase in size when the vector becomes full. Vector with one argument sets up an empty vector with the sole argument specifying the initial capacity of the vector. This constructor sets the capacityIncrement instance variable to zero, ensuring that the capacity of a Vector object is doubled whenever it runs out of space. The final constructor is Vector without any arguments. The size of the vector is set to a system-defined default with any Vector objects instantiated in this way doubling their size when they run out of capacity.

Thus:

```
Vector    smallQ = new Vector(20, 3),
          largeQ = new Vector(),
          medQ = new Vector(1100);
```

declares three Vector identifiers. It declares the first vector smallQ to initially contain 20 elements with the size of the object being incremented by 3 whenever it runs out of space. It declares the Vector largeQ to contain the system default of the number of items initially assumed to be held in the vector and assumes the vector's size will be doubled whenever it runs out of space. The final declaration informs the Java system that the vector medQ will initially contain 1100 elements and will be doubled in size whenever it runs out of space.

There are a large number of methods associated with Vector objects. The aim of this section is not to detail all of them but to briefly describe a small number in order to give you a flavour of the sort of facilities a data structure class will provide within the Java system.

- public void addElement(Object) adds the object which is its argument to the end of the vector object to which it sends the message corresponding to this method. Notice that the parameter of the method is Object; this means that any objects can be held in a vector.

- public int capacity() returns with the capacity of the vector object to which this message is sent. This integer represents the current upper limit of items that can be stored in the object.

- public int size() returns with the current number of objects stored in the vector. This is different to the capacity: the latter represents the current maximum number of elements which can be contained in the vector before the vector is increased; the former represents the number of items actually stored.

- public boolean contains(Object) returns the Boolean value true if the object which is the parameter of the method is currently stored in the vector object which receives the message corresponding to the method.

- public int lastIndexOf(object) searches for the object which is the parameter to the method and returns an index to it if it is found; however, if it is not found, then it returns the value −1.

- public Object firstElement() returns with the first object in the vector object to which the message corresponding to this method is sent.

- public void removeElements() removes all the elements from the object to which the message corresponding to the method is sent. The vector becomes empty.

These, then, are a small selection of methods which are associated with vectors. Before leaving this section it is worth developing some code which involves vectors in order to give you an idea of the power of the class library. The example which we shall use is that of a simple message handler which processes messages associated with a computer in a computer network, stores them in a queue associated with input messages and transfers them to an output queue ready for transfer to another computer. The class will represent the computer and the two queues as three instance variables: a string variable which is the name of the computer and two vectors which contain the messages that are to be stored in the queues. We shall assume that the messages are strings, but will not be concerned with what the semantics of the messages are. For the first time in the book we will include program code which checks whether potential error conditions can occur. This code will set a parameter of the method depending on whether the error has occurred or whether the processing proceeded normally.

The header for the class is:

```
Class MessageSwitch {
  Vector inQ, outQ;
  String computerName;
```

Let us assume a number of methods are required:

- public String getComputerName() returns with the name of the computer which is carrying out the process of switching messages from an input queue to an output queue.

- public void sendIn(String String int) adds a message to the input queue of the computer designated by the second parameter. The third parameter will be set to zero if the correct computer has been sent the message; otherwise it will be set to −1.

- void sendFromInToOut(int String) sends the first message in the input queue of the computer specified as the second parameter to the output queue. If the method was carried out correctly, then the integer parameter is set to zero. However, the parameter is set to −1 if the input queue was empty and set to −2 if the message was sent to the wrong computer.

- public String sentOut(String int) returns with the message which is at the front of the output queue. The queue is readjusted so that this message disappears. The string parameter identifies the computer and the int parameter is set to −1 if the output queue is empty and −2 if the wrong computer has been referenced. If the method was carried out correctly, then this parameter will be set to zero.

- public int noInInQ(String int) returns with the number of items currently stored in the input queue of the computer identified by the string parameter. If the string parameter does not match the name of the computer then the int parameter is set to −1. If the method was carried out correctly then the parameter is set to zero.

- public int noInIOutQ(String int) returns with the number of items currently stored in the output queue of the computer identified by the string parameter. If the string parameter does not match the name of the computer, then the int parameter is set to −1. If the method was carried out correctly, then the parameter is set to zero.

We shall also assume that there is one constructor MessageSwitch(string, int) which sets the computer name and initializes both queues to the value given by its second parameter.

The code for the method is reproduced below:

```
public MessageSwitch(String computer, int initialSize) {
inQ = new Vector(initialSize),
outQ = new Vector(initialSize);

computerName = computer;
}
```

This is fairly straightforward: it uses the Vector(int) constructor associated with the Vector class to initialize the two queues.

The code for getComputerName() is shown below:

```
public String getComputerName() {
return (computerName);
}
```

The code for sendIn(String String int) is shown below; again the code is straightforward:

```
public void sendIn(String message, String computer,
                   int errorOccurred) {
errorOccurred = 0;
if (computer != computerName)
  errorOccurred = -1;
else
  inQ.addElement(message)
}
```

This uses the method addElement associated with the Vector class to add an element to the end of inQ. The code for sendFromInToOut(int String) is shown below:

```
void sendFromInToOut(int errorOccurred,
                      String computer) {

errorOccurred = 0;
if (computer != computerName)
  errorOccurred = -2;
else{
  if inQ.size() = 0{
    errorOccurred = -1;
    else{
      String firstMessage = inQ.firstElement();
      inQ.removeElementAt(1);
      outQ.addElement(firstMessage);
    }
  }
}
}
```

The key processing in this method occurs at the end when the first element of the input queue is accessed by sending the firstElement message; this element is then removed by sending the message removeElement and finally the message that has been removed is added to the end of the output queue by sending it the message addElement – all of these messages are contained in the Vector class.

The two methods which interrogate the input and output queues of the class to determine how many items are in each queue are shown below:

```
public int noInInQ(String computer int errorOccurred) {
errorOccurred = 0;
if (computer != computerName)
  errorOccurred = -1;
  return(null);
else
  return (inQ.size());
}
```

```
public int noInOutQ(String computer int errorOccurred) {
errorOccurred = 0;
if (computer != computerName)
  errorOccurred = -1;
  return(null);
else
  return outQ.size();
}
```

This gives the full class definition as:

```
Class MessageSwitch {
  Vector inQ, outQ;
```

```
string computerName;

public MessageSwitch(String computer,
                     int initialSize) {
inQ = new Vector(initialSize),
outQ = new Vector (initialSize);
computerName = computer;
}

public String getComputerName() {
return (computerName);
}

public void sendIn(String message, computer,
                   int errorOccurred) {
errorOccurred = 0;
if (computer != computerName)
  errorOccurred = -1;
else
  inQ.addElement(message)
}

void sendFromInToOut(int errorOccurred,
                     String computer) {
errorOccurred = 0;
if (computer != computerName)
  errorOccurred = -2;
else{
  if inQ. size() == 0 {
    errorOccurred = -1;
    else{
    String firstMessage = inQ.firstElement();
    inQ.removeElementAt(1);
    outQ.addElement(firstMessage);
    }
  }
}

public int noInInQ(String computer int errorOccurred){
errorOccurred = 0;
if (computer != computerName)
  errorOccurred = -1;
  return(null);
else
  return (inQ.size());
}
```

```
public int noInOutQ(string computer
                      int errorOccurred) {
errorOccurred = 0;
if (computer != computerName)
  errorOccurred = -1;
  return(null);
else
  return outQ.size();
}

}
```

6.3 The I/O class library

We conclude this chapter with a very brief look at the I/O class library since it will be used a little in the next six chapters. The package Java.io contains a number of methods for sending data to different input and output devices and needs to be explicitly loaded into your program using the directive:

```
import java.io.*
```

Interaction with the keyboard and the monitor are the two most common streams that the programmer will use and they are implemented by the instance variables in and out of the System class. Writing or reading to these streams is achieved by methods contained in java.io. The input stream works with bytes so that the statement:

```
System.in.read();
```

will read a byte. Printing is achieved by two methods, print and println. The method print sends the output to a buffer until a new line is issued, while the println method will print its parameters straight away. Both of these methods can take all the basic data types of Java as arguments. For example, if nVal was an int and chVal was a character then:

```
System.out.println(nVal, chVal)
```

will display the integer followed by the character.

6.4 Summary

This has been quite a brief look at one of the packages within the Java library which examined one particular class within the util library. As you will find confirmed in the next two chapters the Java library contains a host of facilities which enable the programmer to reduce drastically the amount of code that needs to be written from new.

CHAPTER
SEVEN
The AWT library

AIMS

- To outline the general functions of the library package.
- To describe some of the graphics elements.
- To introduce the event handling system.
- To introduce graphics contexts.
- To introduce font and colour support.

7.1 Introduction

The Abstract Window Toolkit library (AWT) contains pre-built classes of graphical interface elements. While it is possible to build an interface from scratch using the basic drawing primitives (rectangle, line, text) you will, for simplicity and consistency, mainly rely on the tools that the Java language provides.

The AWT library is a relatively new package and, unlike some of the more established window toolkits and widget sets such as *Motif* and *OpenLook*, can look simple and sometimes dated; although it is worth stating that it compares favourably with much of the interface builder software available on PCs. In general appearance, AWT is similar to the early Motif sets on UNIX hosts.

If you are reading this book sequentially, you will have had some experience of coding in Java and, at this stage, your impression of Java could be similar to that of one of the authors (AF): that it is a powerful and useful alternative to C++ which can be used to address the cross-platform issues that have haunted many large-scale projects. The AWT classes can be difficult and fiddly because there is often little consistency between interface elements that seem to be logically related. In addition there is the feeling of tinkering with the unknown that always comes when trying to write an interface without the use of a GUI builder.

Our approach to writing the interface elements of any code is to strike a balance between bespoke elements and the AWT. Where simplicity and development speed are important, the AWT is a quick way of introducing an interface. When it comes to production systems, we tend to have an artist draw the interface from scratch and we use the image libraries of Java together with some extra code to develop interfaces which look professional and functional. At this stage in the life of Java, applets and applications written using the AWT have a dull appearance that only a developer could love, but until something better comes along, it is all there is available to the developer.

One other way of deploying the AWT is to override the sections of the classes which relate to appearance. On the whole, the parts of the AWT which are behind the scenes are sound and so, by careful use of inheritance, it is possible to create a hybrid set of components which have a better appearance than the raw AWT elements but benefit from the underlying functionality. Whichever method you eventually choose for developing interfaces it is worth investigating the AWT library so that you can make informed decisions about your strategy – after all, there will be occasions where the AWT is perfect for the task in hand; if you are not aware of its potential and limitations you could spend time and money developing a bespoke solution without there being any need for it.

7.2 Overview of the AWT

The AWT can be broken down into groups of related classes. In this section we'll make a quick tour of each group and then return to them later by describing some small examples which illustrate them.

- *Containers*. The AWT provides two types of containers: `Windows` and `Panels`. Both classes are subclasses of the Java `Container` class. The `Window` subclasses include `Dialog`, `FileDialog` and `Frame`. They are generally used to hold other elements such as buttons. Panels are used to group elements together in an existing area of a window.

- *Layout managers*. These are used by containers to arrange embedded elements to a particular model, for example laying the elements out in a grid. The various models are used to ensure spacing or alignment, and include `BorderLayout`, `CardLayout`, `FlowLayout` and `GridLayout`. You will meet a number of these in this chapter. Since the classes implement the `LayoutManager` interface it is possible to write new classes to meet particular problems when the supplied classes are deficient.

- *Control elements*. This group of elements provide the means by which users will usually interact with your applications or applets. They include controls such as buttons, menus, choice selectors, text areas and lines, canvases, simple labels, scroll bars, and lists. They form the backbone of the AWT library and will be the building blocks of most Java applications that require user interfaces.

7.3 The AWT at large

To cover this class library, we'll give a series of example code fragments or small applications to cover specific topics. We won't cover every element in the AWT, but there should be enough to give you a solid foundation and allow you to access the AWT library without fear. When you start to use the AWT you will almost certainly begin to develop your own personal style of writing interfaces but, until that happens, the most effective way to progress is to experiment liberally with the classes until you find something that you like the look of which solves the particular problem in hand.

7.3.1 Containers and layouts

The two groups of classes can be logically described together, since they are closely related in practical use. We'll start by showing you how to create containers and then demonstrate some layout techniques.

Using containers

An AWT window is a top-level window without borders or a title bar. As it stands, it is not entirely useful, except for implementing a pop-up window, but it forms the basic building unit for the window subclasses. The Frame subclass, for example, has borders and a title-bar and is normally used as the root window for building standalone Java applications. Each of the subclasses is associated with a default LayoutManager – for example, Dialog uses BorderLayout.

The following code is a very simple application which displays a frame and sets the title of the window:

```
import java.awt.*;

public class FrameDemo {
  public static void main(String args[]) {
    Frame fr = new Frame("We Love Java");
    fr.resize(200,200);
    fr.show();
  }
}
```

This class just creates a frame, sets the title, sizes the frame (to 200 by 200 pixels) and then maps it to the screen. Once you have an object which is described by a class which is subclassed from the Container class (for example, Frame) then you can add other user interface elements quite easily.

Figure 7.1 Screen shot of simple frame.

To make things even simpler, when you write an applet, the applet itself is subclassed from the `Container` class so you can just add elements as you wish. Earlier versions of the Java language didn't have `Applet` subclassed from `Container`, which made it very difficult to use the AWT components in early applets. The screen shot corresponding to the code above is shown as Figure 7.1.

Once you have created a top-level window (which is implicit in the case of an applet) you can use the `Panel` class to divide up the larger interface into manageable sections.

Placing elements using LayoutManager

We'll follow the model of extending our simple class to include more features. In this subsection, we'll demonstrate some of the ways that the `LayoutManager` interface can be used to place elements automatically. Each class that implements the `LayoutManager` interface will place elements according to some algorithm; for example, `BorderLayout` will use the points of the compass.

We will start with the `BorderLayout` class. Our example code looks like this:

```
import java.awt.*;

public class FrameDemo {
   public static void main(String args[]) {
      Button buttons[] = new Button[6];
      Frame fr = new Frame("We Love Java");
```

```
/* Set the layout manager of the frame */
fr.setLayout(new BorderLayout());
/* Add some buttons */
for (int i = 1 ; i < 6; i++) {
  buttons[i] = new Button("Button " + i);
}
/* Place the buttons */
fr.add("North",   buttons[1]);
fr.add("South",   buttons[2]);
fr.add("East",    buttons[3]);
fr.add("West",    buttons[4]);
fr.add("Center", buttons[5]);
fr.pack();
fr.show();
    }
}
```

The code simply pads out the example for frames that we described in the previous section. We define an array of buttons each of which is created with a numbered string. We also explicitly set the layout model for the frame to BorderLayout by means of the method setLayout associated with frames. We then place each button into the frame.

When using the BorderLayout model each element is placed using a string North, East, South, West, and Center. These strings define where in the frame the objects are placed, following the rough basis of a compass (Figure 7.2).

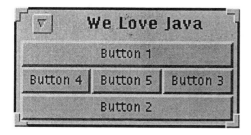

Figure 7.2 A more complex frame.

The element which is placed at the Center location is allocated as much space as has been left over by the other elements. Finally we call the pack() method to shape the frame around the elements and then call show() to display the frame on the screen.

You can see how the elements are placed on the points of a compass. Notice that the first two buttons placed into the frame are expanded to fill the whole of the frame, while the others remain small.

The next layout we'll look at is the FlowLayout. The new code example is:

```
import java.awt.*;

public class FrameDemo {
    public static void main(String args[]) {
        Button buttons[] = new Button[6];
        Frame fr = new Frame("We Love Java");
        /* Set the layout manager of the frame */
        fr.setLayout(new FlowLayout(FlowLayout.LEFT));
        /* Add some buttons                           */
        /* Each executed statement in the for         */
        /* loop forms a string "button i"             */
        for (int i = 1 ; i < 6; i++) {
            buttons[i] = new Button("Button " + i);
        }
        /* Place the buttons */
        fr.add(buttons[1]);
        fr.add(buttons[2]);
        fr.add(buttons[3]);
        fr.add(buttons[4]);
        fr.add(buttons[5]);
        fr.pack();
        fr.show();
    }
}
```

This time when we define the layout for the frame we call FlowLayout, with the parameter set to align the buttons to the left (LEFT is a static variable associated with the FlowLayout class). When we place the buttons we don't need to specify any strings to position them as in BorderLayout, since the class maps them automatically. The display is shown as Figure 7.3.

You can see that the buttons have been laid out in a line. This is not only one of the simplest ways of arranging items, but it is also one of the most useful. The final layout we will describe here is the GridLayout method. The code to demonstrate this is shown below:

```
import java.awt.*;

public class FrameDemo {
    public static void main(String args[]) {
        Button buttons[] = new Button[6];
        Frame fr = new Frame("We Love Java");
```

Figure 7.3 Another frame.

```
/* Set the layout manager of the frame */
fr.setLayout(new GridLayout(3,2));
/* Add some buttons */
for (int i = 1; i < 6; i++) {
  buttons[i] = new Button("Button " + i);
}
/* Place the buttons */
fr.add(buttons[1]);
fr.add(buttons[2]);
fr.add(buttons[3]);
fr.add(buttons[4]);
fr.add(buttons[5]);
fr.pack();
fr.show();
  }
}
```

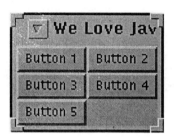

Fig 7.4 A frame using Gridlayout.

The only change in this example is the call to set the layout of the frame. The call to the GridLayout method with arguments (3 and 2) specifies the number of rows and columns in the grid. As you might expect, in the GridLayout model, the elements are arranged into a grid. The display corresponding to the code is shown as Figure 7.4.

We have covered three of the layout models which are supported as a default in Java. The models are simple and easy to work with; however, they tend to suffer from a lack of flexibility and extensibility. In cases where the default models do not meet your requirements, you can write some bespoke classes which implement the LayoutManager interface; however, the details of this are outside the scope of this introductory book.

As an aside it is worth mentioning that it also possible not to use any layout manager and to place components manually. This is done by specifying the layout manager to be null, adding the component to the holder in the normal way and then using the reshape() method to place and size the component in the holder For example:

```
. . .
    holder.setLayout(null);
    Button b1 = new Button("Java!");
```

```
holder.add(b1);
b1.reshape(10,10,20,20);
...
```

The advantage of this is that you get greater control over placement. The disadvantage is that every element has to be placed manually, rather than relying on a layout manager. This has major ramifications when you have to change the user interface; for example, inserting a new element will mean that many of the existing elements will need to be moved and individually recoded.

7.3.2 Control elements

Once you have created a holder for your interface and, optionally, selected a layout method you can begin to add the control elements which will do the real work. In the section we will illustrate some of the elements in sample code.

A simple class to build on

To begin with we will introduce a class which will provide the basis for adding the control elements. This class simply defines a top-level window with a number of panels which we'll use to hold examples of control elements. Remember that panels are used to group elements such as buttons together. Our base class for this section looks like this:

```
import java.awt.*;
public class awtclass {
  Panel topPanel, botPanel;

  public static void main(String args[]) {
    awtclass thisclass = new awtclass();
    // Define the top-level frame
    Frame fr = new Frame("AWT Chapter");
    // Call our method to display the UI elements
    thisclass.doUI(fr);
    // Pack and display the frame
    fr.pack();
    fr.show();
    }

  public void doUI(Frame fr) {
    fr.setLayout(new BorderLayout());
    // Create the panels to hold the UI elements
    topPanel = new Panel();
    botPanel = new Panel();
    // Add the elements to the frame
    fr.add("North",topPanel);
    fr.add("South",botPanel);
  }
}
```

Before continuing it is worth your reading through this code in order to make sure you understand what is does. We create a new frame, then create an instance of this class and pass the frame as an argument to the method doUI which carries out the process of building up the interface elements. Inside the doUI method two panels are created and then added to the frame using the add method. We have used this method before and glossed over the details so it is worth providing a little more detail. Whenever you want to insert an object into a frame (or related container), you will use the add() method. There are two ways that the method can be called. The first:

add(Component)

is the most common, but the second way is:

add(String, Component)

which is required by layout managers that use the string to locate the component, for example the BorderLayout class. The add() method you use is determined by the layout method your holder is using. This is a slightly inflexible approach at first, especially since elements placed using the wrong call will not appear. If you are writing code and your calls to add() don't seem to be working, one of the first things that you should check is that the layout manager you are using doesn't require the string argument. This is especially likely to happen with certain classes which use the BorderLayout class – your code will compile and run, but if you call the wrong version of add() then the components will not appear.

If you build and run this class you won't see much at all. Depending on your development platform you will just see a very small window title. The reason for this is the occurrence of the pack() call near the end of the code which instructs the frame to resize around its components. Since all we have at the moment is the set of panels which will also shrink to nothing the whole of the application disappears.

Adding a menu

The first thing that we will add is a menu bar. This is just a bar which contains menus; these, in turn, contain individual menu items. The procedure for creating menus is somewhat convoluted. First you must create a MenuBar:

MenuBar mb = new MenuBar();

Then you must create a new item for each menu that you want to appear in the menu bar, for example:

Menu m = new Menu("Menu 1");

After this you must create MenuItems for each selectable item that you want to appear in the menu and tell the menu to hold the item:

m.add(new MenuItem("MenuItem 1");
m.add(new MenuItem("MenuItem 2");

Once you have completed adding items to the menu you must add the menu to the menu bar:

```
mb.add(m);
```

Finally, when all of this has been done, you must tell the frame that you want it to use the MenuBar that you have prepared:

```
fr.setMenuBar(mb);
```

This approach is very flexible, but at the cost of extensive coding and very little satisfaction.

The code now becomes:

```
import java.awt.*;
public class awtclass2 extends awtclass {
  public static void main(String args[]) {
    awtclass thisclass = new awtclass2();
    // Define the top-level frame
    Frame fr = new Frame("AWT Chapter");
    // Call our method to display the UI elements
    thisclass.doUI(fr);
    // Pack and display the frame
    fr.pack();
    fr.show();
  }

  public void doUI(Frame fr) {
    super.doUI(fr);
    MenuBar mb = new MenuBar();
    Menu m = new Menu("Menu 1");
    m.add(new MenuItem("MenuItem 1"));
    m.add(new MenuItem("MenuItem 2"));
    mb.add(m);
    fr.setMenuBar(mb);
  }
}
```

There are a number of things to notice about this code. First, awtclass2 extends awtclass which we defined previously, so all the methods and instance variables in this class become available to awtclass2. Second, the method doUI in awtclass2 calls the doUI method in awtclass by using the super facility that we discussed earlier. This sets the frame and the panels previously defined.

If you build and view this code, you still won't see very much. In fact, it is not until the addition of more 'normal' components that the pack() command picks up the minimum sizes of the elements.

Adding a TextArea and a Canvas

We will now continue to add some useful elements to the top panel. We will add a TextArea and a Canvas. A TextArea is a general-purpose text widget which can be used to hold arbitrary text strings. A TextArea comes complete with scroll bars which are linked to the text area. A Canvas is a general-purpose widget which can be used for a whole range of tasks. In this example, we have subclassed Canvas to produce myCanvas, which overrides the paint() method associated with `Canvas` to place a text string into the main area. This is a very simple example of the versatility of the canvas and you will almost certainly find yourself using `Canvas` components to build complex interfaces.

The code to add these two elements to the display looks like this:

```
import java.awt.*;
public class awtclass3 extends awtclass2 {
  public static void main(String args[]) {
    awtclass thisclass = new awtclass3();
    // Define the top-level frame
    Frame fr = new Frame("AWT Chapter");
    // Call our method to display the UI elements
    thisclass.doUI(fr);
    // Pack and display the frame
    fr.pack();
    fr.show();
  }

  public void doUI(Frame fr) {
    super.doUI(fr);
    // Set the layout model for the topPanel
    topPanel.setLayout(new GridLayout(1,2));
    // Add the text area
    topPanel.add(new TextArea("TextArea",5,20));
    // Add the mycanvas item
    topPanel.add(new myCanvas());
  }
}
```

As before, we have extended the class from the previous example. In the `doUI` method we begin by setting the layout for the panel we are going to use. In this case, we initially want a grid with one row and two columns. We then employ the `add()` method to insert a `TextArea` (with initial text set to the string `"TextArea"`) and a `myCanvas`. The code for the `myCanvas` class is included below:

```
class myCanvas extends Canvas {
  public void paint(Graphics g) {
  int w = 180;
  int h = 80;
  g.drawRect(1, 1, w - 1, h - 1);
  g.drawString("Canvas", (w - g.getFontMetrics().
  stringWidth("Canvas"))/2,10);
  }

  public Dimension minimumSize() {
    return new Dimension(200,100);
  }
```

```
  public Dimension preferredSize() {
    return minimumSize();
  }
}
```

This draws a rectangle with its top left hand point at an *x* coordinate and *y* coordinate which are both offset by one pixel from the origin (the top left hand corner of the screen). The third parameter of drawRect is the width of the rectangle in pixels, while the fourth parameter is the height. The method drawString has three parameters: the string to be drawn, the *x* offset of the string and the *y* offset of the string measured in pixels from the origin. The method minimumSize returns a Dimension which is simply an object that contains an *x* and *y* coordinate. The code:

```
(w - g.getFontMetrics().stringWidth("Canvas"))/2
```

is used to position the string in the centre of the rectangle.

```
g.getFontMetrics
```

returns with a font metric object which gives details of the font being used and stringWidth then calculates the width of the string.

We simply override the methods we need to generate a simple subclass which displays a string in the canvas object. Our canvas subclass is very simple but by carefully tying in the paint() method with user interaction it is possible to create very sophisticated tools within the interface.

Adding a Button, *a* TextField, *a* Choice *and a* CheckBox

The last set of additions to the interface will be some small user interface items: a Button, a Choice, a TextField, and a CheckBox. The code is shown below:

```
import java.awt.*;
public class awtclass4 extends awtclass3 {
  public static void main(String args[]) {
    awtclass thisclass = new awtclass4();
    // Define the top-level frame
    Frame fr = new Frame("AWT Chapter");
    // Call our method to display the UI elements
    thisclass.doUI(fr);
    // Pack and display the frame
    fr.pack();
  }

  public void doUI(Frame fr) {
    super.doUI(fr);
    // Add small things at the bottom.
    botPanel.add(new TextField("TextField"));
    botPanel.add(new Button("Button"));
    botPanel.add(new CheckBox("Checkbox"));
    Choice c = new Choice();
    c.addItem("Choice Item 1");
```

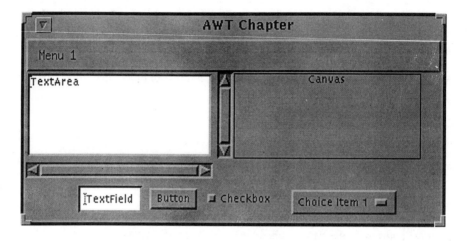

Figure 7.5 A screen with widgets.

```
    c.addItem("Choice Item 2");
    c.addItem("Choice Item 3");
    botPanel.add(c);
  }
}
```

In the doUI method, we simply employ the add() method to insert elements into the panel. Starting with the TextField we create an instance with the default text value of "TextField". A TextField is a single line text holder which is similar to the TextArea widget we introduced earlier, although it is much simpler since there are no considerations regarding multiple lines of text or multiple viewing positions. We then proceed to add a Button, with the label on the button set to be the string "Button". As you can see, adding this kind of element is very simple and is a great contrast to the process of adding a MenuBar. We also add a CheckBox in the same manner and then create a Choice. A Choice is a pop-up list of options, only one of which can be selected at any time. Once the Choice is created, we use the addItem() method to create the items that will appear in the pop-up menu. Finally, the `Choice` is added to the `Panel`. At this point, the interface is as shown in Figure 7.5.

7.4 The event system

You may have noticed that while we have created several interface elements none of them carry out any processing. In Java the mechanism for handling events from interface elements is handled separately from creating and displaying the elements. This is a flexible approach which, once mastered, enables the developer to create powerful and adaptable code. The Java system acts as the event dispatcher and passes the event to the `handleEvent` method of the component – for example, a button – which has generated the event. The default `handleEvent` method for components (which of course can be overridden) switches on the type of event and calls an appropriate method for dealing with it. The default specific handlers (for example, `handleMouseDown` and `handleMouseExit`) are simple methods which return a Boolean false. If any of the methods used to handle events returns false, then the event is passed to the parent components and the whole process is repeated, until a handler is found which returns true (and optionally performs some action), or until the event has been passed to and refused by the top-level window.

7.4.1 Approaches to handling events

When writing methods to handle events, there are several points at which your code can override the standard methods. You should experiment with various approaches and settle on the one which you find fits best with your interface design and coding practices. Two of the approaches to overriding are discussed below.

The `handleEvent()` *method*

This is the method which is called by the Java system and handles the event directly. By default this method in a `Component` or related subclass looks like this:

```
public boolean handleEvent(Event evt) {
  switch (evt.id) {
    case Event.MOUSE_ENTER:
      return mouseEnter(evt, evt.x, evt.y);
    case Event.MOUSE_EXIT:
      return mouseExit(evt, evt.x, evt.y);
    case Event.MOUSE_MOVE:
      return mouseMove(evt, evt.x, evt.y);
    case Event.MOUSE_DOWN:
      return mouseDown(evt, evt.x, evt.y);
    case Event.MOUSE_DRAG:
      return mouseDrag(evt, evt.x, evt.y);
    case Event.MOUSE_UP:
      return mouseUp(evt, evt.x, evt.y);
    case Event.KEY_PRESS:
    case Event.KEY_ACTION:
      return keyDown(evt, evt.key);
```

```
    case Event.ACTION_EVENT:
      return action(evt, evt.arg);
  }
  return false;
}
```

The method is passed an event as the parameter. The Event class has a variable which defines what type of event it is, and this is used by the handleEvent method as a switch variable when selecting an appropriate target method. The Event class also defines a set of variables (for example, Event.MOUSE_ENTER, Event.KEY_ACTION) which are the set of Events that the Java system can issue and each statement in the switch-body checks to see if the event is one that the handleEvent class knows a suitable target for.

Notice that when a match is made, it is left for the target method to return the Boolean value to the method calling handleEvent. It is this approach which allows the cascading of handlers returning either true or false responses. If the type of event does not match any of the handlers that handleEvent knows about, the method returns false and the event will be passed to the parent component.

If we look at the default method for, say, keyDown we can see the whole of the picture:

```
public boolean keyDown(Event evt, int key) {
  return false;
}
```

You can see that if this method is not overridden, then it will simply return false to handleEvent(). Since all of the methods in the Component class are defined in the same manner, it can now be seen why our code samples for the previous sections in the chapter do not do anything when the interface elements are manipulated.

Since the handleEvent() method is the parent method of all the event handlers in the Component class (and therefore all subclasses, including the user interface elements in the AWT library), it is possible to handle some or all of the event control directly in this class. Instead of switching to other methods based on the type of event, it would be possible to write the code to process events on a per-component basis and concentrate the code into one method. Although this is possible, it does not provide a modular approach to handling the events. It is suitable for a small number of interface elements in an application or applet but the coding complexity which is encountered with larger numbers of interface elements is significant and difficult to manage.

The action() *method and friends*

A better approach to handling events is to leave the handleEvent() method alone and override specific event handlers, such as action(), handleMouseExit() and handleMouseLeave(). As we saw above these methods, by default, simply return a Boolean false and cause the event to be passed to the parent component. By simply redefining the specific handlers which are required for the interface elements which have been used it is possible to minimize effort and code complexity. The methods that you should consider using include:

- `action()`. This is called when an interface element is manipulated, such as a Button being pressed.

- `mouseDown()`. Called when the mouse button is pressed over a component.

- `mouseDrag()`. Called when the mouse is moved over a component while the mouse button is pressed.

- `mouseEnter()`. Called when the pointer enters a component.

- `mouseExit()`. Called when the pointer leaves a component.

- `mouseUp()`. Called when the mouse button is released.

The majority of the events are self-explanatory and are related to the operation of the mouse and mouse-pointer. The method which most often causes confusion is `action()`, which is invoked by the Java system when a user interface element is manipulated.

The reason that confusion arises is that if the event handling is implemented within an instance of the `Frame` class which is parenting several user interface components, then all events caused by all of the components are sent to the `action()` method in the `Frame`. It is then the responsibility of this method to determine which component has sent the event and deal with the event accordingly. Of course, it is possible to have each user interface component handle events directly, but since a subclass of each class must be created for every type of element that handles events differently, the class hierarchy can soon become huge and difficult to maintain. In the next section we will illustrate a simple solution to this problem.

Handling events using the `action()` *method*

The approach that we use is to break the event down into the type of element that sent the event and then process the specific event to determine which element of that type was responsible. This approach provides a reasonable and flexible approach to coding the method. It retains event control in a high-level window, without pushing the code down to the subclasses and bloating the class hierarchy with large numbers of classes which exist only to handle events; this is more an issue when writing an interface for an applet, where each class must be separately loaded over the network – a situation where a large number of classes can significantly delay the loading and execution of your code.

We have written a simple applet with an interface similar to the one in the examples so far in this section. The code looks like this:

```
import java.applet.Applet;
import java.awt.*;

public class evui extends Applet {
  Panel botPanel;
  public void init() {
    setLayout(new BorderLayout());
    botPanel = new Panel();
    add("South",botPanel);
    botPanel.add(new TextField("TextField"));
```

```
        botPanel.add(new Button("Button 1"));
        botPanel.add(new Button("Button 2"));
        botPanel.add(new CheckBox("Checkbox"));
        Choice c = new Choice();
        c.addItem("Choice Item 1");
        c.addItem("Choice Item 2");
        c.addItem("Choice Item 3");
        botPanel.add(c);
    }

    public boolean action(Event evt, Object arg) {
        if (evt.target instanceof Button) {
          String str = (String) arg;
          if (str.equals("Button 1")) {
            showStatus("First Button!!");
          } else {
          if (str.equals("Button 2")) {
            showStatus("Second Button!!");
          } else {
            return false;
          }
        }
        return true;
      } else {
        if (evt.target instanceof CheckBox) {
          showStatus("CheckBox: " + (Boolean) arg);
        } else {
          if (evt.target instanceof TextField) {
            showStatus("TextArea: " + (String) arg);
          } else {
            return false;
          }
        }
        return true;
        }
    }
}
```

This example simply illustrates how to handle events. Before discussing it, it is worth restating that it involves an applet and that more details on applets can be found in Chapter 10. All you will need to know about applets to understand this example is that it inherits from Component and that the method init is executed when an applet is started up.

We start by building a limited interface with two Buttons, a TextField and a CheckBox in a Panel. Since this is an applet it inherits from Component and so has methods for add() and action(). When an event is sent from any of the embedded components the default event handling methods called by handleEvent return a Boolean false. This means that the events rise through the interface hierarchy until they are sent to the `Applet handleEvent` method, which calls our `action()` method as shown in the code above.

When an event is sent to this method the code tries to establish what type of object has caused the event to be sent by using the `instanceOf` operator against the target variable of the event. This variable contains a reference to the object which sent the event. Once the type of object has been determined the code then handles the individual objects.

The `arg` parameter is of type `Object` and what it contains will depend on the type of element that has been executed. For example, if a button has been pressed it will contain a string which identifies the button, if a checkbox has been manipulated it will contain a Boolean value which will be true or false depending on whether the checkbox has been set or not. Once the type of user interface element has been determined a cast is needed to extract the value of `arg`.

The `arg` parameter is used to see which button has been pressed. The `arg` parameter is an arbitrary one. This means that it is set according to the object which caused the event. You can see how this operates when the `CheckBox` is altered. The parameter which was cast to a `String` for the `Buttons` must be regarded as a Boolean for the `CheckBox`. Similarly, the `TextField` uses the `arg` parameter to pass the text it holds.

If there were more interface components to be handled then it would make sense to pass off the event to another method responsible for handling all components of a given type, so that the method `handleButtonEvent()` is called once `action()` has identified that a button has caused the event to be sent through the system.

When writing code to handle events, it is worth making a big effort to select an approach which concentrates the handlers in a limited number of components without creating huge methods which will prove difficult to maintain. The event mechanism is very flexible and can be used to create useful event handlers with only minimal coding, but the way that the handlers are placed against components is of paramount importance for the long-term maintenance of the code.

7.5 Graphics

The `Graphics` class is an abstract graphics device which is used in the `Applet` class. Rather than define a graphic class for every type of client machine, Java defines an abstract class which the local Java system translates to the real graphics device when graphics operations occur.

The `Graphics` class is of most importance to the writing of applets, since almost all applets will modify their appearance using Graphics contexts. The only exception to this is the AWT components which we have covered in this chapter, which operate in a slightly different manner.

7.5.1 Using Graphics in a basic applet

When using the `Applet` class, the Java system creates a default Graphics context and this is passed to the `update()` and `paint()` methods. Here is a simple example:

```
import java.applet.Applet;
import java.awt.Graphics;

public class simpleApplet extends Applet {
  public void paint(Graphics g) {
    g.drawRect(10,10,100,75);
  }
}
```

In this example a rectangle is drawn at offset (10,10) from the origin into the Graphics context. We can also draw text and images, using the `drawString` and `drawImage` methods. In fact all of the main graphics primitives are supported, including line, arc and polygon as well as different types of rectangle. Since `Graphics` inherits directly from `Object`, there is no direct support for events. Instead you must use the parent object to receive events generated from the Graphics context. This is not entirely consistent with the rest of the AWT elements, but if you are following an event handling approach such as the one we outlined in this chapter, then you will not need to worry about it.

7.5.2 Double buffering

It is also possible to create an offscreen Image and Graphics context and use them for screen buffering. Buffering the display is useful when you have a series of discrete operations to apply to the display which consume a long period of time. When applying a large number of operations the Java system will update periodically. This means that the user is presented with a partially complete display. Performing the operations on a display which is not shown to the user and then copying the final work to the main display leads to two positive things happening: first, it prevents the display updating before the tasks are complete and, second, stops the display flickering as the context is manipulated.

An applet which draws a large number of lines to the display is shown below:

```
import java.applet.Applet;
import java.awt.*;

public class singleBuffer extends Applet {
  public void init() {
  }

  public void paint(Graphics g) {
    for (int x = 0; x < size().width; x += 2) {
      g.drawLine(x,0,x,size().height);
    }
    for (int y = 0; y < size().height; y += 2) {
      g.drawLine(0,y,size().width,y);
    }
  }
}
```

The code in the first for loop draws vertical lines which are the height of the applet display until the end of the width of the display has been met. The drawLine method associated with the Graphics class has four arguments: the first two represent the start position of a line while the remaining two represent the end position of a line. The second loop draws horizontal lines.

In this code, the paint method draws a large number of lines directly to the display. On some machines (notably slower client machines) the amount of time that is taken to draw a large number of graphics operations will mean that the screen suffers from flicker as the system updates the screen. On faster machines, this may not happen; however, it is wise not to make assumptions about the hardware at the client end – even when you think you know who will be using the software.

The code for an applet which uses an offscreen Image and Graphics is displayed below:

```java
import java.applet.Applet;
import java.awt.*;

public class doubleBuffer extends Applet {
    Image offScrImage;
    Graphics offScrGr;

    public void init() {
        offScrImage =
        createImage(size().width,size().height);
        offScrGr = offScrImage.getGraphics();
    }

    public void paint(Graphics g) {
    for (int x = 0; x < size().width; x += 2) {
        offScrGr.drawLine(x,0,x,size().height);
    }
    for (int y = 0; y < size().height; y += 2) {
        offScrGr.drawLine(0,y,size().width,y);
    }
    g.drawImage(offScrImage,0,0,this);
    }
}
```

In this version, the Init() method creates an Image and then gets the graphics context (also sometimes called a surface) associated with it. When the paint method is called the graphics operations are performed on the offscreen context which is not subject to being displayed on the screen and coinciding with system updates. When the lines have been drawn, the whole of the offscreen image is copied into the default Graphics context by the drawImage method (notice that the offscreen Graphics occupies the whole of the offscreen Image) and the display updates smoothly. This approach to screen management is especially useful with animation and with tasks which generally take a long time or require a large number of screen operations.

7.6 Fonts and colour

The AWT also provides support for fonts and colours.

7.6.1 Font support

In Java there are two classes which relate directly to font support, the `Font` and `FontMetric` classes. The `Font()` method is usually the most frequently used, while `FontMetric` is required when information about an existing instance of `Font` is needed.

The `Font` *class*

The `Font` class defines the font itself, including the font family, size and style. For example, to create a font in Courier at 12 point and in Bold you would use:

```
someFont = new Font("Courier", Font.BOLD, 12);
```

The first parameter to the constructor is a string which defines the font family. The next parameter is a static variable from the `Font` class which defines the font as being bold. Finally, the last integer is the size of the type.

By default, the Java system guarantees that the *Helvetica, TimesRoman, ZapfDingBats, Dialog, DialogInput* and *Courier* families are always available. The *Dialog* family relates to a native font on the client system which is the standard for the system to use in dialog with the user. For each of the default families the sizes 8, 10, 12, 14, 24, and 36 points are always available. It is possible to specify other sizes than the default and, if the client system supports font scaling, then this will be used to generate the type. However, if the client system does not implement a method for font scaling, then the nearest available size will be used instead of the size that has been specified. This means that if an interface has been designed expecting type to take a certain amount of screen space, then changes in font size at the client system can make applications and applets look very strange and not at all as intended.

Once an instance of `Font` has been created, it can be used to define the appearance of text in a display. For example, in an applet the following would be possible:

```
public void paint(Graphics g) {
    Font someFont = new Font("Courier", Font.BOLD, 12);
    g.setFont(someFont);
    g.drawString("Some Text!",10,10);
}
```

In this example, the `paint()` method defines a new font and then asks the Graphics context to use the font for further graphics operations. The next operation uses text and displays a String in the context. Because the font for the context was set prior to the call to drawString using the setFont method the text will be drawn using the font that was created.

The FontMetric *class*

The FontMetric class can be used to obtain information about a particular font. This information is most useful when the display of an application or applet requires the accurate positioning of components or when text needs to be formatted in a particular manner. The FontMetric constructor requires an instance of Font as a parameter. For example:

```
Font someFont = new Font("Courier", Font.BOLD, 12);
FontMetric someFontMetric = new FontMetric(someFont);
```

Once an instance of FontMetric exists, it is possible to use the methods of the class to return information about the font. Some of the methods in the class include stringWidth(String) and charWidth(char) which return the pixel widths of strings and characters in the font that was used to create the instance. As an example of using these methods imagine that you required the title of a file to be centred in a window. If the user loads the file from a dialog, then there is no way of knowing the file name in advance and therefore no way of knowing what the required offset is to ensure that the name of the file is centred as expected. However, by creating an instance of FontMetric, it is a simple matter to determine the width of the filename using stringWidth() and then centre the string based on the width of the parent window. Other related methods return the height of a font and the ascent and descent of a font.

7.6.2 Colour support

The Color class encapsulates RGB colours. The colours are used to define the appearance of text, graphics primitives and UI components. To create a Color, there are several constructors which are supported.

- *Color(int, int, int)*. This creates a Color with each of the ints repesenting a value for one of the red, green and blue channels.

- *Color(int)*. This creates a Color with the bits of the integer representing the values of the channels.

- *Color(float, float, float)*. This creates a Color with the channels being defined by the floats in the range 0.0 to 1.0.

So, for example, to create a colour where all three channels are set to 100:

```
Color myColor = new Color(100,100,100);
```

However, most of the time there will not be a need to define colours with such precision, and so the Color class defines a number of standard colours for general use. The range of colors is black, blue, cyan, darkGray, gray, green, lightGray, magenta, orange, pink, red, white and yellow. To use one of these predefined colours, for example green, use the following constructor:

```
Color myColor = new Color(Color.green);
```

Once you have defined a colour, you can use it in your interface code. For example:

```
public void paint(Graphics g) {
      Color myColor = new Color(Color,green);
      g.setColor(myColor);
      g.fillRect(10,10,100,100);
}
```

Once a colour has been set, any subsequent operations will be performed using this colour. Consequently, it makes sense to group operations that require the same colours and fonts together in your code to avoid switching more than you really need to.

When using colour in your interface, remember that the Java colour support is not device independent, and some colours will look radically different on a range of client machines. If colour accuracy is important to you then you should either select a set of colours which vary from machine to machine, catering to the differences between the hardware, or consider implementing a device-independent imaging method. At the time of writing, no commercial packages exist to handle such a requirement, but as the demand for Java grows it is an area that will attract further development effort.

CHAPTER
EIGHT
The java.net library

AIMS

- To provide an overview of the network support within Java.

- To outline the network library classes.

- To build and analyse simple network software.

8.1 Introduction

One of the key packages in the Java system is the `java.net` library. This provides support for accessing the network both as a client accessing remote services and as a server providing services to remote clients.

The role of the network in the life of the Java language is critical. The most popular application areas for Java code will be those supported by mixed-platform environments where the ability to access remote information and services will be of prime concern. The `java.net` package includes support for creating clients and servers, as well as classes for related requirements, such as those connected with network addresses.

8.2 A tour of the package

The `java.net` package includes all the tools you will need to implement network support. The library is small and compact but requires a basic level of understanding before it can be used effectively. We will explain as much as is required to implement simple services; however, it is worth pointing out that this text is not the place for a detailed explanation of network issues and we will not hesitate to sacrifice accuracy for clarity when we cover the basic topics. By the end of this chapter you should have sufficient knowledge to write code that will enable you to implement network functions seamlessly into Java applications and applets.

8.2.1 The common protocol

One criticism which has been made against the network support within the Java package libraries is that the only protocol which is available is TCP/IP, which is not always available as part of the standard operating system software in non-UNIX environments.

While it is true that some platforms have better support for other protocols, the selection of IP for the Java libraries is reasonable given that it is the de facto protocol for the Internet and has been ported to a whole range of platforms. In addition, supporting a range of protocols which are not uniformly available on all platforms which can run Java would inhibit the intrinsic cross-platform nature of the Java language and limit the cross-connectivity which makes Java such a useful language.

However, there are bound to be problems which require Java and the use of a protocol other than TCP/IP. In these cases all is not lost: it is possible, albeit challenging, to write methods which implement other protocols. By using native methods it is also possible to take advantage of existing system libraries to manage network connections. The final chapter of this book contains more details of native methods and the implications of using them. While it is possible to create such support for your Java applications, our advice is to stick with the TCP/IP support within the standard Java libraries wherever possible; this level of support will be sufficient for the majority of development efforts.

8.2.2 Software and servers

Java allows the developer to create network connections in a range of ways. This makes embedded Java applets far more flexible than just vanilla HTML pages. While some applets will be self-contained and require no external support, most complex applications will rely on external servers and services to enrich the application/applet environment. The way that connections are handled is at the discretion of the developer, ranging from connections which the user fully controls and understands, through to connections that happen 'behind the scenes' without user intervention.

In addition, subject to security settings, Java code can connect to any arbitrary server available from the end-user machine. The final part of this chapter provides more information about security models and network connections and the concluding chapter of the book contains a general discussion of security and Java. There is no requirement to limit access to a single machine or to a single network, especially from a Java application. In particular, the Java network libraries do not limit the developer to using only HTTP to access external services and handlers can be created for any service which uses IP as a transport.

8.2.3 Some simple examples

The examples that we give in this chapter will concentrate on establishing and managing network connections. We will not focus on what to do with the data that is generated, except in an abstract manner. There are two reasons for doing this: first, because this chapter is about the network libraries only and, second, because there are so many uses for network connections that we could not possibly do justice to them.

The code that we will introduce to illustrate the `java.net` library will typically do simple tasks – after all, we are not concerned with what the application does aside from the network implications. The thing to remember when looking at these examples is that you should take the network aspects of the code and extend them to your own environment. For example, in order to extend a simple server which sends the time to network clients to carry out a more useful task, you should be able to replace the code which handles generating the time with code to carry out other tasks such as accessing a file with little effort. Once you have a set of classes which handles networking in a generic manner it is relatively trivial to add additional functionality which meets your project goals.

8.2.4 Possible applications

Even though we can't realistically provide examples for every kind of server, it is worthwhile giving some sample uses for servers generally. The Java packages can be used to write a diverse range of servers limited only by resources and the imagination of the development team.

Examples include gateways to databases, proxy servers to navigate through firewalls, feedback systems for large-scale systems, mediators for network games, mail servers and so on – the list is endless.

One thing to consider when embarking on developing a Java server is avoiding writing something which already exists in another language. While there may be compelling reasons to port functionality to a Java applet or application – for example, writing a cross-platform mail reader – there is little point in writing the accompanying server if another application is already available. Not only will you incur expense by performing the development, but you will create a new program with the bugs and problems that immature software always suffers from. If there is a mature, stable and usable server package available, then do not hesitate to use it. While the clients may benefit from a Java client there is no reason why the code that they use cannot be written to work with the existing servers and, in many ways, it makes client development simpler since the server is a known quantity.

8.3 Writing a server

We'll start our descriptions of client–server functionality with the server end of things. Our goal will be to write a simple server that will accept network connections and then write back any strings that the client sends in. It's a simple goal. However, it serves as an excellent way of introducing the libraries. For the reader impatient to see big applications, we would advise you to imagine that instead of simply returning a string the server carries out some major set of functions such as accessing a huge database, making several complex and involved queries and then returning the string.

8.3.1 The cost of using Java for servers

Java is not always the best language for writing servers. One of the biggest problems is the delay that is incurred while the Java run-time software loads and interprets the Java code. This means that if a server crashes and then is restarted, there is a significant delay before service is restored. This is not always a problem. However, if high availability and fast response are important to your application, then Java may not be the best of choices. This may not be a problem when full compilers are available for Java but, currently, it presents a challenge to developers.

Of course, there is a cost in not using Java as the server. The development team must write in different languages with potentially different approaches to networking. Java has an excellent network library which may not be matched in other languages, and since Java is cross-platform, it is possible to deploy the server software on a range of platforms – a feature that should not be underestimated.

The bottom line is that you should carefully consider the language to use on any project and be sure that the final selection is the most appropriate for your particular resources and problems. Don't be seduced by the hype that surrounds a language: it is always the case that programming languages have strengths and weaknesses and that a so-called general-purpose language is not always as general as intended.

8.3.2 Introducing the first iteration of the server

This first version of the server will just wait for a connection and then write the string received from the connection to the out channel of the server process. When the string has been printed out the application will quit. As a rule, it is only possible to have servers running as part of Java applications because of the security constraints imposed on applet code by the Web browser which embeds the Java run-time system. Further details on writing applications can be found in Chapter 11.

The code for the server is shown below:

```
import java.lang.*;
import java.net.*;
import java.util.*;
import java.io.*;

public class server1 {
    public static void main(String args[]) {
    /* Create a new instance of the simpleServer */
    simpleServer ss = new simpleServer(6001);
    }
}

    class simpleServer {
  ServerSocket sock;
  Socket conn;
```

```
BufferedInputStream instream;
String str;

simpleServer(int port) {
  try {
    /* Try to be a server on this port */
    sock = new ServerSocket(port);
    System.out.println("Started on port " + port);
    conn = sock.accept();
  } catch(Exception e) {
    System.out.println("Err: " + e);
    System.exit(1);
  }

  try {
    /* Create the stream to the socket */
    instream = new
    BufferedInputStream(conn.getInputStream());
  } catch(Exception e) {
    System.out.println("Err: " + e);
    System.exit(1);
  }
  /* Read line from the socket and then
  write it out */
  str = this.getline();
  System.out.println("Str: " + str.trim());
}

public String getline() {
  StringBuffer strbuf = new StringBuffer();
  int tmp;
    do {
    try {
      /* Try to read from the stream */
      tmp = instream.read();
    } catch(Exception e) {
    return(null);
    }
    if (tmp == -1) {
      /* There is nothing to read */
      return(null);
    }
    if (tmp != 0) {
      /* Add character to StringBuffer */
      strbuf.append((char)tmp);
    }
    } while (tmp != '\n');
      /* Return the String of the StringBuffer */
```

```
            return(strbuf.toString());
      }
}
```

If we compile this file and run the server, we can then telnet into port 6001 and type a string. The string is printed out on the server output and then the server exits. It is worth walking through the code to explain what is happening. The first class, `server1`, just contains the `main()` method that all applications have to implement. The class creates a new instance of `simpleServer` and passes the port we wish to use as an argument. All of the work happens in the `simpleServer` class. Looking at the constructor, we can see that the first line of code is:

```
sock = new ServerSocket(port);
```

This creates a new `ServerSocket` called `sock`. What is a socket? Well, without going into much detail, a socket is a combination of a host and a port. A host is a (possibly) remote computer which supports the TCP/IP protocol and a port is the part of the computer that you talk to for a given service. So certain ports are used for sending email, starting terminal sessions and even playing games. You can think of a port as a way of telling the computer which software or service you would like to use.

The `ServerSocket` creates a network connection on the machine which is prepared to accept connections from client machines in order to provide some kind of service. The number that is passed as an argument specifies which port we want to use. In order to let clients access our simple service the client software must have some prior knowledge of the port number that we are using. Well-known services have a set of ports which are universally recognized and ports that have a number less than 1024 are considered 'special' on many implementations of TCP/IP and require system privileges to be used. The danger in selecting a port at random is that if your software is later moved to another server, it is possible that another piece of network software is already expecting to use the port that you have selected and your software will die reporting that the port is in use.

The best way of dealing with this is to provide a mechanism for allowing the user to specify an alternative port on the command line which can override the default that the software uses. At the moment, we have created the socket connection for the server but nothing else will happen. We need to tell the socket that it should accept a connection when one arrives. This is done with the call:

```
conn = sock.accept();
```

This tells the `ServerSocket` that it should wait for a connection. Because it is impossible to predict when a connection request will arrive from a client, making the call blocks the thread of execution until a connection is made to the port. Until this happens no other lines of code are processed. This is fine when the server is expected to cope with only one client, but if there are multiple clients, having the entire execution halted until another client arrives is not workable – we will return to this problem later in the chapter and show you a solution. Notice that the call to `accept()` is grouped with the `ServerSocket` call, so that if there are problems establishing the port the code doesn't send a message to an object which could not be created. If there are problems in establishing the `ServerSocket`, then the error is printed to the `out` channel and the application exits by means of the code:

```
System.exit(1)
```

The argument 1 to the call of exit enables the system to provide an error code which gives an indication of the problem.

The next few lines of code create the required streams to let us read from the socket. When these lines of Java are executed, we already have a connection established from a client. We know this because the call to `accept()` blocks execution until this is true. In this example, we have chosen to use a `BufferedInputStream` from the `java.io` package. We have to catch the exceptions because the call could generate a problem. The alternative would be to declare that our class can throw the same exception, but this approach has the cost of losing the resolution which is provided by catching exceptions at the point in the code where they are thrown.

If the application has successfully created the `ServerSocket`, accepted an incoming connection request and dealt with the I/O streams, we can then read a line of input from the socket connection. This line of input will be the line that the user has typed. We have defined a separate method called `getline()` to handle this task. In essence, `getline()` reads a byte from the stream we have associated with the socket (it is not possible to read and write directly to sockets – instead you must associate a stream using the `getInputStream()` and `getOutputStream()` methods). If the byte is equal to –1 then there is no input from the user waiting to be read. If the byte is not equal to 0, then we make a cast from the integer value of the byte to a char and place the character into a StringBuffer. When the character matches `"\n"` (which is the code for the return key) we send back the String representation of the StringBuffer. At this point `simpleServer` prints out the line that `getline()` returned and since there are no other lines of code to execute the application exits.

8.3.3 Extending the server

The first example has illustrated the basics of writing a very simple server. The first step is to create a ServerSocket which will be used to accept incoming connections. The next stage is to accept a connection on the ServerSocket and to process the input appropriately. In our example we just used the standard telnet to test out the server and typed in strings from there. We will come to writing clients later in this chapter. So, we now can write lines to the server `out` channel but what about the client? Also, what happens if we want to deal with more than one line of text? The next example covers both these cases. Because we are going to handle multiple lines of text, we'll also add support so that the user can type 'bye-bye' to terminate the connection.

The constructor for `simpleServer` has the following lines to supervise reading the line and printing it out. The rest of the constructor remains the same with `getline()` still being used to handle reading from the connection.

```
/* Read line from the socket and then write it out */
do {
   str = this.getline();
   this.putline("You said: " + str);
   System.out.println("Str: " + str.trim());
} while (!str.startsWith("bye-bye"));
```

The first change is that we are now using a do-while loop to handle reading from the connection. As long as the string returned from getline() does not start with "bye-bye" then the loop keeps reading lines of text. When the string does start with "bye-bye" the loop is terminated and the application exits since there is no more code to execute. We have also added a new method to handling writing strings to the client, called putline(). The Java code for this is:

```
public void putline(String line) {
   byte tline[] = new byte[1024];

   line.getBytes(0,line.length(),tline,0);
   try {
   conn.getOutputStream().write(tline,0,line.length());
   }
   catch(Exception e) {
      System.out.println("Err: " + e);
   }
}
```

The purpose of this method is to take a string, convert it into bytes and then write those bytes out to the network connection. The first line of code places a byte representation of the whole string into an array of bytes. These bytes are then written out to the client.

You might like to compile and test the code at this stage. Using telnet to connect to port 6001 you can type a series of lines each terminated with a CR and see them echoed back to the screen. If the string you type begins with "bye-bye", the whole of the string is echoed back and then the connection closes as the application exits. It is worth saying that it is not good practice to allow socket connections to close when the application exits. A preferable method is to close the socket explicitly – we will do this in later examples.

8.3.4 Handling multiple clients

So far both examples in this section have handled only one client. In this section we will introduce a technique for handling multiple clients. The way we will do this is to have each client connection handled by a different thread (if you are not familiar with the notion of threads and multiple lines of execution, then you should take the time to read Section 5.3.8). In this way, it appears to each client that it is the only user of the system since the fact that it is a multi-user server is hidden from it. The source code looks like this:

```
import java.lang.*;
import java.net.*;
import java.util.*;
```

```java
import java.io.*;

public class server3 {
  static int port;

  public static void main(String args[]) {
    try {
      port = Integer.parseInt(args[0]);
    } catch (Exception e) {
      port = 6001;
    }
    /* Create a new instance of the simpleServer */
    simpleServer ss = new simpleServer(port);
  }
}

class simpleServer implements Runnable {
  ServerSocket sock;
  Socket conn;
  int port;
  Thread kicker;

  simpleServer(int port) {
          this.port = port;
          this.start();
  }

  public void start() {
    if (kicker == null) {
      try {
        /* Try to be a server on this port */
        sock = new ServerSocket(port);
        System.out.println("Started server on
        port  " + port);
      } catch (Exception e) {
        System.out.println("Err: " + e);
      }
      kicker = new Thread(this);
      kicker.start();
    }
  }

  public void stop() {
  }

  public void run() {
    while (kicker != null) {
      try {
        conn = sock.accept();
        new connectionHandler(conn);
      } catch(Exception e) {
```

```
        System.out.println("Err: " + e);
        System.exit(1);
      }
    }
  }
}
class connectionHandler implements Runnable {
  Socket conn;
  Thread kicker = null;
  BufferedInputStream instream;
  String str;

  connectionHandler(Socket connin) {
    conn = connin;
    this.start();
  }
  public void start() {
    if (kicker == null) {
      kicker = new Thread(this);
      kicker.start();
    }
  }
  public void stop() {
    try {
      conn.close();
    } catch (Exception e) {
      System.out.println("Err: " + e);
    }
    kicker = null;
  }
  public void run() {
    try {
      /* Create the stream to the socket */
      instream = new
      BufferedInputStream(conn.getInputStream());
    } catch(Exception e) {
      System.out.println("Err: " + e);
      System.exit(1);
    }
    /* Read line from the socket and
    then write it out */
    do {
      str = this.getline();
      this.putline("You said: " + str);
      System.out.println("Str: " + str.trim());
```

```
  } while (!str.startsWith("bye-bye") && kicker !=
    null);
    this.stop();
}

public void putline(String line) {
byte tline[] = new byte[1024];
line.getBytes(0,line.length(),tline,0);
try {
  conn.getOutputStream().write(tline,0,line.length());
} catch(Exception e) {
  System.out.println("Err: " + e);
}
}

public String getline() {
StringBuffer strbuf = new StringBuffer();
int tmp;
do {
  try {
    /* Try to read from the stream */
    tmp = instream.read();
  } catch(Exception e) {
    return(null);
  }
  if (tmp == -1) {
    /* There is nothing to read */
    return(null);
  }
  if (tmp != 0) {
    /* Add the character */
    strbuf.append((char)tmp);
  }
} while (tmp != '\n');
/* Return the String representation */
return(strbuf.toString());
}
}
```

The source code is quite detailed so you should take a moment to make sure that you understand how it works. The basic principle is that each Socket is handled in a separate thread and new Sockets are created from another thread which monitors the ServerSocket.

In this server it appears to each client that it is the only client using the server, even though there could be several other users. You will also notice that when the user types a string starting with "bye-bye" the thread is stopped and the socket is closed cleanly using the close() method. As we said earlier in this chapter, sockets should be closed cleanly wherever possible – especially in a server which is maintaining multiple sockets.

A logical extension of this server would be to have the input of one client sent out to all of the other clients in the manner of a broadcast system. Looking at the way that the server above is written, you should be able to see that the simplest way to do this would be to create a method which keeps track of all of the open sockets and can be asked to write out strings to all but the sender socket.

8.3.5 Other tasks with sockets

So far we have shown you how to build a basic server in several iterations. When deploying the server code in your own projects, there are hooks to handle the application-specific processing as required. In this section we will look at some of the other methods which are related to sockets.

Identifying the client

While some servers will be available to the whole of the Internet, others may contain information or services which could be restricted to clients from particular sites or from a certain list. The socket class provides a mechanism for obtaining the address of the client that it is connected to.

Here is a code fragment which illustrates how to get the IP address of a client:

```
. . .
ServerSocket ss = new ServerSocket(3000);
Socket sock = ss.accept();
InetAddress addr = sock.getInetAddress();
System.out.println("Address: " + addr.toString());
. . .
```

This code creates a `ServerSocket` which is listening to port 3000 (for brevity we have omitted the exception handling which is required) and then `accept()` is called which will block the thread of execution until a client connects to the port. When a connection is made, the socket is created and then we make a call to `getInetAddress()` which returns the address in the form of an `InetAddress`. We convert the address to a String and then print it out. Instead of just printing it we could have put some further processing in, for example to make a comparison to check the address matches a predefined set of rules.

The `InetAddress`

This is the first time that we have used the `InetAddress` and it is sufficiently useful to be worthy of some coverage. The `InetAddress` is an object which is related to an IP address; it can be thought of as the call-sign that computers using TCP/IP will use to identify themselves. Like call-signs, IP addresses can be changed (within some constraints which are beyond the scope of this book) and therefore it is worth remembering that checking that the IP address of the client matches an address in the ruleset is not a guarantee that everything is fine. However, for simple security and usage logging, getting the IP address from the socket is sufficient.

So what can you do with an IP address? IP addresses are typically associated with hostnames. For example, the address 206.26.48.100 is associated with the machine called 'java.sun.com'. The network package provides support for looking

up names based on numbers and numbers based on names. Here is a simple code
fragment to illustrate the point:

```
. . .
    ServerSocket ss = new ServerSocket(3000);
    Socket sock = ss.accept();
    InetAddress addr = sock.getInetAddress();
    System.out.println("Address: " + addr.getHostName());
. . .
```

This is very similar to the previous fragment, with the exception that when we print
out the line of information we make a call to the getHostName() method; this
returns a String containing the name. This is more useful for screening hosts than
working with 'raw' IP numbers. For example, if we only wanted to allow access
from hosts which are part of the Sun network we could look for hostnames which
end with 'sun.com' or 'sun.co.uk' instead of having to maintain a list of the
network ranges which Sun uses.

It is worth noting that the call to getHostName() returns the name which was
returned from the local name services implemented on your machine. For example,
if the code was executed on a Sun, then the name returned to the call will vary
depending on whether the information came from the local files, the NIS service or
the DNS. Equally possible is the chance that the client has not been registered in
the name services properly and so there is no entry available at all. When basing
code decisions on something as potentially variable as hostnames it is advisable to
make sure that the information that is returned from the call is the information that
you are expecting, especially if granting access has some financial or security
implications.

It is also possible to perform the operation in reverse, taking the name of a
machine and obtaining the IP address. This is done through the getByName()
and getAllByName() methods which return the addresses associated with a
hostname. The getAllByName() method returns all of the IP addresses that a
machine has registered; typically this is applicable to large server machines which
require multiple network connections for increased speed or robustness or service.

One other useful method which is associated with InetAddress is
getLocalHost() which returns the IP address of the local machine. This is
useful for all sorts of applications, not least of which is having a network client
report the IP address of the machine it is using for logging purposes.

8.3.6 Summary of server applications

This section has shown you how to build moderately complex servers using Java.
The examples described have focused on the mechanism of creating the server
process and managing connections, with little emphasis on the overall functionality
of the server. The point of this approach is to remove the extraneous issues of
additional functionality for the sake of clarity and simplicity of code. It is a small
matter to take the example server and add functionality which is specific to your
application requirements.

We have also discussed the benefits and costs associated with writing a server
process in Java. The primary cost is that the interpreted nature of the language

means that the overall latency of the system will be unsuitable for some requirements. The advantages of using Java can be quite compelling, especially the ability to deploy an identical server application onto a whole range of platforms with no changes to the source code.

When writing Java applications the developer has access to the Thread support as we have shown in the example above and can use a familiar language to develop both the server and the applet for a system solution. When writing a large-scale server the attractions of the language and the problems associated with using it both become more significant. Our advice in this matter is to choose the best tool for the problem and the project – this includes considering the abilities of the developers. The long-term maintenance of the server will be a time-consuming task and an inappropriate selection of programming language will only make this more so.

8.4 Writing an applet

The previous section covered the use of the network package to develop a server process for a Java application. Java also supports network access for applets. In this section we will illustrate the use of the network package within applets.

8.4.1 Applet security

As mentioned briefly at the start of this chapter, network access from applets is subject to some constraints. The most significant limitation is that applets can only make network connections to the host that they were downloaded from. This constraint is imposed by a Web browser which operates a strict security policy. Each browser is allowed to implement a different security model or to allow the user to switch between models; at the time of writing the browser that is most likely to have the majority of users, Netscape Navigator, will implement a heavily constrained model which is not modifiable by the user.

There have been some releases of code which allows the developer to bypass the security model by taking control of network connections that were intended for other purposes and were therefore not subject to the same constraints as applet socket connections. While these approaches may work, we would advise against using them for two reasons: first, such security loopholes are likely to be addressed as Java products become more stable and may make your code break in later releases of the system and, second, subverting other connections without the express knowledge of the user violates any trust that the user has in the software. Applet developers are constrained within a tightly controlled environment, and violating the rules undermines user confidence in the applet and in Java as a whole.

8.4.2 Our first look at a client

A simple example of a client will be described in this section. This client will connect to a port and then print out whatever output the server produces. This is not very useful for interactive services such as telnet or ftp but does work with the daytime service which simply prints out the current time and exits. Our code will make a socket connection to the server and then read back a line of output which will be printed to the standard channel out. Here is the code for it:

```java
import java.lang.*;
import java.net.*;
import java.util.*;
import java.io.*;

public class simpleClient {
  static int port;
  static String host;

  public static void main(String args[]) {
    try {
      host = args[0];
      port = Integer.parseInt(args[1]);
    } catch (Exception e) {
      host = "localhost";
      port = 13;
    }

    /* Create a new instance of the simpleServer */
    simpleHandler ss = new simpleHandler(host, port);
  }
}

class simpleHandler {
  BufferedInputStream instream;
  Socket conn;

  simpleHandler(String host, int port) {
    try {
      conn = new Socket(host,port);
      instream = new
      BufferedInputStream(conn.getInputStream());
    } catch (Exception e) {
      System.out.println("Err: " + e);
      System.exit(1);
    }
    /* Read line from the socket and then
    write it out */
    String str = this.getline();
    System.out.println("Str: " + str.trim());
  }

  public String getline() {
    StringBuffer strbuf = new StringBuffer();
    int tmp;
    do {
      try {
        /* Try to read from the stream */
        tmp = instream.read();
      } catch(Exception e) {
        return(null);
```

```
        }
        if (tmp == -1) {
            /* There is nothing to read */
            return(null);
        }
        if (tmp != 0) {
            /* Add the character */
            strbuf.append((char)tmp);
        }
    } while (tmp != '\n');
    /* Return the String */
    return(strbuf.toString());
    }
}
```

If you have read the preceding section, this code should make sense to you. The arguments are used to supply a hostname and a port to connect to. For example, to access the day/time server on the local UNIX machine, it would be possible to type:

```
java simpleClient localhost 13
```

and the output would be the date and time. Because the arguments are expected to be a String and an int representing the hostname and the port, using the names of the service will not work. For example:

```
java simpleClient localhost daytime
```

would not work because the call to Integer.parseInt() would generate an exception and the default settings would be used. If this were a real-world application and not an example, it would be a good idea to give the user some indication that the arguments that have been supplied have failed and the defaults are being used. If this is not done, the user could make any kind of mistake and not notice that the software has defaulted to other parameters.

Once the arguments have been processed, we create a new instance of a class called simpleHandler which will do all of the work. The first thing that simpleHandler tries to do is to open a network connection to the specified host, using the arguments passed from main(). The next line of code tries to establish an input stream from the socket connection in much the same manner that the server examples did in the preceding section. Since both of these calls could generate exceptions we have used a try...catch statement which will either succeed and the execution of the code will continue, or fail and it will exit reporting the exception to the user by using println().

Once the connection has been established, a call is then made to the getline() method which was first used in a server class and then the line that is returned is printed. In the case of the daytime service this will be the current time and date from the viewpoint of the server.

One of the things that you should note is the amount of replicated code which is shared between the server examples and the client examples. This is a deliberate ploy: we could have written the code to look completely different, but using code which is very similar has the benefit of illustrating the close ties between servers and clients. This is something that should be expected, considering that both types of application are written using the same classes from the same package. This similarity is a great strength of the `java.net` package, mainly because it uses well-understood principles developed in one area that can be effortlessly deployed in the other.

In fact, the basic principles which apply to servers are exactly the same as those which apply to clients. The essence of the network package is to create a socket (either using a ServerSocket in a server or directly in clients) and then to create the input and output streams using the `getInputStream()` method and the `getOutputStream()` method. Once these steps have been taken, it is possible to read and write to the network connections using the methods that we have already illustrated. With this in mind, it is a small matter to create a set of classes and methods which deal with the nitty-gritty of managing network connections, thereby increasing the amount of code that can be reused in a project.

We should also note that the `sun.*` package hierarchy includes a network library that replicates a good deal of the functionality of the `java.net` package and often includes classes that are more flexible and require less coding to reach the same level of support. However, since Java ports to other platforms are only required to implement the `java.*` packages there is no guarantee that a target system will be able to use the classes in those packages. We have deliberately chosen not to illustrate the use of these packages for that reason – after all, this book is about the generic Java language and as far as possible is not tied to any specific implementation.

8.4.3 Making constrained connections

We have already mentioned the limitations that are imposed on network connections made by applets. However, since it is possible that applet code will be available from a number of servers other than the original distribution point, how is it possible to make connections? One approach is to hard-code the network address of each server into different versions of the applet. Clearly this is a clumsy and inelegant solution. In this section we explain how to obtain the name of the machine that the applet was downloaded from. This can then be used to make a connection that will not fall foul of the security model.

The `Applet` class contains a number of methods which return information about the document that an applet is embedded in and we will use these to get the information. The following example is an applet which determines the host from which it was downloaded and then makes a connection to the daytime service, displaying the results using `paint()`. The code is shown below:

```java
import java.applet.*;
import java.net.*;
import java.io.*;
import java.awt.*;

public class safeConn extends Applet {
  Socket conn;
```

```
int port = 13;
String host;
BufferedInputStream instream;
String time;

public void init() {
  try {
    URL tt = new
    URL(this.getDocumentBase(),"somefile");
    host = tt.getHost();
  }catch(Exception e) {
    System.out.println("Err: " + e);
  }
  try {
    conn = new Socket(host,port);
    instream = new
    BufferedInputStream(conn.getInputStream());
  } catch (Exception e) {
    System.out.println("Err: " + e);
    System.exit(1);
  }
}

public void start() {
  /* Read a line from the socket and
  then write it out */
  time = this.getline();
}

public void paint(Graphics g) {
  g.drawString("Host: "+host+" Time: "+time,10,10);
}

public String getline() {
  ...
  /* As before in examples */
  ...
}
}
```

The most significant lines in the context of this chapter are:

```
URL tt = new URL(this.getDocumentBase(),"somefile");
host = tt.getHost();
```

The first line creates a new URL which comprises the document base of the applet (that is, the Web page into which the applet has been embedded) plus a spurious String which is only used to satisfy the parameter requirements of the class. The next line asks the URL for the host element; this is returned as a String. After that, the code is a simple adaptation of the `simpleClient` class illustrated above ported to be a simple applet.

One potential problem with using this technique to get the hostname is that when pages are loaded from disk (using the 'Load File' option or similar) the hostname will be returned as an empty String. This will generate exceptions if passed directly to Socket. Be aware that users may have local copies of your class files, and code accordingly.

8.4.4 Guidelines for applets and applications for client–server applications

The same basic guidelines apply to both servers and clients. For example, it is always preferable to close a socket explicitly using the `close()` method rather than let it be closed when the application dies or when the connection times out. This is especially important with an applet which must ensure that all open sockets are handled appropriately when the applet is unloaded and reloaded.

Equally, when using network connections, it is essential to keep the user informed of what the applet is doing and why. Recently, there has been increased awareness of the potential of malicious software and it is prudent both for the prolonged life of your code and the reputation of you and your organization if the user knows what connections are being made and why. We would also advise you to avoid hijacking other connections to bypass the security model for much the same reason. There is no justification for not keeping the user informed of progress and functionality and a carefully considered approach to this will pay dividends.

8.5 General considerations

Having discussed some of the specific issues surrounding using the `java.net` package we will now move on to some of the more general issues. These are considerations that are not directly related to the coding of a project, but should be considered when the overall design of the system is being developed.

8.5.1 Network bandwidth constraints

One of the biggest problems facing Java and related technologies is the limited capacity of the Internet. Java invites users to download and manipulate a rich content set which can include images, sound clips and motion video, in addition to the requirement to download the class files associated with the execution of the code.

When designing an applet, you should consider carefully the impact of poor network quality on your application. For example, if your system consists of an applet which feeds back user response to a remote server controlling the animations that are transmitted to the applet, what impact will poor performance have? In this instance it is easy to imagine that network congestion will delay the user feedback to the server by several seconds. This will frustrate the users as they provide the same feedback again – and when the server gets the messages the action will be executed twice.

Equally, from an attention-span perspective, not many users are going to wait an hour for your meticulously crafted full-motion video to be downloaded over an already crowded network. As a developer, you have but a limited period of time from when the user clicks on the link to your applet to losing interest to show your wares – regardless of whether your content is commercial, educational or recreational. If you want your applet to be viewed, then carefully consider how you can minimize the amount of network resources you will consume.

One approach that is being considered on a project one of us is involved with is to have the user install the majority of bespoke classes in advance of using the applet. However, this approach is not suitable for every application; this project is supporting many tens of thousands of users and the applet code will frequently be reused. Another approach is to optimize the structure of the code to use as many components as possible from the standard Java packages. While this may force a slightly more generic appearance on applets, it does significantly reduce the network demand.

Whatever way you decide to optimize your applet it is worth doing. The amount of time it takes for a user to become bored is very small, and to capture the imagination in spite of generally poor network access is a skill which is worth honing.

8.5.2 Good behaviour

Another aspect of using the network library is to ensure that the user has control over the network processes. For example, if you wrote some code which played an audio stream over the network as it was downloaded you should also take precautions to ensure that the user can control what could be an irritating behaviour. If the audio stream accompanied a transcript of a speech, a user visiting the software in a shared office may well want to switch off the audio and concentrate on the text. In our experience, there is no other aspect of control in software which gets more overlooked or underestimated than network connections. When writing any kind of code, make sure that the user has control and not the developer. Users who get tired of software will not revisit it.

8.6 Summary

In this chapter we have covered the use of the `java.net` package. This allows a developer to create and manage network connections. We explained how to build a server and demonstrated that the same principles can be used to create functional clients. Throughout the chapter we focused on the package and not on the 'back-end' functionality that would tailor the code to specific applications.

We have discussed the basic steps that are required to make use of the network classes and given examples of each one. We have also discussed the limitations that the security model imposes on network connections and the implications this has on code design. We have provided a method to determine which server supplied the Web page to the browser and therefore which machine the applet can connect to without violating the security rules, and we have advocated not violating those rules with regard to user trust and breakable code.

Finally, we have discussed a few points which are worthy of consideration when planning network-dependent code. After reading this chapter, you should be able to implement both server and client functionality into Java code and have an understanding of the general approach taken by the Java system. We feel that the network package is one of the most flexible and important elements of the Java system, and we fully expect to see it become an essential tool in Java development – especially in applet development. Using the network classes enables a Java applet to reach out beyond the confines of the Web browser and create an environment where the user can access information in a coordinated model, restricted only by the user's capacity to absorb data.

CHAPTER
NINE
The Java Development Kit

AIMS

- To describe the process for compiling and testing Java code.

- To outline the functionality of the Java development tools.

- To describe how to add applets to HTML pages.

9.1 Introduction

This chapter does not cover the Java language directly but, instead, focuses on the background information that a developer needs to know in order to develop Java applications and applets. We will outline the essential information required to make the most of the tools which are supplied as part of the Sun Java Development Kit (JDK). The examples given in this chapter are based on the Sun JDK distribution for the Sun Solaris operating system – although most other platforms will operate in a similar manner. We have not chosen to give specific examples for other operating systems simply because we would not be able to create a complete list. Certainly, between the completion of the manuscript for this book and final publication, announcements are expected for a range of platforms and operating systems such as the Macintosh range. We have selected the Sun JDK as the development environment because it is freely available and is stable. At the time of writing several commercial development companies have made announcements regarding Java support in commercial products. At this stage it is unclear which development kit will be dominant, if any. Since the majority of early Java developers will be using the Sun JDK, we have elected to cover that package.

9.2 First steps

This section will show you how to take a Java file and compile it. This will allow you to work through any of the examples shown in this group as well as allowing you to access and work through any code fragments that are available for downloading on the Internet or any of the commercial networks.

9.2.1 Compiling a Java source file

The basic sequence for compiling a Java code file is to create the file, either by typing in the code or by downloading the code from another site, and then instruct the compiler to process the file. The compiler will take the source file and produce a file which either can be used by a browser or the appletviewer or is a standalone application.

Let's take the standard HelloWorld Java application and step through the compilation process. In this example we will describe an application rather than an applet; however, the process for compilation is just the same. The code is:

```
public class HelloWorld {

    public static void main (String args[]) {
            System.out.println("Hello World");
        }
}
```

Creating the source file

As a developer you can use a text-editor or word processor to create your source code files as long as the saved files are in ASCII format. Source files must end with the .java extension and, by convention, the name of the file is the same as the name of the class which is defined within the file, so we would create a file called 'HelloWorld.java' to contain the source in the example above.

It is important to point out that you can only have one public class per Java source file – although it is quite acceptable to include as many non-public classes as you like.

The convention of naming files after classes is an important one. As the amount of code required for a project increases, the importance of a consistent naming system to handle a large number of files becomes increasingly vital for keeping track of classes.

So, for this example, we create a text file called HelloWorld.java and type in the simple example as above. Note that the name of the file is case-sensitive to match the class name.

Compiling the source file

Once you have constructed a source file you can use the compiler to translate the Java instructions into byte-codes. These will later be used by the Java interpreter.

When the compiler compiles a Java source file it writes out a file named after the class that has been processed with .class appended. This is another reason for naming the source files after the class names, since the compiler will create files named after classes regardless of the naming strategy you have adopted. The one-to-one mapping of classes to sources and classes to compiled class files is useful for keeping track of large amounts of code.

The Java compiler is called javac in the Sun JDK. It is invoked simply by typing :

```
javac <filename>.Java
```

If the JDK has been installed correctly, the compiler will be in your search path and will not have to be specified explicitly. If your shell returns an error reporting that the javac binary cannot be located, you should return to the installation instructions and ensure that you have followed all of the steps laid out. Some readers will look to this book to help diagnose installation and configuration problems, but even with the best will in the world we just can't cover the range of platforms that Java will support. The best place to look for guidance in this area is the documentation which is supplied with the JDK and the Sun Java Web servers.

So, for our example, we just type:

```
javac HelloWorld.java
```

The compiler will take the source file and generate a byte-code file called HelloWorld.class.

Dealing with syntax errors

The Java compiler, as with most compilers, will perform syntax checks on the source code as part of the compilation process. These check for syntax errors and ensure that you have created source code which conforms to the definition of the Java language. So, for example, if instead of typing this line in our example:

```
public static void main (String args[]) {
```

we typed:

```
main (String args[]) {
```

and recompiled it, the javac compiler would report the following error:

```
HelloWorld.java:4:  Invalid  method  declaration;  return
type required.
  main (String args[]) {
      ^
  1 error
```

This error indicates that a method in Java must declare what will be returned to the calling method. Even methods that do not return anything must explicitly say so by using the void keyword. You can see that the compiler has also stated that the error has been encountered in line four of the source file. Since blank lines are taken into account this may not be the fourth line of code. The Java compiler tries to continue compiling after encountering an error, so that as many problems can be identified in one pass as possible. However, this may mean that the same error can generate a whole raft of errors as the compiler finds related problems further into the source file. For example, instead of declaring a String correctly we could have typed:

```
sTring someString;
```

and then compiled the source file. Not only would the compiler complain about the real error but it would also generate an error each time that the String was referenced. For example, if `someString` was assigned a value from calling a method which returned a String, the compiler would complain about an invalid cast between `String` and `sTring`. Most compilers do this and it is not something specific to the Java system, but it is worth looking at the errors that are generated from a source file and seeing how many of them are caused by one problem being encountered over and over again.

In addition to errors, the Java compiler can also issue warnings. A common warning is creating a file which contains a public class that is not named after the file. The compiler will continue to compile after a warning, but it is an indication that the developer is not following the guidelines that the compiler expects to work with. In our experience it is worth fixing the problems that the warnings disclose, if only to prevent you becoming desensitized to real errors when they are reported.

Syntax errors are, of course, the simplest to handle and report. After all, the design of the Java language is well defined and the compiler knows what the rules are. When source code does not conform to these rules there is a clear case of an error and the compiler can make a clean-cut decision about syntax based on the relatively simple model of the language definition.

There is another kind of error which a compiler rarely detects and that is a conceptual flaw in the design of the program. This can be thought of as the developer writing code which is *syntactically* correct but which is flawed in the logic of the design. You will encounter these errors more frequently than you would like and you will often have to trace the progression of your code through execution to determine what is happening.

There are two main approaches to debugging code in this manner. The first, and most basic, is to insert lines of code at key points in the source code which print out a line of information regarding the progress of the execution or possibly the value of a variable. These lines would typically be moved by the developer as the problems are narrowed down to a specific area of the code. This approach is effective for simple problems in small amounts of code, but does not scale up to handling complex problems in large code bases. The other approach is to use a debugger. This allows the developer to control the execution of the program manually on a step-by-step basis and check the way that methods are called and the value of variables at each step of progression.

Dealing with syntax errors

In order to make use of the Java debugger `jdb`, you must compile your source code using the `-g` flag for the javac compiler. This flag allows the compiler to build into the final class file the required information that `jdb` will use to debug the file. To use the debugger, you simply call the binary and specify the Java target. So, for example, if we wanted to debug our simple example, we would first compile the .java file using the debug flag for the compiler:

```
javac -g HelloWorld.java
```

and then call the debugger with:

```
jdb HelloWorld
```

The model of operation for this type of debugger is to specify a break-point somewhere in the code. A break-point is a point in the source code which will cause the debugger to stop execution and hand over control to the developer. Exceptions that are not caught by methods, or are unexpected, are also considered as break-points so the debugger will stop there as well. The use of break-points lets the debugger run the program automatically until the execution reaches the area which interests the developer. At that point, it is possible to step through the execution of the code, one line at a time, to see in greater detail what is happening. Because, after each line is executed, the debugger can read the value of any variable it is a useful way of seeing where design problems manifest themselves.

9.2.2 Running Java code

Once you have created a Java file and compiled it so that there are no syntax errors you will want to run the code. We have covered the general debugging concepts before this section because they fit more comfortably with the compilation process. However, only the syntax errors will have been detected and fixed by the time that the compiler generates a usable class file, so any conceptual errors which you have made will not show up until you try to run the software. Some errors may take hours or weeks of use to show up, because the problems increment slowly and the effect takes some time to become noticeable, or because the code which generates the problems is so deeply tucked away into the program structure that it is not often called during normal use. Regardless of this, you will still need to run the code.

Running an application

To run an application you will need to call the Java run-time interpreter and ask it to process the class file that you have compiled. If your application consists of multiple classes, and hence has multiple class files, you need only enter the name of the class which contains the main() method.

Continuing with our example, to run the HelloWorld application we would type:

```
java HelloWorld
```

Notice that we did not need to tell the Java interpreter that this is a class file. The java binary knows that this is the case and, in fact, will not run if you specify the .class part of the file name. When your application requires access to additional classes the Java interpreter will take care of loading them. The class files in the same directory as the class which has been passed to java and the default Java packages will be available to the interpreter automatically. However, if you have a development structure which spans multiple directories and includes packages which you have written yourself, then you need to set the CLASSPATH environment variable to include all of the places that you want the run-time system to look for additional classes.

There are some interesting arguments that can be supplied to the Java interpreter. We shall describe them here:

`-debug`

This allows the Java debugger to attach itself to the Java session. When you start a session with the `-debug` flag a password is displayed which must also be used by the remote debugger.

`-cs`

When this flag is used, the Java interpreter checks the class files against the source files and recompiles any classes which have been modified. The recompiled classes are then loaded. While useful, this can take some time to happen especially in projects with large amounts of source code.

`-noasyncgc`

This flag disables the automatic garbage collection to free up resources occupied by objects which are no longer in scope. Under other circumstances, the garbage collector runs as a background thread which is executed in parallel with the main system and program threads.

`-verbosegc`

Causes the garbage collector to print out a message to the standard channel out every time memory is freed from objects which are no longer in scope.

`-verify, -noverify`

Controls the operation of the code verifier.

`-verbose`

Asks the interpreter to print out a line to the standard output for each class that is loaded.

In addition to the `javac` interpreter, there is also a non-optimized version which is invoked by calling 'java_g'. An additional flag which applies to this is '-t' which prints out a trace of the instructions as they are executed.

Running an applet

There are two ways of viewing applets. The first is to use a Java-compatible browser such as Netscape Navigator 2.0 (which at the time of writing is available as a public-beta). The second is by using the Appletviewer which is shipped as part of the Sun JDK.

Both the browser and the Appletviewer work in much the same way. A page of HTML containing references to applets (we will discuss these references in detail later in this chapter) is loaded and then the class files and associated resources (images, sound, and so on) are located and loaded, as the applet code is executed. The fundamental difference between a browser and the Appletviewer is that the browser will display all of the HTML that it understands – this includes text, Java code and images – whereas the Appletviewer ignores all of the HTML tags except for those which are Java applets. The Appletviewer then loads each of the applets and associated resources and displays each of the applets in a separate top-level window.

To use the Appletviewer you must create an HTML file which references your applet. You can place other entities into the HTML file but the Appletviewer will ignore them. A simple file to view our HelloWorld applet would look like this:

```
<HTML>
<HEAD>
<TITLE> Appletviewer Test </TITLE>
</HEAD>
<BODY>
<APPLET CODE="HelloWorld.class" WIDTH=150 HEIGHT=25>
</APPLET>
</BODY>
</HTML>
```

We will not discuss the basics of HTML at any length, except to cover the extension of HTML which allows applets to be embedded into Web pages. The example above simply defines an HTML document which has a title of 'Appletviewer Test'. In the body of the Web page the tag that interests us is <APPLET>. This is the agreed extension to HTML which allows Web page writers to include references to applets in pages. We have used the most basic form of the tag:

```
<APPLET CODE="HelloWorld.class" WIDTH=150 HEIGHT=25>
</APPLET>
```

The first word in the line 'APPLET' is self-explanatory. In developmental alpha versions of the Java system the tag used to declare Java applets was APP. You may still see some references to this as the alpha release of the software will take some months to disappear completely. The next word is CODE. This flag tells the browser which class file to load. In this case we have chosen to use the HelloWorld.class file that we compiled earlier. It is important to remember to put the .class suffix after the name of the class you wish to load. The name of the class is the top-level class in your applet. Other classes which are called or defined by your top-level class will be loaded automatically. The next two arguments are used to define the amount of browser window space that the applet will occupy. These tags have been made compulsory in the beta release and are included so that browsers such as Netscape can determine the layout of a Web page before waiting for all of the classes and resources to load and the applet to initialize. The cost of this is that you may find that some of the methods in the Applet class relating to size are not implemented correctly in all the browsers supporting Java. The final tag </APPLET> defines the end of the tag for this applet.

These five small elements define the minimum amount of HTML that is required to include an applet into a Web page. There are some other tags which can be used, as well as a mechanism for passing arguments into applets using HTML, but we will return to this topic later for a more in-depth coverage. For the moment, it is sufficient to understand that this small amount of HTML will specify to the Appletviewer (or a browser) that a Java applet is embedded into the page.

Having created the HTML file, we now need to have the AppletViewer load the applet and execute it. It is not possible to load an applet directly into the AppletViewer without creating and loading an HTML page. Having created a file such as the one above, it is possible to load the file by calling the viewer with the name of the file as the argument:

```
appletviewer myfile.html
```

This approach assumes that the file is located in the current working directory. It is also possible to have the viewer load and process a page of HTML containing applet references from a remote machine by specifying a URL as the argument in the place of the local file name, for example:

```
appletviewer http://host.domain.com//some/path/myfile.html
```

Naturally, this assumes that the remote machine is running as a server for HTML pages and that your machine is allowed access to the page that you specify. If both of these are true, then the Appletviewer will load the HTML page, looking for APPLET tags. For each tag that is found the viewer will try to download and execute the applet – each in a separate top-level window.

There is only one command line option which can be specified to the Appletviewer, and that is '-debug' which allows the jdb debugger to connect to the process and perform debugging remotely.

9.3 Other JDK tools

So far we have discussed the Java compiler (javac) which takes source code and generates byte-code class files. We have also touched on the debugger (jdb) which allows the developer to trace the execution of Java code to track down programming problems. In the last section we described the basics of the Appletviewer, which allows the developer to test out an applet without needing to use a browser. There are other tools in the JDK, but in our experience the ones that we have already described are those that are the most commonly used. The remaining tools are included in this section.

9.3.1 Native method support – Java

This tool generates the header files for use in native methods that are written in C. Native methods are discussed in more detail in the last chapter of this book, but at this stage it is sufficient to say that native methods are methods which are written in another language (for example, C), but called within Java applications.

9.3.2 The Java disassembler

The JDK also includes a Java disassembler which can be used to obtain information from compiled class files. The first thing to note about the disassembler is what it can't do, namely take a piece of compiled Java and generate the source code for the classes. In theory it would be possible to analyse the byte-codes which are generated by the compiler and then reverse-engineer the results to create a form of the sources, but it is our opinion that the amount of effort this would require to render a mildly useful form of the source code will ensure that this is very rarely done.

The disassembler is called javap and we will illustrate its use in this section. For this we will need a sample class to work with. The class we have created is as follows:

```java
class myClass {
  static int a = 1;

      public static void main(String args[]) {
              myClass mc = new myClass();
  }

      public void methodA() {
              int b = 2;
              System.out.println("b: "   + b);
              this.methodB(b+1);
  }

      private void methodB(int i) {
              System.out.println("i: "   + i);
      }
}
```

This is a very simple Java application which prints out two lines of output and then exits. The static int a is used for illustration only and is not used in the code. The first step is to put this class into a file and then compile it. We will call the file myClass.java following the naming scheme which we described at the start of this chapter.

The file must first be compiled:

```
javac myClass.java
```

The javac command takes the Java source code and produces the byte-codes which are used by the Java run-time system, either as a standalone interpreter or as a part of a Web browser. Once the code has been successfully compiled, you may want to execute the code to make sure that it behaves as expected. To run the program all you need to do is type:

```
java myClass
```

This piece of sample code is an application and will not run in a browser or with the Appletviewer. When running the compiled code, you should see the following:

```
b: 2
i: 3
```

The next stage is to use the disassembler to look at the compiled code in more detail. If used without any arguments javap takes the compiled code and prints out a list of the public files and methods which are in the class. So if we pass the disassembler over our example class with no arguments:

```
javap myClass
```

you will see the following output:

```
Compiled from myClass.java
class myClass extends java.lang.Object {
    static int a;
    public static void main(java.lang.String []);
    public void methodA();
    public myClass();
    static void <clinit>();
}
```

The first line of the output shows what file contained the source code that generated the class. In our case we used the filename myClass.java, and so this is reflected in the output.

The next line shows the class definition. In our example, the class myClass did not extend anything, but if you look back in this book you will see that all classes either extend another class or extend java.lang.Object which is the basic building block for the whole of the Java language. In our example, because we have not explicitly extended from another class, we inherit automatically from Object.

The next line shows the presence of the (unused) static integer, and the next four lines show the methods that exist in the class. There are two things to notice: the first is that the disassembler has listed a class, clinit, which is not in the source code above; the second is that methodB is not listed at all in the output. Why is this? Well, the additional class clinit is added by the system for internal use and the private methodB is not displayed because the default set up with javap is to list only the public methods. There is a command line argument that can be supplied to javap to list both the private and protected methods in a class in addition to the public ones. The flag is -p and if we call javap again using the flag:

```
javap -p myClass
```

we see the following:

```
Compiled from myClass.java
class myClass extends java.lang.Object {
    static int a;
    public static void main(java.lang.String []);
    public void methodA();
    private void methodB(int);
```

```
  public myClass();
  static void <clinit>();
}
```

As you would expect, much of the output is the same, with the addition of the extra line which lists the private methodB.

Javap is also capable of listing the instructions which comprise the Java byte-codes, using the -c flag on the command line. So if we call javap as:

```
javap -c myClass
```

we see the following result:

```
Compiled from myClass.java
class myClass extends java.lang.Object {
static int a;
public static void main(java.lang.String []);
public void methodA();
public myClass();
static void <clinit>();

Method void main(java.lang.String [])
0 new #5 <Class myClass>
3 dup
4 invokenonvirtual #11 <Method myClass.<init>()V>
7 astore_1
8 aload_1
9 invokevirtual #10 <Method myClass.methodA()V>
12 return

Method void methodA()
0 iconst_2
1 istore_1
2 getstatic #16 <Field java.lang.System.out
  Ljava/io/PrintStream;>
5 new #3 <Class java.lang.StringBuffer>
8 dup
9 invokenonvirtual #18 <Method
java.lang.StringBuffer.<init>()V>
12 ldc #1 <String "b: ">
14 invokevirtual #15 <Method
java.lang.StringBuffer.append(Ljava/lang/String;)Ljava/lang/
StringBuffer;>
17 iload_1
8 invokevirtual #9 <Method
java.lang.StringBuffer.append(I)Ljava/lang/StringBuffer;>
21 invokevirtual #13 <Method
java.lang.StringBuffer.toString()Ljava/lang/String;>
24 invokevirtual #17 <Method
java.io.PrintStream.println(Ljava/lang/String;)V>
```

```
27 aload_0
28 iload_1
29 iconst_1
30 iadd
31 invokenonvirtual #8 <Method myClass.methodB(I)V>
34 return

Method void methodB(int)
0 getstatic #16 <Field java.lang.System.out
Ljava/io/PrintStream;>
3 new #3 <Class java.lang.StringBuffer>
6 dup
7 invokenonvirtual #18 <Method
java.lang.StringBuffer.<init>()V>
10 ldc #2 <String "i: ">
12 invokevirtual #15 <Method
java.lang.StringBuffer.append(Ljava/lang/String;)Ljava/lang/
StringBuffer;>
15 iload_1
16 invokevirtual #9 <Method
java.lang.StringBuffer.append(I)Ljava/lang/StringBuffer;>
19 invokevirtual #13 <Method
java.lang.StringBuffer.toString()Ljava/lang/String;>
22 invokevirtual #17 <Method
java.io.PrintStream.println(Ljava/lang/String;)V>
25 return

Method myClass()
0 aload_0
1 invokenonvirtual #14 <Method java.lang.Object.<init>()V>
4 return

Method void <clinit>()
0 iconst_1
1 putstatic #12 <Field myClass.a I>
4 return

}
```

This lists the byte-code instructions for all of the methods. A discussion of what the byte-code instructions represent is beyond the scope of this book, but an idle glance over the output from javap reveals a surprising amount of information to the casual user. We do not recommend that developers spend time understanding the byte-code system unless there are very good reasons, such as implementing a Java system on a new platform, but javap does provide a useful tool for working at that level. One of the benefits of the Java system is that there is no need for most developers to understand the intricacies of the underlying system: if you are working at that level then you are probably doing something wrong or have selected the wrong programming language.

9.3.3 API documentation

If you have downloaded a copy of the JDK, you will be familiar with the style of the API documentation in HTML. All of the API pages follow a similar and clear format which summarizes information at the top of the page and then provides more detail further down the page. The JDK provides a tool to assist in the production of documentation for classes in a format which matches the Sun API HTML pages. Unlike the previous tools, the documentation generator (javadoc) works with source files and not with compiled class files.

The basic method for generating the documentation is to call javadoc with the name of the source file:

```
javadoc myClass.java
```

Javadoc will load and process the file and then write out an HTML file to the local directory called <classname>.html. The output from this process is pretty basic. A better solution is to include comments in the source file that javadoc can understand and therefore add to the HTML output. The comments which javadoc can work with start with @. Extending our example, if we added the following lines to the Java source code file before the class definition:

```
/**
 * A class used for illustrating javadoc
 * For example:
 * <pre>
 *      javadoc myClass.java
 * </pre>
 *
 * @version 1.2 21st November 1995
 * @author  Adam Freeman
 */
class myClass {
   ...
```

then the documentation produced would be as shown in Figure 9.1. The forward slash and double star identifies comments that can be used in automatic documentation generation tools.

The codes have been interpreted and formatted in the output file. It is important to provide all of the information that someone using the class might need to know, without providing extraneous information. javadoc will only document methods in the class that are available for external use, and it is possible and desirable to document the methods as well as the class as a whole. The following is an example:

```
/**
 * Prints the value of the int to the standard out
 *
 * @param someint The integer to print out
 *
 */
public void someMethod(int someint) {
   ...}
```

Class myClass

```
java.lang.Object
   |
   +----myClass
```

class **myClass**
extends Object

A class used for illustrating javadoc For example:

```
javadoc myClass.java
```

Version:
    1.2 21st November 1995
Author:
    Adam Freeman

Constructor Index

• **myClass**()

Method Index

• **main**(String[])
• **methodA**()

Constructors

⬤ **myClass**

```
public myClass()
```

Methods

⬤ **main**

```
public static void main(String args[])
```

⬤ **methodA**

```
public void methodA()
```

Figure 9.1 An example of `javadoc` documentation.

This comment, immediately before the method, allows `javadoc` to provide information about how the method should be used and what it does. The '@param' tag is one of three such tags which can be used in method comments:

```
@param parameter-name description
```

This adds a reference for a parameter to the method comment. The name of the parameter should be the descriptor and not the type.

```
@return description
```

This adds a return section, which describes the value that the method will return.

```
@exception class-name description
```

This adds a 'Throws' entry which lists the exceptions that the method may throw. It is important to specify the fully qualified exception name since `javadoc` will automatically create a hot-link to the documentation for the exception that the method could throw.

The value of using `javadoc` to automatically document usage details for your developed classes cannot be underestimated. Not only will `javadoc` provide a documentation format which is consistent with other classes that you write but also with the Sun API specs. In addition, using the tags within the source file imposes a level of comments which is both plentiful and consistent across multiple source files. If you are considering permitting other developers to access your package library, then it is our advice that you consider the use of `javadoc` to be essential before shipping the code to other sites.

9.4 HTML tags

This section will cover the essentials of using HTML to embed applets into Web pages as we promised at the start of the chapter. You have already seen the basic building blocks which are used to tag Java code, namely:

```
<APPLET>, CODE, WIDTH, HEIGHT and </APPLET>
```

Using these tags it is possible to include applets into Web pages. The example we gave above was for the HelloWorld applet which is discussed at length in the next chapter. The HTML tags to embed this into a Web page were:

```
<APPLET CODE="HelloWorld.class" WIDTH=150 HEIGHT=25>
</APPLET>
```

To recap, the first `APPLET` tag states to the browser (or the Appletviewer) that this is a Java applet. The next tag, `CODE`, tells the browser that the code for the applet can be found in the `HelloWorld.class` file.

There are other tags that can be used when embedding an applet. The `CODEBASE` tag specifies where the browser should locate the class file which is specified with the `CODE` tag. It is also possible to pass arguments to applets through

HTML. This is of most use when the Web pages are being generated dynamically through CGI (Common Gateway Interface) or when one applet is likely to be widely used and is therefore capable of supporting a range of operation modes. The way of doing this is to include PARAM tags between the <APPLET> and </APPLET> tags, like this:

```
<APPLET CODE="HelloWorld.class" WIDTH=150 HEIGHT=25>
   <PARAM NAME=param1 VALUE=value1>
   <PARAM NAME=param2 VALUE=value2>
</APPLET>
```

Within the applet code that is invoked by this HTML it is possible to read these values. For example, in the init() method of the example class we could have changed the line which prints out 'Hello World' to read the value of param1 and print that out instead. The code to do this is shown below:

```
String str = getParameter("param1");
System.out.println(str);
```

This line of code gets the value of the parameter called param1 (listed in the example above) and then prints out the value of the string holding the parameter. One thing to be careful of is cases where your code expects to receive a parameter through HTML and it has not been added. This is most likely to happen if others use your code. One simple way of handling this is to check the value that has been returned from the call to getParameter() and supply a default value if there is nothing available from the Web page. For example:

```
String str = getParameter("param1");
if (str == null) {
   str = "HelloWorld!";
}
System.out.println(str);
```

This small change ensures that the value has been initialized with something – even if the Web page that called the applet failed to specify a value. Supplying a default value is a very useful strategy, especially when not initializing a variable correctly could cause exceptions later in the execution of the applet code.

9.4.1 Non-Java browsers

It is possible to include tags between the <APPLET> and </APPLET> tags in the HTML page. HTML that is included here will be displayed by browsers which do not recognize the <APPLET> tag and therefore do not support Java applets. This facility can be used to include explanatory messages or even screen-shots of Java applets to non-Java browsers; this is an important feature since a large number of browsers will not support Java for some time to come. As an example of this feature, consider the following HTML code:

```
<APPLET.....>
<blockquote>
<hr>
```

```
<em>
You are using a browser which does not support Java.
If you had a Java-aware browser, then you would
currently see the HelloWorld applet at work...
</em>
<hr>
</blockquote>
</APPLET>
```

Java-compatible browsers will recognize the `APPLET` tags and load the applet, but other browsers will skip the `APPLET` tags and display the text instead. We strongly recommend taking advantage of this facility when writing Web pages that will embed Java applets, not least because seeing a nearly-empty screen because an applet should be there is disconcerting to the user unless there is an explanatory message.

9.5 Summary

We have described the system facilities for carrying out common tasks such as compiling Java code and including Java code within HTML documents. Many of these facilities look like those available in a UNIX-based system. However, as more and more implementations of Java are made we expect different instantiations of these facilities together with extra facilities which may be specific to the host system.

CHAPTER
TEN
Building an applet

AIMS

- To describe the major events in the life cycle of an applet.

- To introduce the concepts of event handling and drawing the applet.

- To outline the basic use of threads within applets.

- To introduce the basics of applet user interface support.

- To build a sample applet to demonstrate some of these new topics.

10.1 Introduction

At this point you should understand the differences between an applet and an application. In short, applications are standalone while applets conform to rules which allow them to be 'hosted' in a Java-compatible browser. This chapter focuses on applets and the differences that arise from requiring a host.

There are some subtle differences between writing an applet and writing an application. When working with a standalone application, the developer can make arbitrary decisions about pretty much any aspect of his or her code. When writing an applet it is essential that your code conforms to the applet standard so that your work can be executed within a Java-compatible browser. Of course, it is possible to write an applet which conforms to the letter of the applet class while still being a 'bad' example of coding because it fails to operate within the spirit of the hosted system. To help you write code that will cooperate with the Java system, we will describe some pointers during the chapter that should assist you in writing better applets.

10.1.1 'Hello World' revisited again

As with the previous chapter, we'll use the standard issue 'Hello World' building block and extend the code to introduce new concepts. For an applet, the code looks like this:

```java
import java.awt.Graphics;

public class HelloWorld extends java.applet.Applet {
  public void init() {
    resize(100,100);
  }

  public void paint(Graphics g) {
    g.drawString("Hello World!",5,20);
  }
}
```

The first line in the applet 'imports' the awt.Graphics library into the applet file. Chapter 7 describes the AWT library in more detail.

You can see from the declaration of the class that the HelloWorld class inherits from the Applet class. The Applet class itself inherits from classes within the AWT library which means that applets can make use of interface components when constructing interfaces. We'll cover this in more detail later in the chapter.

Because this is a very simple applet there are only two methods. The first method in the code, init, is always called by the system to allow the applet to prepare for execution. In this example, our applet just increases the amount of browser page space from the system default that it occupies. The second method is called by the system when the applet is asked to display itself on the screen. This could be because the applet has just been loaded or because the browser has been uncovered from under another window. In this applet, all we do is draw our string into the Graphics context at the specified pixel coordinates.

10.2 Introducing some essential applet methods

Real applets won't be as simple as the 'Hello World' example above. An applet can perform a whole range of tasks including games, advertising, spicing up a home page and simulating a real-world situation. Clearly the limits of an applet's functionality are the limits of the developer's imagination. Because applets are typically embedded in pages of HTML, there is a need for applets to coexist in a peaceful manner. To this end the Applet class defines a set of methods which applets can override to allow code to be hosted happily in a browser. To start off, we'll look at a group of methods which control the 'life cycle' of an applet.

10.2.1 Methods to control the life of an applet

The Java system needs a way to control the execution of an applet. The system needs to tell an applet when it has been loaded into the page or when it has been unloaded. The core set of such methods is described briefly below:

- `init()`. This method is called by the Java system to initialize the applet each time that it is loaded or reloaded.

- `start()`. The Java system calls this method when the applet is loaded and the applet can begin executing its main task.

- `stop()`. When the user leaves the page or exits from the browser the system will call this method. The applet should suspend any outstanding tasks and threads.

- `destroy()`. This method is the last chance that an applet will have to clean up before it is unloaded from the browser. All tasks should be stopped and any threads halted.

The `HelloWorld` class doesn't need to override all of the methods. Typically, the `init()` method should be used to prepare the applet for the main task ahead by performing work which only needs to be done once in the lifetime of the applet, for example allocating storage for arrays.

The `start()` method performs the applet's work or establishes other objects to do the work. Most applets that override `start()` will also need to override `stop()`. The `stop()` method should be used to prevent the applet consuming system resources when the applet is not active – for example, halting a demanding graphics routine when the user moves on to a different browser page.

One of the most common ways of redefining `start()` is to create a thread which runs as a background process and then use a call to `stop()` to halt the thread at the start of the next loop. This means that the thread doesn't die immediately after `stop()` is called; however, for most applets this won't be a big issue. If your applet uses a thread with a very time-consuming main loop you should consider breaking up the code so that the thread checks for `stop()` being called more frequently. The effect of letting a thread (or any other similar object) live long after the user has moved on is to slow down the client machine. If the user encounters several such ill-behaved applets then the client can be ground to a halt.

Many applets don't bother to override the `destroy()` method, because their `stop()` method puts the applet into a state suitable for being unloaded. This is an acceptable approach because the Java system guarantees to call `stop()` prior to calling `destroy()`.

10.2.2 Adding life-cycle methods to the `HelloWorld` class

So, let's build on the `HelloWorld` class to include examples of the life-cycle methods. To keep things simple, we will just have the class print a line to the standard output when each of the methods is invoked. You should spend some time loading, reloading, and unloading the applet until you are happy that all of the methods are called and, more importantly, the methods are called in the correct order. The revised class is shown below:

```java
import java.awt.Graphics;
public class HelloWorld extends java.applet.Applet {
  public void init() {
    System.out.println("Applet: system
                       has called init()");
    resize(100,100);
  }

  public void paint(Graphics g) {
    g.drawString("Hello World!",5,20);
  }

  public void start() {
    System.out.println("Applet: system
                       has called start()");
  }

  public void stop() {
    System.out.println("Applet: system
                       has called stop()");
  }

  public void destroy() {
    System.out.println("Applet: system
                       has called destroy()");
  }
}
```

At this point you should compile the applet and view it in a browser. Play around with the page and watch the output as you load and unload the applet code. Each time one of the methods is invoked, the applet just prints out a line using the System class library detailing the method. If all is well, the methods should be called in the following order when the applet is first loaded: init(), start(), stop(), destroy().

10.3 Drawing and handling events

So far our HelloWorld class has been simple: there has been no interaction with the user and we have only displayed a single string on the browser page. The rest of the information has been sent to the standard out. Real applets are going to want to change their appearance and receive input from the user. Happily, the Applet class supports both of these requirements.

10.3.1 Drawing to the screen

There are two main methods that you will need to know about to handle drawing to the browser page, paint() and update().

By default, the paint method is used by the applet to draw its representation onto the browser page and the update method is used when part or all of the applet needs to be refreshed. If you don't override these methods by means of inheritance then your applet will inherit the following:

```
public void update(Graphics g) {
  g.setColor(getBackGround());
  g.fillRect(0, 0, width, height);
  g.setColor(getForeground());
  paint(g);
}

public void paint(Graphics g) {
}
```

So you can see that the `update` method just paints a rectangle the size of the applet in the background colour which is typically the colour of the browser page; it then resets the applet screen to the colour it was before and calls `paint`, which by default does nothing.

Most of your display code will go into the `paint` method. There are occasions when the `update` method is useful. We will cover those later in the chapter.

10.3.2 Adding drawing methods to the `HelloWorld` class

To illustrate a simple example using these methods, we'll extend the `HelloWorld` class to draw a filled 3-D rectangle into which we'll place the 'Hello World!' string.

The revised code is shown below:

```
import java.awt.Graphics;
import java.awt.Color;

public class HelloWorld extends java.applet.Applet {
  public void init() {
    System.out.println("Applet: system
                        has called init");
    resize(100, 100);
  }

  public void paint(Graphics g) {
    g.setColor(Color.red);
    g.fill3DRect(5,5,95,95,true);
    g.setColor(Color.black);
    g.drawString("Hello World!",5,20);
    System.out.println("Applet: system
                        has called paint");
  }

  public void update(Graphics g) {
    super.update(g);
    System.out.println("Applet: system
                        has called update");
  }
```

```
public void start() {
   System.out.println("Applet: system
                       has called start");
}

public void stop() {
   System.out.println("Applet: system
                       has called stop");
}

public void destroy() {
   System.out.println("Applet: system
                       has called destroy");
}
}
```

The code:

```
g.fill3DRect(5,5,95,95,true);
```

displays a three-dimensional rectangle at the pixel points specified with the fifth parameter with the rectangle casting a shadow.

So what have we added? Well, we have imported another class, `java.awt.Color`. We need this because our rectangle must be a different colour to our text in order for us to be able to read it. We've redefined the `paint()` method to:

(1)   set the colour to use to red (using the `Color` object);

(2)   draw a 3-D rectangle which is slightly smaller than the applet area;

(3)   set the colour to use back to black;

(4)   draw our string using the colour black;

(5)   print out a line saying that the method has been called.

We've also added an `update()` method. You'll recall from previous chapters that the `super` variable refers to the superclass, so we are invoking the `update()` method contained in the `Applet` class which we listed earlier in this section. After invoking the superclass method, our `update()` call goes on to write out a status line.

10.3.3 Improving drawing performance

We mentioned in Section 10.3.1 that you usually won't need to override the update method. One of the exceptions to this rule of thumb is when your applet requires improved graphics performance. By default, the `update()` and `paint()` methods affect the whole applet and cause the whole of the Graphics context to be redrawn. This approach becomes unacceptable when your applet only wants to update a small section of the screen.

As an example, consider a simple applet which draws a ball bouncing around inside a box. By default, every time the ball moves the whole of the applet must be redrawn. All that is really needed is for the area that the ball has moved out of and the area that the ball has moved into to be handled. This type of selective updating can be done with the judicious use of the `paint` and `update` methods.

10.3.4 Handling applet events

Previous chapters will have introduced you to the idea of events. In this section we'll discuss some of the events that are defined in the `Component` class and inherited by the `Applet` class and, therefore, by your applet as well.

As you might expect there is one method which handles all incoming events and acts in the manner of an exchange to route the event to the appropriate specialist method. This routing method is called `handleEvent()`. Although it is possible for you to override this method, it is more important for you to realize that the method exists for the moment.

Some other methods that you'll encounter include:

- `mouseDown()`, `mouseUp()`. These methods inform the applet that the mouse button has been pressed or released.

- `mouseEnter()`, `mouseExit()`. These methods inform the applet that the pointer has entered or left the browser page.

- `mouseDrag()`, `mouseMove()`. These methods inform the applet when the mouse is moved with either the button pressed (`mouseDrag`) or the button released (`mouseMove`).

- `keyDown()`. This method notifies the applet that the user has pressed a key.

In general this set of seven methods will form the core of the events that you are interested in. Be careful when typing screen updates to user events to ensure that you make the most efficient use of the `paint` and `update` methods. The flow of events, particularly with those related to mouse motion, can be so fast that the screen updates will cause the applet to 'flicker'. While it is possible to override the `handleEvent` class you should consider if it is essential before doing so.

10.3.5 Adding event handling to `HelloWorld`

To demonstrate the event methods, we'll extend the `HelloWorld` class to have two extra features. When the mouse moves over the area of the applet, we'll have the string move with the cursor, and when the user presses a key, we'll append the key character to the string.

The code to do this is:

```
import java.awt.Graphics;
import java.awt.Color;
import java.awt.Event;

public class HelloWorld extends java.applet.Applet {
    int sx,sy;          // The coordinates of the string
```

```java
StringBuffer hw;    // The string to display
public void init() {
   sx = 5;
   sy = 20;
   hw = new StringBuffer("Hello World!");
   System.out.println("Applet: system
                       has called init");
   resize(100, 100);
}


public void paint(Graphics g) {
   g.setColor(Color.red);
   g.fill3DRect(5,5,95,95,true);
   g.setColor(Color.black);
   g.drawString(hw.toString(),sx,sy);
   System.out.println("Applet: system
                       has called paint");
}


public void update(Graphics g) {
   super.update(g);
   System.out.println("Applet: system
                       has called update");
}


public void start() {
   System.out.println("Applet: system
                       has called start");
}

public void stop() {
   System.out.println("Applet: system
                       has called stop");
}

public void destroy() {
   System.out.println("Applet: system
                       has called destroy");
}

public boolean mouseMove(Event evt, int x, int y) {
   sx = x;
   sy = y;
   repaint();
   return true;
}
```

```
public boolean keyDown(Event evt, int ch) {
    hw.append((char)ch);
    repaint();
    return true;
}
}
```

As you might expect by now we have had to import the `java.awt.Event` class
so that we could override the event-based methods. We've used two ints to hold the
coordinates of the string (the initial values are defined in the `init` method).

Because we are going to be appending characters to the `"Hello World!"`
string, we've declared a `StringBuffer`, which is also initialized in the `init()`
method. The `paint()` method then converts the StringBuffer to a String and plots
it at the coordinates held by the two integers (`sx` and `sy`). The method `toString`
converts a `StringBuffer` to a `String` which is expected by `drawString`.

The `mouseMove` method simply takes two coordinates of the pointer as
supplied by the system and sets the int values. The `repaint()` method is called
to have the applet redrawn. As an aside, this simple applet would benefit from
overriding the `update()` method. Currently, `update()` calls `paint()` and the
whole of the applet is drawn. A more effective way to do this would be just to
redraw the area that the string has left and then call `drawString()` to place the
text in the new position. Clearly, if such a simple applet can benefit from this
technique, larger and more complex drawing operations should certainly be
optimized.

The last remaining method we've added takes the `keyDown` event and appends
the character to the `StringBuffer`. Because the `keyDown` method receives the
character in the form of an int, we have made an explicit cast to a char and then
appended to the StringBuffer. If we had not cast in this manner, `StringBuffer`
would append the integer value directly.

It is worth pointing out that the call to `repaint()` in `mouseMove` and
`keyDown` causes the system to call the `update()` method which, by default,
clears the graphics context and then calls the `paint` method.

In this simple applet, there is no support for handling special case characters,
such as the delete key. We can extend our `keyDown` method quite simply to
demonstrate one possible technique:

```
public boolean keyDown(Event evt, int ch) {
    switch (ch) {
    case(8):   // This is the delete key
        if (hw.length() > 0) {
            hw.setLength(hw.length() - 1);
        }
        break;
        default:   hw.append((char)ch);
    }
    repaint();
    return true;
}
```

In this example, if there are any elements in the StringBuffer when the delete key is pressed, then the StringBuffer is made smaller by one character. When any other key is pressed, the character matching the integer representation is appended to the StringBuffer as before.

10.4 Using threads in applets

One of the most common problems introduced into applets is excessive code in the init() method. The reason that this causes a problem is because the browser waits for the init() method to return before continuing to the next applet. So, if an applet which executes all of its code in the init() method is at the top of the page, no other applets will be loaded until after the first applet has returned from the method.

10.4.1 Threads are our friends

One solution to this issue is to create a thread and move as much of the code from the init() method to the thread as possible. This model forms a good general principle: if an applet performs an intensive task then you should arrange for the code to be placed in a thread and have the task executed in the background.

As stated previously there are two main approaches to adding threads to your applet or application. The first way is to subclass the Thread class and override the relevant method (usually you can just override run() and expect the default methods to do the right thing) and the second is to provide a runnable interface in your class. If you do this and provide a handle to your runnable interface then the threads you generate will use the run() method defined in your class.

10.4.2 Making sure your threads die with your applet

You should ensure that your applet can stop any running threads when the system calls stop() or destroy() (remember that if your stop() method prepares your applet for unloading then you can effectively ignore the destroy() method). If you let your threads run wild then the client machine will be slowed and, in the case of processor-intensive tasks, this could be a considerable problem. One simple way of making sure that your threads die is to use a variable known as a **sentinel** which is checked with each iteration of the thread. For example:

```
public class SomeThreadClass implements Runnable {
   Thread kicker = null;

   public void start() {
      kicker = new Thread(this);
      kicker.start();
   }

   public void run() {
      while (kicker != null) {
         ...
```

```
        }
    }

    public void stop() {
        kicker = null;
    }
}
```

In this simple example, the class `SomeThreadClass` implements the `Runnable` interface. When the system calls `start()`, the thread is created and inherits the `run()` method of `SomeThreadClass`. Each iteration of the thread checks to see that the `Thread` object is not null and continues to loop (remember that passing a handle which refers to an instance of the class implementing the `Runnable` interface means that the thread uses the `run()` method we've defined). When the applet is about to be unloaded the system calls the `stop()` method and the thread is set to null. This halts the thread operation the next time that the `while` statement is encountered. This approach of stopping the thread at the next convenient moment is fine unless the main section of the thread takes a particularly long time to complete. If that is the case then you should consider either using multiple threads or checking the state of the thread more frequently. However, there is a point where checking the state of the thread too frequently will consume more system cycles than would be used by letting the thread complete a full iteration – so experiment with your code and find a balance that seems a reasonable trade-off.

10.4.3 Scheduling threads within applets

The `Thread` class contains a method `setPriority()` which enables a programmer to give a thread a priority value; and it is sometimes tempting to use it to set the priority of threads to a maximum and never to yield the CPU. Sometimes, this is not a problem, but it will often affect the whole of the Java system and quite possibly the client machine as well.

Not only should you consider the effect of prioritizing the threads in your applet relative to other threads in the same applet, but you should also consider the impact of your threads on the system as a whole. Threads running at high priority in tight code loops which never yield the CPU are irritating at best and can destroy any interactive elements of other applets – or even of your own applet. So, try to select an appropriate priority value and use the scheduling system to your advantage.

One constructive way of using high priority threads is when you need a periodic display update of a code-intensive loop. By scheduling the thread at a higher priority for the display than for the calculations you can be sure that when the display thread wakes, the system will execute that thread in preference to the calculation thread(s) thus ensuring that the display is updated. When the display thread sleeps, the system will run the calculation threads and keep beavering away.

If you are running multiple threads, you should give some serious thought to your priority assignments. While it is possible to ignore the whole issue and let the system run with the default assignments, it is possible to streamline the operation of your applet considerably by careful selection of priorities and thread design. There is no benefit in running multiple related threads at the same priority, because the system will simply execute the peer threads in rotation, waiting for each thread to yield the CPU. Some systems will switch between equal priority threads, but since you can't rely on this feature to be available on all of the architectures which support Java you should not design code around its availability.

10.4.4 Adding thread support to the `HelloWorld` class

To illustrate the principles of threads and thread scheduling we'll provide two examples. The first example shows the effect of running two threads at different priorities performing the same task. In addition, there is a third thread which periodically wakes up and displays the current values. We'll use both methods of implementing threads, starting with subclassing the `Thread` class for the counting threads. The class is very simple and looks like this:

```java
public class myThread extends Thread {
    int value = 0;

    public void run() {
    while (value < 1000000) {
      value++;
      }
    }

    public int getValue() {
        return value;
    }
}
```

The `myThread` class extends the `Thread` class and only needs to override the `run()` method. In this method, the class simply increments a counter until it reaches a reasonably large number. If you are going to run this code on a particularly fast machine you might need to increase the ceiling for the counting if your system can reach the goal before the display thread wakes up.

Instead of extending the `HelloWorld` class any further, we've subclassed it to produce the `ThreadHelloWorld` class which is listed below:

```java
import java.awt.Event;

public class ThreadHelloWorld extends HelloWorld
                implements Runnable {

    myThread counter[];    // The threads which will count
    Thread dispthread;     // The thread which will display

public void init() {
    sx = 5;
    sy = 20;
    hw = new StringBuffer("Hello World!");
    counter = new myThread[2];
    /* Start the counter threads */
    for (int i = 0; i < 2; i++) {
      counter[i] = new myThread();
```

```
      counter[i].setPriority(i+1);
    }
    /* Start the display thread */
    if (dispthread == null) {
      dispthread = new Thread(this);
      dispthread.setPriority(Thread.MAX_PRIORITY);
    }
    System.out.println("Applet: system has called init");
    resize(100, 100);
}

public void run() {
    while (dispthread != null) {
    printVals();
    try {
    dispthread.sleep(10);
    } catch (InterruptedException e) {
    /* Do nothing */
      }
    }
}

public void printVals() {
    int cval[] = new int[2];
    /* Get the current values from the threads */
    for (int i = 0; i < 2; i++) {
      cval[i] = counter[i].getValue();
    }
    /* Write out the values */
    System.out.println("Thread 1: " + cval[0] +
                       " Thread 2: " + cval[1]);
    /* See if we should stop the threads */
    if (cval[0] == 1000000 && cval[0] == 1000000) {
      stop();
    }
}

public void stop() {
    /* Stop the counting threads */
    for (int i = 0; i < 2; i++) {
      if (counter[i].isAlive()) {
        counter[i].stop();
        counter[i] = null;
      }
    }
    /* Stop the display thread */
    if (dispthread.isAlive()) {
      dispthread.stop();
      dispthread = null;
```

```
        }
    System.out.println("Applet: system has called stop");
}


public boolean mouseDown(Event evt, int x, int y) {
    /* Start the counting threads */
    for (int i = 0; i < 2; i++) {
      if (!counter[i].isAlive()) {
        counter[i].start();
      }
    }
    /* Start the display thread */
    if (!dispthread.isAlive()) {
      dispthread.start();
    }
    return true;
  }
}
```

We have just extended the HelloWorld class to include some basic threads and
have altered the init() method to create the threads we require. Notice that the
priority of the two counting threads is low and that one thread will have a higher
priority than the other. Notice also that the display thread has been given maximum
priority.

Because our class implements the Runnable interface we have to supply a
run() method. In this case we simply obtain and write out the current values of
the counters and then sleep for a fraction of a second. When the counters reach the
target value the threads are stopped. You'll notice that the targets are defined both
in the myThread class and in the ThreadHelloWorld class. This is somewhat
redundant, because the display thread has a higher priority than the counting
threads and the system will execute that thread whenever it wakes. However, while
redundant we always like to make sure that each of our threads is capable of
yielding in case we get the scheduling wrong. In this case there is the additional
reason for the ThreadHelloWorld class checking that both counters are at the
target which requires some additional checking in the myThread class. The rule of
thumb is that you can never be too careful with terminating threads.

We've also added another event method, which we use to start the threads off.
When the mouse button is pressed within the applet area the threads are started and
the whole thing is kicked off. The counter threads start up and the display thread
starts the sleep/wake cycle.

So what happens? Well, as you might expect, the counter thread with the higher
priority holds the CPU when the display thread is asleep. Periodically the display
thread wakes up and is executed, displaying the current values of both threads.
Only when the higher priority counting thread has finished counting will the system
execute the other counter. So what you see is output which shows the first counter
at zero until the second counter hits the target. At that point, the second thread is
allowed to start counting.

So, we hear you asking, why bother with the priority at all? Why not just let everything run at the same level? Well, let's try it. If we change the line in the `ThreadHelloWorld` class from:

```
counter[i].setPriority(i+1);
```

to:

```
counter[i].setPriority(2);
```

and run the applet again, you should see one of two things. If you are on a UNIX system you'll probably see both counters increasing together, although not always in equal amounts. If you are on some other system, then you won't see any difference from the first version of the code.

And this is the problem with not deliberately scheduling. For something as simple as a counter in the example it doesn't matter which of the threads reaches the target first. But in some situations where the completion of one thread prior to the start of another is critical it isn't possible to assume that the client system will divide up the time evenly between threads of the same priority: even systems which do slice up time are not required to do so evenly or consistently. So if thread sequencing is important to your code strategy then ensure that you make full use of the priority system.

10.4.5 Summary of thread use in applets

- Whenever an applet has a time-consuming task to perform, you should use threads. This is especially true when the tasks would be included in the `init()` method, because the browser may not be able to move on to the next applet until your method has returned.

- Make sure that your threads are able to stop when required. You should do this by writing checks at convenient points in your code to ensure that the thread is still required.

- Make sure that your threads are considerate. Your code will have to share a common set of resources on the client machine and the more compliant the applet code the better all of the applets will perform.

- Make proper use of the thread scheduling facilities. Do not assume that the end system will allocate time slices to threads of the same priority.

10.5 Adding an interface to an applet

In this section we will use classes from the AWT library to add a simple interface to our threaded `HelloWorld` class. In this case, we will display the progress of the counting threads in a `TextField`, add a start button to initiate the thread sequence, and add a selector which will allow the user to view the threads performing with the same priority or different priorities.

10.5.1 Adding a TextField

So, to start with let's add the TextField and some general support code. The class looks like this:

```java
import java.awt.*;
public class UIHelloWorld extends ThreadHelloWorld {
  TextField textfield = new TextField(20);
  Panel topPanel,bottomPanel;
  public void init() {
    super.init();
    /* Create two new panels */
    bottomPanel = new Panel();
    topPanel = new Panel();
    /* Set the layout model for this element */
    setLayout(new BorderLayout());
    /* Add the two panels to this element */
    add("South", bottomPanel);
    add("North", topPanel);
    /* Set the layout model for the top panel */
    topPanel.setLayout(new BorderLayout());
    /* Add a label to the panel */
    topPanel.add("North", new Label("Results",
    Label.CENTER));
    /* Add the text area to the top panel */
    topPanel.add("South", textfield);
  }
  public void printVals() {
    int cval[] = new int[2];
    /* Get the current values from the threads */
    for (int i = 0; i < 2; i++) {
      cval[i] = counter[i].getValue();
    }
    /* Set the text in the field to the current values
    */
    textfield.setText("Thread 1: "+cval[0]+" Thread 2:
                      "+cval[1]);
    /* See if we should stop the threads */
    if (cval[0] == 1000000 && cval[0] == 1000000) {
      stop();
    }
  }
  public void paint(Graphics g) {
  /* Do nothing */
  }
}
```

We override the `init()` method so that we can define the interface elements. We also make a call to the superclass `init()` method to ensure that anything we might need to make use of later is ready.

We start the interface by creating two panels. The first will hold the `TextField` to display the progress of the counting threads and the second will hold the start button and the selector. We then set the layout style for this applet, and add the two panels to the applet display.

For the rest of this subsection, we will concentrate on `topPanel` to which we set the layout style, add a simple label and add a `TextField`. In order to have the progress displayed within the applet we have to override the `printVals` method. Instead of printing the string to the standard `out`, we set the text content of the `TextField`. The final change required for this stage is to override the `paint()` method to do nothing. If you look at the final iteration of the `ThreadHelloWorld` class, you will see that the `paint` method places several things into the applet display. Since we no longer require these elements, we want the method to do nothing. At this first stage the applet should produce the display shown in Figure 10.1.

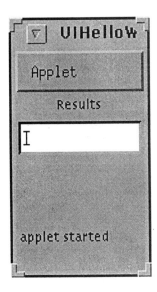

Figure 10.1 Screen shot of applet.

10.5.2 Adding the start button

We will now extend the code to have a start button. Instead of clicking on the applet area to start the threads we will have a button which has to be clicked on. The code for the extension class looks like this:

```
import java.awt.Button;
import java.awt.Event;
public class UIHelloWorld2 extends UIHelloWorld {
  public void init() {
    super.init();
    // Add the button to the lower panel
    bottomPanel.add(new Button(" Start! "));

  public boolean action(Event evt, Object arg) {
    if (" Start! ".equals(arg)) {
      /* Start the counting threads */
      for (int i = 0; i < 2; i++) {
        if (!counter[i].isAlive()) {
          counter[i].start();
        }
      }
    }
```

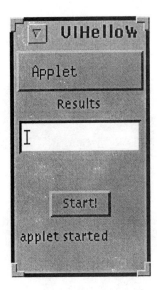

Figure 10.2 Screen shot of applet.

```
    /* Start the display thread */
    if (!dispthread.isAlive()) {
        dispthread.start();
    }
    return true;
  }
  return false;
}
```

In the `init()` method of this class, we call the `init()` method of the superclass and then insert a button into the lower pane that the superclass created. We also need to create a handler for the event that will be generated when the button is pressed. Although it is the only object which is likely to generate an event to be passed to the `action()` class, it is still good programming practice to check that the event we are processing is in fact sent from the button. In this case if the event is from the button, then we start the threads using the same code that was previously used in the `mouseDown` method. The applet should display Figure 10.2.

10.5.3 Adding the selector

The final element that we are going to add is a `Choice` that will allow the user to select the two models of thread priority that were discussed in Section 10.4. We just need a simple two-option `Choice` which we'll use to set the priority of the threads prior to execution. The code for this is:

```
import java.awt.*;
import java.lang.Thread;
public class UIHelloWorld3 extends UIHelloWorld {
Choice c;
public void init() {
  super.init();
  // Set the layout of bottomPanel
  bottomPanel.setLayout(new BorderLayout());
  // Add the start button to p1
  bottomPanel.add("North",new Button(" Start! "));
  // Add the choice
  c = new Choice();
  // Add the two options to the choice
  c.addItem("Equal Priority");
  c.addItem("Unequal Priority");
  // Add the choice to the frame
  bottomPanel.add("South",c);
}
public boolean action(Event evt, Object arg) {
  String tmpstr;
  if (" Start! ".equals(arg)) {
    tmpstr = c.getSelectedItem();
    if (tmpstr.equals("Equal Priority")) {
```

```
        counter[0].setPriority(counter[1].getPriority());
      }
      /* Start the counting threads */
      for (int i = 0; i < 2; i++) {
        if (!counter[i].isAlive()) {
           counter[i].start();
        }
      }
      * Start the display thread */
      if (!dispthread.isAlive()) {
        dispthread.start();
      }
      return true;
    }
    return false;
    }

}
```

In this class we inherit from the original `UIHelloWorld`. In the `init()` method we invoke the method from the superclass and then add the buttons as we did in the previous example. We then create the `Choice` and add the two elements that we want the user to pick from. The first element that we add to the choice will be the default that is displayed unless an explicit call is made to select another.

As you might have expected, we have overriden the `action()` class. There are two ways that the user selection can be handled. The first involves taking the event generated when the user selects from the `Choice` and setting the threads appropriately. The second way which we have adopted here is simply to check the value of the selected item prior to starting the threads.

When adding interface elements to applets, make sure that the final interface is usable. One of the problems that plagues programming and seems particularly prevalent with applets is poor design. Your applet could be used by a huge number of people and it is worth paying serious consideration to the human factors involved in your system. If you are writing applets for commercial or large-scale deployments, you should engage in a serious human factors evaluation. Increasingly, the worth of your company will be judged by applets and Web pages, and the more usable and suitable your applets are the better the perception of your company will be.

CHAPTER ELEVEN

Building an application

AIMS

- To describe the differences between an application and an applet.

- To describe a simple application.

- To outline the advantages and disadvantages of using applications.

11.1 Introduction

The difference between applets and applications should be clear to you by this stage of the book. To make it even clearer, applications are standalone, requiring only the presence of the Java run-time interpreter, and are self-contained. Applets, by contrast, are dependent on a host, typically a WWW browser, to support execution and to handle the more direct interfaces with the underlying client system.

This chapter is about applications, which are the most well-known type of code, although paradoxically the first wave of Java code is likely to be almost entirely applets as developers experiment with the possibilities that the applet provides. However, applications written in Java should not be ignored and will solve some problems where applets are not appropriate.

Naturally, since Java is the language used in both applets and applications, both share a common set of characteristics which embody some of the strengths of the

Java system. However, there are some differences which are important and so we'll take the time to tell you when you should be using an applet and when an application would be better suited.

11.1.1 Introducing an application

We'll introduce applications using the minimal Hello World approach. As you will have seen before the Hello World code simply prints the string "Hello World" to the output. In the case of a Java application this is the standard output: the command line interface which was used to start the application off.

Here is the code for the Java version of Hello World:

```
public class HelloWorld {
      public static void main (String args[]) {
            System.out.println("Hello World");
      }
}
```

Applications are required to define a static method called main. The Java system guarantees to call this method with the arguments that were supplied as the command line passed as the sole parameter with it being up to the application to process the arguments and act accordingly. In our simple application, there are no arguments, and the only line of code in the main() method prints out a String to the output of the system.

The main method is the basic building block of a Java application, as it is with some other programming languages such as C. The main method is the core of an application, and it is from here that your code will allocate resources, load external entities and generally control the flow of the application. In Java, the main method is defined as static. This means that it is associated with the class rather than with an instance of the class.

Using the command line arguments

Our first example doesn't make use of the fact that the system will pass on the command line arguments that were given to the application when it was called. The command line arguments are whatever the user has typed after the name of the application; for example, if the user types:

```
java myApplication fast yellow loud
```

at the system prompt, then the Java run-time interpreter executes the Java class called myApplication.class (which will contain the class for your application) and the words 'fast', 'yellow' and 'loud' will be passed on to the main method in the application. These arguments are typically used to specify optional behaviour within the application. For example, the argument -fast might ask the application to use a faster algorithm to process images in preference to the slower but more accurate algorithm that the application would use by default. The use of the minus sign in arguments is not a requirement, but is common on some systems, especially UNIX. It doesn't really matter how you process the arguments that the user supplies to your application as long as the arguments make sense to the user and the user is given a clear and reasonable message when incompatible or unsupported arguments are given, ideally with a list of the arguments that are supported. Some systems, again notably UNIX, lean towards using single letters. However, the use of more friendly arguments, such as:

```
grep -nocase socket myApplication.java
```

may look more useful and will not require the user to consult the help system before use. The downside is that lengthy arguments tend to be tedious to repeat frequently, and an application which may require a large number of arguments becomes a real chore to use.

Our advice is to support a flexible combination of both one-letter and full-word arguments whenever possible. For example, the example given for myApplication could support both -fast and -f to indicate that the user wants to use the fast algorithm. By carefully choosing your arguments it is possible to create a usable system which is both friendly for novices and quick for experienced users.

This system fails when you have a large number of arguments; for instance, if we wanted to have arguments to specify a fast algorithm -fast and to make the application write out the final production file -final, how do we implement both arguments as single letters? Do we have -final implemented as the next free letter of the alphabet -g? The answer is an emphatic no. If your application requires more than a few arguments then you should seriously consider implementing an interface to allow the user to select options on-screen. The use of huge lists of command line arguments is an unwarranted abuse of your users' time and patience and should be avoided at all costs.

Given that you do require some arguments, how do you process them? Let's illustrate this by extending the HelloWorld example from earlier in the chapter. The code looks like this:

```
public class HelloWorld2 {

  public static void main (String args[]) {
    for (int i = 0; i < args.length; i++) {
      System.out.println("Arg " + i + ":" + args[i]);
    }
  }
}
```

If you run and compile this code and then execute it as:

```
java HelloWorld2 Java is cool!
```

you should get the following output:

```
Arg 0:Java
Arg 1:is
Arg 2:cool!
```

You can see that the new code takes each argument that has been passed to the application and prints it out on a new line, indicating which argument it is. The number of arguments passed to the method can be obtained by using the `length` method.

Handling real command line arguments

What if you want to do something with the arguments? Let's take the example given above for specifying that the type of algorithm used is to be faster than the default. The code to handle this is as follows:

```
public class HelloWorld3 {

   public static void main (String args[]) {
      String algorithm = "slow";
      for (int i = 0; i < args.length; i++) {
         if (args[i].startsWith("-f")) {
            algorithm = "fast";
         }
      }
   System.out.println("Algorithm: " + algorithm);
   }
}
```

In this example, each argument is checked to see if it started with '–f'. This includes arguments such as '–fast' and '–f', but also would match the arguments '–fish' and '–friday'. Another approach would be to explicitly look for the supported arguments '–f' and '–fast'. If an argument matches, then the algorithm is changed from the default slow algorithm to our faster option.

Conflicting options

One last thing to watch out for when handling arguments is always to specify a default behaviour. Instead of requiring the user to specify one of '–fast' or '–slow' to select an algorithm, define a default behaviour and only require the user to override this when needed. If you don't do this, you will have to cope with the possibility of the user calling both arguments, one after the other, which will require a good deal more supporting code and effort on your behalf to ensure that the behaviour that the user expects is what is really happening inside your application.

11.2 Applications life cycle

You saw in Chapter 10 how the Java system creates a 'life cycle' for applets. At key points in the life of an applet, certain methods are guaranteed to be called by the system. These key points allow the developer to design an applet which will cooperate with other applets and the Java host system, as well as providing a general model for designing an applet. Applications are not required to cooperate with other applications in the same manner. This means that if you implement a method that would be called automatically in an applet, you must arrange to have this method called manually in your application. Some of the applet methods may not be directly related to the operation of your application but others are more useful, especially the Runnable interface.

The main() method has already been introduced as the core of an application, and it is from here that methods must be called (although, of course, methods can be called by other methods which were, in turn, called from main). If you wish to define a life cycle for your application, main is the method you should start from.

Why would you require this kind of execution model? After all, when your application is closed by the user the thread of execution is ended. Well, while it is true that most applications will not require the kind of rigorous model that the Java system demands of an applet, there is a need to ensure that any external resources are handled cleanly when the application exits. For example, if an application connects to a remote server to perform some kind of search, then it is far better, and preferable, to ensure that the server knows that the client has been closed by the user as soon as possible in order to avoid consuming valuable resources by performing a search for a client that is no longer able to take the results. Equally, if an application shares information with other applications, or provides some kind of service, then the code should take precautions to ensure that when the thread of execution is terminated the dependent resources are released cleanly. The advantage of the model imposed by applets is that developers are required to implement at least the basics of the life cycle in order to have code executed. Our advice is to follow a similar model when writing applications.

11.2.1 Using threads in an application

When using threads in an applet the Java system provides a certain amount of support for starting threads if the applet subclass implements the Runnable interface. For example, when your applet has been sent the call to the init() method, a call will be made to the methods that make up the Runnable interface, which will allow you to ensure that your threads are running and stopping when they are supposed to. The reason that a Java browser does this is to ensure that threads are killed or suspended when a page of HTML (including applets) is no longer on screen or is reloaded. None of this is required with an application – after all, once the user has called the application from the user interface or the command line interface the code will be executed until all the intended functions have been completed or the user terminates the execution.

Therefore, applications wishing to implement threads must make sure that they are executed from the main() method. The most effective way of handling threads in an application is to provide separate classes which extend the Thread class and which are created and managed from the main application class. A simple example is shown below:

```
class appThread {

public static void main (String args[]) {
    new myThread("One").start();
    new myThread("Two").start();
    }
}
```

```
class myThread extends Thread {

    public myThread(String str) {
    super(str);
    }

    public void run() {
        for (int i = 0; i < 10; i++) {
            System.out.println("Thread "
                                + getName() + " :" + i);
            try {
                sleep(100);
            } catch (InterruptedException e) {
            }
        }
    }
}
```

In this code, the top-level class appThread creates and starts two instances of the myThread class. myThread extends the Thread class and so we only have to call the super method to instantiate it and then implement run() in order to provide the code to be executed in the thread. By passing a string to myThread (and so to the Thread, by the use of super), we call a constructor which defines a name for the thread. Then, in the run() method we determine which thread we are by calling getName(). This is one approach; another approach would be to pass a String to myThread, which is then made available to other methods in the class. We prefer the method in the example because it maintains a level of consistency with the constructor for the subclass and the superclass. If you compile and execute this example, you will see each of the threads counting up from zero to nine, with the output being interleaved as the sleep() statements free up the logical execution stream for the other thread.

This example illustrates how to start threads. As we have already mentioned, you should make some effort to ensure that when threads die or an application exits, any resources such as network connections and files are closed cleanly. You can see from the example that threads can be started in the normal manner, and equally threads can be stopped by calling the stop() method. If this method has not been overridden, then the default behaviour is to stop the execution of the thread.

11.2.2 Dual-purpose code

One other reason for implementing methods which define a life cycle for an application is that it is possible to write code that can be executed both as an applet and as a standalone application. At the time of writing this book the most compelling reason for doing this is the lack of a stable browser to display applets. Other reasons might be to extend cross-platform support to platforms which may have a browser but not a run-time system, or which have a run-time system but no browser.

However, while the idea of writing code which can be run both as an application and as an applet may be appealing, there are some important differences between applets and applications which should be seriously considered. Before discussing these issues it is worth introducing a simple example which can run both as an applet and as an application:

```
import java.applet.Applet;
import java.awt.*;

public class dualCode extends Applet {

  public static void main (String args[]) {
     Frame f = new Frame("Dual Applet/Application");
     f.setLayout(new FlowLayout());
     dualCode dc = new dualCode();
     dc.init();
     f.add("Center",dc);
     f.resize(100,100);
     f.show();
  }

  public void init() {
          setLayout(new FlowLayout());
          add(new Button("Button"));
  }
}
```

When this code is run as an applet the first method that is called is init(). The init method simply defines the layout model for the applet and creates a button. However, when the code is executed as an application the first method that is called is main(), as we have described at the start of this chapter. In this example, main creates a new top-level Frame, called f. The main method sets the layout model and creates a new instance of the example class – this is done because main() is static. Then, the new instance of the example class, dc, is added to the Frame f. The Frame is then resized and displayed. So, once the Frame is displayed the code operates in the same manner regardless of whether it is being executed within the hosting environment of a browser or as a standalone application. However, while this looks like a perfect solution and makes you wonder why Java even bothers to differentiate between applets and applications, there are some severe constraints on using this approach.

The problems arise when differences in functionality between applets and applications make the use of the same Java code impossible. As an example, the security model imposed on applets by the browser means that opening network connections is very constrained, while an application can open and manage connections freely. Therefore, in order to write code which can function as both an applet and an application, it is necessary to write to the lowest common feature set. In the case of network connections this means imposing the constraints of the browser security model on applications as well as applets and in the process severely limiting the functionality of the resulting code.

The next section discusses some of the differences between applications and applets. Each can be regarded as an obstacle in writing dual-purpose code. However, if you find that the requirements of your project are served by the constrained feature set that allows the generation of dual-purpose code, then using this technique can be an elegant and simple solution to reaching a larger number of users on a wider range of platforms, as well as facilitating development of applet code in the absence of browsers.

One final word on using dual-purpose code: make sure that you test it both as an applet and as an application before shipping the final product to your users. It is easy to fall into the trap of assuming that calls which work for one type of model will work for the other, even though at the back of your mind you are retaining the fact that there are some features and library calls that are not dual-functional.

11.3 Differences between applets and applications

Although applets and applications are both written in Java and have access to the same library packages, there are some significant differences between the functionality available in each. In this section we will discuss some of the more important differences and the impact this has in making the decision to develop either an application or an applet. It is very easy to be seduced by the charm of developing an applet which can be downloaded and executed on the fly. However, there are some limitations to applets. These are primarily imposed by security models adopted by Java-compatible browsers which make applet development unsuitable for some requirements.

11.3.1 Loading images

Loading images into applications is extremely difficult. Applets rely on the `getImage()` method to pull in an image from a URL. Unfortunately, this method does not work with applications, even if the application class extends `Applet`. The reason for this is that the `getImage` method always makes a call to `getAppletContext()`, and `getAppletContext()` calls the stub of the applet, which is defined automatically when an applet is hosted by a browser, but is not set in an application. Consequently, calls to `getImage` within an application will generate an exception. There is a short-term solution to this problem, reported to the *comp.lang.java* group, which is to import:

```
import sun.awt.image.URLImageSource;
```

at the start of the code and then use the call:

```
img = Toolkit.getDefaultToolkit().
createImage(new URLImageSource(url));
```

to load in the images. While this is a workable solution, the use of the sun.* packages is not recommended, since not all implementations of Java are guaranteed to implement the Sun libraries, and so your code could well break on some Java systems. Java implementations are only required to supply the java.* hierarchy, which means that betting on the availability of a package that may not be included in the port that a client is using is a recipe for disaster in the long term. In general, it is very strongly recommended that developers use the java.* classes wherever possible, as adopting this approach will ensure that code makes the most of the Java cross-platform support.

11.3.2 Applet security limitations

Because the model of applet execution includes the dynamic loading and running of unknown code from anywhere on the network, there is the chance that malicious code will be written which will try to abuse the local client machine in some manner. Therefore, the designers of Java have implemented a security model for applet execution which limits what an applet can do with the local system. These limitations are important components in deciding between developing application code or applet code for a particular application. Although an applet can make calls to the libraries which have been constrained for security reasons the results from these calls will not be as expected. The following subsections discuss the limitations that the security model imposes on applets.

The local file system

For security reasons, applets have very limited access to the local file system. In fact most of the basic file operations which are available to an application (including checking if a file exists, and seeing what type of file it is) are not available to applets. In addition, the use of the `FileInputString` and `RandomAccessFile` libraries is constrained and applets cannot create new file handlers in the I/O packages. The reasons for this are sound – after all, the thought of an unknown applet having unlimited access to the local file system would compromise system security. The Java security model defines a series of Access Control Lists. If the file that your code requires is not on the list, then you cannot:

- check for the existence of the file
- read the file
- write the file
- check the file type
- check if the file is a directory
- get the timestamp from the file
- check the file size
- create a directory
- name the file.

Since your applet code cannot define the files in the access list the access you can have within applet code is almost non-existent. Therefore, if you need access to files on the local machine, you must write an application. At the time of writing, the definitions of the control lists are vague, especially as the browser that will almost certainly have the greatest distribution (Netscape) has yet to decide on an implementation model. However, regardless of the model that Netscape adopts, it is not possible to assume a given security model on a browser without making assumptions about which browser the user is running – and making this kind of assumption eats deeply into the cross-platform nature that makes Java a flexible language.

Network connections (sockets)

Applets are unable to open network connections to arbitrary hosts. In fact, an applet can only make connections to the host from which it was downloaded. This does pose some problems regarding scalability for large-scale systems, since one machine must be responsible for delivering applets using HTTP as well as maintaining services for all of the other aspects of applet operation. While this model prevents connections being made to 'hidden' hosts (that is, hosts that the user has no knowledge of), it does mean that one machine has to deliver a complete range of services to all clients instead of adopting an approach of separate machines running specialized services.

In addition, applets cannot create socket factories. Socket factories are the handlers which process incoming socket connections and process the raw data from the network layer. By removing the ability to create socket handlers the designers of the Java system have removed the possibility that malicious code can use this route to subvert network streams. Again, however, there is a direct separation between the functionality of the Java libraries and the functionality of the Java applet.

Library loading/linking

Applets are not allowed to access packages in the `sun.*` library. These functions contain classes which could potentially be used for subverting local functionality. Additionally, applets are not allowed to create new class loaders. The class loaders that are supplied as part of the Java system run a comprehensive series of checks before allowing a class to be referenced, and therefore allowing an applet to create new loaders would defeat the notion of that aspect of the security system.

Applets are not allowed to link libraries using the `System.loadlibrary()` call, which is not the case with applications. Also, applets cannot modify the AppletSecurityManager which implements these rules, for much the same reason.

The creation of classes in the `java.*` library is also not permitted. This prevents applets from creating packages which contain subversive code to be called by other (benign) applets loaded later by the user.

Local system processes

Applets cannot define native methods. These are methods which are written in another language and compiled to machine code. The lack of native methods means that malicious applets cannot define methods which the Java system cannot manage or analyse. Stopping forked processes prevents applets starting processes which are outside the control of the Java system (for example, starting a process which deletes files in the user space).

In addition, applets cannot manipulate threads which are not part of the applet thread group. While this does not reflect directly on the functionality of an application (which doesn't require the same notion of thread control), it is an important limitation of the scope of thread control within the browser space.

Summary of applet security constraints

There has been considerable criticism of Sun for limiting the functionality of applets to this extent. With the current security models available, there are some projects that will be unable to run within Java without access to some of these features. However, at the time of writing, the Java developers are proposing a system whereby trusted libraries can be identified and allowed additional access to some or all of the Java system. Until this time, however, some of these constraints will severely impact the scope of Java applets.

11.3.3 Creating servers

Applications can be written to support server functionality using the network libraries. Applets, however, do not support this, and the use of the `accept()` and `listen()` calls is not permitted. This has been done to stop applets bypassing the constraint of only opening connections to a single remote host (where the applet was loaded from) by becoming servers and accepting connections from 'hidden' machines.

11.3.4 Summary of differences

Most of the differences between applets and applications exist because of the important requirement to provide a reasonably secure mechanism for executing unknown applet code, while minimizing risk to the local machine. Other differences, such as loading images into applications, can be regarded as design deficiencies in the Java system. These may well be addressed in later releases of the Java environment or by the availability of third-party libraries.

In essence, it is important to consider the needs of a specific project before deciding to develop either an applet or an application. The novelty value of developing applets is not sufficient motivation when the demands of the system require access to facilities that the security model denies to applets; equally, working around the limitations that an application inherits from the bias of the Java packages towards applet development may render some application initiatives useless. As has been mentioned previously, the first wave of Java development is expected to be centred on applets, although this may change with time.

11.4 Application limitations

One other topic worthy of note is the latency incurred when a Java application is started. Because the compiled Java byte-codes are interpreted and then executed in the Java virtual machine there is a period of time which elapses between the start of the execution and the Java code being executed. For most applications this is not important. For example, it doesn't matter if a simple game or a spreadsheet takes an additional ten seconds to start before being available to the user. However, there are systems which cannot tolerate the latency of the interpreter. As an example, consider a large-scale network system which has a series of synchronized servers. When a server crashes, the lag between the server being restarted and the server code rejoining the other servers in providing functionality can be very significant.

Another, smaller, issue with using applications is that if path names to external files and resources are hard-coded into the classes, then the different file structures on different platforms will cause the code to break unless it is specifically ported. For example, the file:

```
/home/adam/development/java/project/images/someimage.gif
```

on a UNIX host will not be the same as:

```
C:\users\adam\development\java\project\images\someimage.gif
```

on a Windows NT host. This also doesn't take into account the limitations that some operating systems impose on file names (for example, Windows 3.1). One approach to addressing this is to have the path to the resource files specified as an argument or contained in a separate configuration file, but neither approach is entirely without limitations. This does affect the cross-platform nature of Java in a small but significant way, since there will be few applications that will run without requiring access to some external data or resources. When developing an application, our advice is to make as few assumptions as possible about the underlying file system in order to preserve as much interoperability as possible.

11.5 Adding user interface elements to applications

It is easy to add elements from the AWT library to applets, mainly because the Applet class inherits from the AWT hierarchy. Applications do not automatically provide a mechanism for doing this, and so it is the responsibility of the developer to create a suitable holder for the user interface elements. There are many approaches to doing this and, in fact, there are many approaches to writing applications in general. Our approach, which we have developed with both Java and other languages, is to keep the amount of code in the main() method to a minimum and create a separate class which contains the bulk of the code for the 'body' of the application.

Our preferred approach is to keep the main() method as simple as possible and use it only to maintain top-level control within the application as a whole, although often these high-level tasks which affect the whole of the application can also be pushed down into other classes.

As an example of adding AWT elements to applications, consider the following:

```
import java.awt.*;

public class uiApp {

    public static void main (String args[]) {
```

```
            frameClass fc = new frameClass("UI Demo");
    }
}
```

In this class, the only method is `main()`. The only line of code in the method creates a new instance of the `frameClass` class. The class that is called looks like this:

```
class frameClass extends Frame {

  public frameClass(String str) {
     super(str);
     addElems();
     resize(100,200);
     show();
  }

  public void addElems() {
               setLayout(new FlowLayout());
               add (new Button("Button 1"));
               add (new Button("Button 2"));
               add (new Button("Button 3"));
               add (new Button("Button 4"));
     }
}
```

At this stage in the book, you should understand most, if not all, of the code in this class. The constructor which has been called from the first class calls `super` with the string as an argument. Since this class inherits from `java.awt.Frame` this has the effect of creating a top-level frame with a title set to the string passed into the method from `main()` in the other class. At this point another method `addElems()` is called which defines the layout model for the frame and then inserts four buttons which are named sequentially. In fact, although these buttons are created by four separate lines of code, there is no reason why a simple loop could not be used. Once the buttons have been added, the constructor resizes the main window and then maps it to the display. At this point, of course, the buttons have no actions attached to them, since we have not overridden any of the methods which handle incoming user events. Since the same AWT elements are being used for applets as well as applications, the technique remains the same for processing external input. You will find more specific details in the chapter on applets (Chapter 10).

11.6 Summary

This chapter highlights the differences between applications and applets. We decided to approach applications in this manner for two reasons: firstly, because a large number of similarities exist between writing an applet and writing an application – a chapter covering a ground-up tutorial for application writing would duplicate a large amount of the material covered in the previous chapter. Secondly, since most Java developers will start writing applets and only switch to applications when confronted by one of the limitations discussed in this chapter, we felt it made some sense to concentrate on applets initially, and then detail what other information is needed to write an application. Having read the initial chapters – especially the applet chapter (Chapter 10) – the information in this chapter should be sufficient to allow you to write an application with little difficulty. The most important part of this chapter is the section that describes what an application can do that an applet cannot and, equally, what an applet can do that an application cannot.

This chapter should make clear that there are many similarities between applets and applications, and that one of the differences is the lack of external calls which are provided for applets by a browser. We have also introduced the notion of code that will execute as both an applet and an application and made clear the advantages and disadvantages that this technique involves. Finally, we described the additional information required to use AWT elements and threads in an application. Although the same libraries are used in both applets and applications, applications require some 'glue' code which compensates for the lack of external messages and inheritance which is implicit with an applet.

At the end of this chapter you should be aware that applications written in Java embody much of the flexibility of an applet, but do not incur the same security limitations that are required for applets. However, this developmental freedom comes at the price of losing the ability for a Java-compatible browser to load Java code dynamically and execute it. By writing applications you must arrange to have the user download the compiled application beforehand; users would typically expect to have access to the source code if the code is not commercial or is unsupported. However, applications written in Java will be developed and, while possibly not as attractive to developers as writing applets, application development can produce powerful and flexible code using the Java package libraries allied with the cross-platform support that Java provides as a function of using byte-codes.

CHAPTER TWELVE

Java internals

AIMS

- To outline the way that Java code is compiled.

- To outline the implications of the Java virtual machine.

- To outline the security aspects of Java.

- To describe the benefits of applets and applications.

12.1 Introduction

This chapter outlines some of the internal workings of the Java system. So far we have described the Java language and you will almost certainly have used the Java compiler, loaded applications using the Java interpreter and viewed applets using a Java-enabled browser. This part of the book will examine how the Java system works internally.

12.2 The compilation process

Unlike normal platform-dependent compilers `javac` doesn't compile your code into machine code. The problem with machine code is that it is generally specific to one machine – for example, a binary file compiled on a Sun SparcStation won't be able to run on a Macintosh. In some languages, even though the binary files are incompatible across platforms, the source code is sufficiently generic to be recompiled on different target platforms; unfortunately, most language libraries are not the same on different platforms. This means that the developers have to write branches into code to cope with the range of target platforms. As the code becomes more complex, the risk of introducing bugs into one version of the code greatly increases.

12.2.1 Byte-codes

When you compile Java code using javac your code is not compiled into machine code. Instead it is compiled into 'byte-codes'. These are a translation of the source code into an intermediate format which can be transported to any platform running the Java interpreter. Unlike machine code the byte-codes are platform independent and can be run on any platform using either a standalone Java interpreter (for Java applications) or an interpreter embedded into a browser (for Java applets).

When you execute Java code it is via an interpreter. Unlike fully compiled machine code, Java byte-codes are not ready to run immediately; they require interpreting. Unfortunately, there is a performance cost in doing this since interpreting code involves a degree of latency when the interpreter first loads the class files and a general speed loss as the code is executed. One possibility is to send over the source files and skip the compilation stage, but although this is the method used by languages such as TCL/TK the transmission of source code over the network does not meet the design goals of Java. Java aims to provide a secure mechanism for handling remote executables with a large amount of the functionality of the security features relying on the byte-codes. In addition, companies who invest large amounts of resources into developing Java applications are not keen to send the raw source which represents their capital investment into a world where it can be copied.

12.2.2 Just-in-time compilers

One drawback with using interpreters is the general performance cost. While the majority of interactive applications spend most of their time waiting for input from the user, some applications require high-performance access to computing facilities. To this end, Sun are committed to supply 'just-in-time' compilers. These will compile the intermediate byte-codes into machine code. You might think that this would be something that Sun would avoid doing, given their commitment to platform independence. This is true: part of the strength of Java is its platform independence. By compiling the byte-codes into platform-dependent binaries, the benefits of cross-platform/platform-neutral computing are sacrificed in favour of performance. This tends to illustrate the problems that face languages like Java. Specific requirements can be met but at a cost to some of the benefits of the general system; in this case that of performance verses platform independence. However, the just-in-time compilers should also be able to load in streams of byte-codes from the network and then compile them for extra performance at the client machine. This means that there is a wait while the client machine compiles the byte-codes but after this the software runs at full speed. This preserves some of the benefits of the byte-code system at the same time as supporting faster applications.

12.3 The Java virtual machine

Another reason that Java implements byte-codes is that the Java system relies on a virtual machine (VM). The idea of a VM is that a virtual computer is specified and the programming language is written to access the logical functions and devices of the virtual machine. Then, each platform which implements the VM specification is responsible for translating the functions and devices of the VM into native support. So, for example, a Java VM for the Sun Solaris is responsible for mapping the graphics primitives from the Graphics class to the local system libraries.

12.3.1 The basics of a virtual machine

The idea of a VM is one which has intermittently appeared in computing, perhaps the most successful example being the UCSD Pascal system. The benefits of using a VM is that it enables the Java system to be be ported to a large number of platforms by simply outlining the functions of the byte-codes and leaving the implementation details to the software engineers. Because the Java machine implements a set of logical or virtual services and devices, there is no need for the Java language to supply libraries for specific types of device (for example, network cards) or to cater for the internal dependencies of specific platforms (for example, byte ordering). The specification for the Java VM lays out the abstract specification and it is then the job of each implementer to translate this correctly.

The use of a VM provides a common development environment which is consistent across software and hardware systems, allowing both the developer and the user to deal with a single, common system and avoiding the complexities of moving between disparate platforms.

Java includes a full VM specification which is precise enough to outline what functions Java implementations should support, but also avoids specifying exactly how these functions should be implemented. By leaving the details to the developers of the Java ports there is a greater scope for Java systems to take full advantage of client platforms *without* the restrictive influence of an overly detailed specification. It also enables the developer to implement Java functions independently of Sun and allows the differentiation of commercial Java ports; this is sure to be good for the life of Java in the long run.

Is it a good idea to allow developers loose with something so important? There are good and bad sides to this. The bad side is that there is no guarantee that all of the features will be implemented correctly – at least until some standard test suites are produced which facilitate exhaustive analysis. But it is good that the specification is sufficiently open to encourage innovation and competition, two things which will benefit the Java community in the medium to long term. The presence of such a thoughtful and open specification should also serve to allay fears that Sun wish to exclusively control the deployment and future of Java since, as the number of independent ports of the Java system increases, the amount of control that Sun and SunLabs can have on the language diminishes.

12.3.2 The downside of a virtual machine

There are costs associated with using a virtual machine. Firstly, if the VM is being designed to run across several platforms there is a tendency for the specification to gravitate towards the lowest common denominator. For example, if the VM were initially intended to run on high-end 3-D workstations as well as low-end PCs, the specification will realistically have to dispense with the additional functionality offered by the workstations in favour of specifying a set of features which the PCs can implement as well – after all, there is no value in a VM which is too restrictive in terms of requirements, because no one will implement a port. Secondly, there is little scope for change or adapting new features into the VM.

As an example, the Java VM specification does not include any built-in support for 3-D graphics. This effectively means that until the Java language is extended to support 3-D graphics in the core language set, Java cannot be effectively used for complex 3-D graphics applications. Also, because the Java language and VM specifications will be implemented on a wide range of platforms, unless all platforms can support 3-D either the support will not be added or some platforms will no longer be supported by Java – both of which would be far from ideal.

Native methods

Java tries to solve this problem by supporting native methods. Native methods are Java instance methods or class methods which are written in a language other than Java, for example C or C++. The native method is declared in the Java code and then developed in another language. Dynamically loaded libraries are used to load the code into the Java environment space; the header files are generated for the target language from the Java code in order to facilitate the passing of arguments.

The advantage of using native methods is that it addresses the inherently static nature of the Java VM by allowing developers to write external code which can take advantage of new system features which were not incorporated in the Java language. Native methods can also be used to access system libraries which may not be available to the Java system, perhaps accessing some system specific features that are not supported on other platforms. Native methods can also be used to increase performance in the absence of a full compiler, especially for computationally intensive code which spends large periods of time in complex loops. The performance benefit comes from the fact that the native methods have been fully compiled into machine code and will consequently run at full speed.

As with everything, though, the use of native methods entails a cost. In the case of Java, native methods are not cross-platform because they are fully compiled binaries or machine code which have been built for a specific type of hardware running a specific version of the operating system.

If a development effort relies heavily on native methods for support, it is worth considering selecting another language for the project. Java has many strengths, but it is our opinion that native methods should be considered a very short-term fix to address extendibility issues, and should not generally be used if a more flexible alternative is available. Native methods erode so much of what is good about Java and require the developer to have prior knowledge of the hardware which is available at the client end. The use of native code also reincarnates the problems associated with machine code which we touched on at the start of the chapter.

While native methods are in principle a good thing they should be used sparingly and avoided in order to preserve the aspects of Java which make for flexible platform-independent computing.

12.3.3 Using other programming languages to create byte-codes

There is an active discussion at the moment about the possibility of using programming languages other than Java to generate compiled byte-codes which will run in the Java run-time interpreter. Developers who have extensive experience in languages such as Smalltalk and C++ want to take advantage of the large potential user base for Java without having to learn a new language. The logic of the argument is that since the Java compiler takes Java source code and translates it into platform-neutral byte-codes, it should be possible to write other compilers which take source code written in other languages and generate the same byte-codes. These could then be passed to the Java run-time system embedded in Web browsers.

In principle, this is technically possible although challenging for the compiler designer. The Java run-time system expects byte-codes that are related to the Java language. This would mean mapping, say, all of the C++ libraries to equivalent Java packages and ensuring that all of the C++ types are mapped to Java types. While it is possible to do this, it would result in a less functional version of C++ for use with the Java run-time system since, effectively, Java provides a subset of C++ in many respects. Facilities such as multiple inheritance which are supported in C++, but not in Java, would have to resolved, as would access from C++ code to Java libraries installed in the Java distribution on the client machine.

However, if there is sufficient demand for this type of compiler, and therefore a sufficiently profitable market niche, then it is certain that some development houses will embark on creating such tools. At the moment, we do not know of such efforts but, given that it is technically achievable, we fully expect such products to emerge as the user base for the Java run-time system increases.

12.4 Memory management

In languages such as C and C++, developers are directly responsible for managing memory – allocating, keeping track of, and freeing blocks of storage. Poor management of memory leads to memory leaks where memory is consumed by code which allocates storage space but never releases it after it has been used, gradually consuming more and more memory. This leads to application crashes.

One of the strong features of Java is that calls such as *malloc* and *free* which grab and free space in other languages are not required. Once a Java object has been defined the Java system takes responsibility for tracking its status and ensuring that there is sufficient storage space available. Once the object goes out of scope and is no longer required the Java system ensures that the storage space it was using is freed up. This automatic process is known as **garbage collection**; it removes the responsibility from the developer.

In Java, garbage collection is handled by a low priority thread. Other systems which implement automatic garbage collection do it by executing the collection activity at odd moments, potentially impairing the responsiveness of interactive applications; this is especially true of non-threaded systems where the application will block user activity while garbage collection is handled. Because the thread runs at a priority which is lower than the developer can set, garbage collection never interferes with application threads and only runs when there are no outstanding thread activities. This ensures that there is a reasonable chance that at any moment there will be sufficient free memory for the application to allocate storage. We use the term *reasonable chance* because the garbage collection thread will only run when the application has no outstanding threads or tasks. This means that a thread which makes a large number of allocations (for example, using a large vector) and does not yield control of the CPU to other threads can potentially exhaust the storage facilities. The best way to address this potential problem is to design your code carefully to avoid monolithic threads and to pass up the CPU whenever possible.

It is worth pointing out that garbage collection is only initiated by the Java system when the host has exhausted its memory resources. This has the effect that on workstations with large amounts of memory garbage collection may not be performed throughout the life of a Java application or applet.

In addition Java enables the developer to write methods known as destroyer methods which will be executed prior to an instance of a variable going out of scope and therefore being collected as garbage. This allows the developer to keep track of the number of instances of a particular class or to ensure that external resources are closed down in a clean manner.

Java also supports the `Vector` class which we detailed in Chapter 6. This is a self-sizing holder of generic objects. This enables the developer to use storage without needing to know in advance how many objects will require storage. This is more flexible than specifying the size of an array in advance with the new facility. The only consideration that the developer must make is that the Java application or applet will still be constrained by the amount of physical memory that the client system possesses. For large workstations and servers with large amounts of memory this may not be an issue, but since Java will also be supported on platforms such as PCs which typically have very small amounts of memory it is something which should be integral to the design of any Java code.

12.5 Applets vs applications

Having seen how to write applets and applications, which one should you choose for your project? Should you adopt the applet paradigm and load your classes over the network or choose the application model and make your code standalone?

12.5.1 What an applet is good for

If you need to have as wide a range of platform support as possible, you should write applets. The reason for this is that browsers which implement Java are far more numerous than standalone Java interpreters. Since Netscape 2.0 supports Java, it follows that before long the majority of Web users will possess a browser which supports Java, thus establishing a potentially huge audience for your code. In addition, Java-compatible browsers can dynamically download Java class files from Web servers, allowing you to make changes to your code without having to redistribute disks or CDs to your clients. If you need to load resources from the network, you should write applets; although it is possible to write application code to support the same set of functions as a browser, it is not worth reinventing the wheel. If you want to embed your Java code into HTML pages, you need to write applets.

12.5.2 What an application is good for

Although applets may look a good proposition there are still problems that are best solved by writing an application. If your code needs to make unusual access to local client resources or to a range of remote servers, the security model implemented in Java-enabled browsers will be too restrictive for your needs.

If you don't want your code to be downloaded from the network, an application may be more suitable. The support Java provides for adding user interfaces to applications as well as applets means that you can build fully functioning applications without working against the restrictions imposed by browsers.

If you need to develop native methods, applications are the best route. If you need to compile your Java code into machine code for performance reasons, applications run somewhat faster than applets hosted in large browsers.

The final choice between an applet and application will be based on a range of factors, but it is worth carefully considering which model to follow before committing your development efforts. Although applets may appear to be simpler and more attractive, the role of the application is significant and should not be underestimated.

12.6 Java security

One of the most promising aspects of the Java system is the ability of Java-compatible browsers to import code from remote servers and execute it. Clearly, a key design goal of the Java language and the Java-compatible browser is to ensure that this can be done in a secure manner.

The potential for bad code deliberately to disrupt local machines, to copy local files to remote hosts or to copy remote files to local hosts is such that the design of the Java security system has been considered at great depth.

The most documented security implementation is that of the Sun HotJava browser, which implements a layered approach to security, instead of favouring a monolithic system. The layers are: the Java language and compiler, byte-code verification, class loader verification, and local system protection. In this section we will look briefly at each layer and discuss the general security of the Java browser.

12.6.1 The Java language and compiler

Some of the language design features of Java add additional security to the system as a whole. For example, pointers can be used in C++ to manipulate client systems and casts from one type to another are not checked in C or C++. Because Java does not implement pointer arithmetic (it implements true arrays) it is not possible to use them at all, let alone illegally. Equally, the use of the cast operator is checked to see if the casting of the first type to the second is legal. If it is not, the code cannot be compiled.

The compiler goes to some lengths to ensure that the byte-codes which are produced are safe and legal, and will refuse to compile code which does not meet the strict Java language rules.

12.6.2 Byte-code verification

While the Sun compilers are trustworthy, what is to stop someone writing a 'bad' compiler which modifies the output of byte-codes for some hidden purpose? This is especially likely considering that Sun are actively encouraging the development of development environments and Java systems.

To stop this happening the browser applies a range of tests to the code fragments before they are executed. The range of tests includes checking for faked pointers, ensuring that the code does not try to access the local system illegally, and checking that objects are correctly used, that all objects are called legally, and that the general state of the Java system remains stable.

The checking of code fragments is one of Java's strongest security features. The overall security of the system benefits from the layered approach to security since defective code must be sufficiently complex to pass all levels of testing before it is executed.

The code fragments are verified before they are passed to the class loader by the verifier. This process ensures that the code doesn't cause overruns or underruns and that no illegal assignments or casts are performed.

12.6.3 The class loader

Once the code fragment has been passed by the verifier, it is passed to the class loader. The class loader ensures that classes do not violate the rules by spoofing the system into using classes which are not part of the core Java system and ensures that each class is in a unique namespace which is not violated by other downloaded classes. This checking is performed at run-time and ensures that the state of the Java system is not affected.

12.6.4 Local system protection

The final layer of explicit security is the set of strict access controls that are placed on Java applets. The Java browser examines calls from classes to the local system and checks to see if they are to the small section of the system which the Java system needs to access. If an applet makes a call to a file which does not exist or to a file which is outside the area of the Java system, the user is presented with the information and the choice of either permitting or denying the request.

This policy aims to ensure that Java applets cannot write to or read from files which are not directly part of the Java system, including personal documents and system-wide files. Some browsers will implement a system of Access Control Lists which define the areas of the file system that the Java code can read and write, and these can be overridden by the user specifying additional areas in environment variables. The key idea to remember is that the Java applet cannot change the lists and therefore developers should not assume that the user has set up the access lists correctly prior to code execution.

12.6.5 The cost of security

The cost of this kind of security is a restriction of the type of functionality which can be included in applets. The Sun HotJava browser includes support for varying the level of security applied to downloaded classes, but commercial browsers are not required to follow the same model and, consequently, commercial and political pressures will ensure that a more restrictive security policy is implemented for the majority of browsers.

The scope and depth of the Java security system aims to protect the user from malicious damage while allowing the execution of code fragments from a range of unknown sources. At the same time the tight security could be seen as limiting to the developer. In the long term it is better that the Java system be oriented towards security instead of flexibility since the importance of security on the large networks is increasing and the publicity surrounding the potential for loss and damage is becoming greater.

Consequently, even if the strict security system does restrict the developers to certain models of access the interests of the Java community as a whole are best served by strong fences and thorough tests.

12.7 The future of Java

As with any new system, there has been a large amount of hype surrounding Java. Some commentators have stated that it will revolutionize the Internet and will, in a short time, be the sole language used in the development of network-based applications. Others have postulated that it will be the death of the Internet, requiring users to consume ever increasing amounts of valuable network bandwidth to download large applets along with the associated images, motion video and sounds. Other commentators have speculated that Java will be the only programming language in use within two or three years. In our opinion none of these will turn out to be true. It is our expectation that Java will be a very important tool in the future for both general-purpose programming and the Internet; however, it is important to remember that Java is a programming language, with the associated demands that any programming language places on the developer – namely an appreciation of programming logic and the time and resources to embark on development efforts.

Most of the users on the Internet are not programmers. They do not have the capabilities or the inclination to develop the skills that are required to produce program code in an object-oriented language. They do not have access to the powerful machines that are required to compile and debug anything but the simplest Java code. In our opinion this is a good thing. The Internet should be focused on content and not be populated by technically oriented programmers alone.

Where does this leave Java? We maintain that Java will change the Internet and any subsequent networks which supersede the Internet. But we have also seen that other languages which embody some of the features of Java have been released amidst a rage of hype, have not been adopted and have gradually faded away. What is there about Java that convinces us both that Java is here to stay?

12.7.1 Java's secret weapons

Java does have some special attributes which we believe will help it survive in the real world – away from the research labs and universities.

Cross-platform support through Netscape Navigator

There have been other object-oriented languages which were targeted specifically at cross-platform design. However, Sun has achieved a major success by having Netscape incorporate Java into the very popular Netscape Navigator browser. Netscape browsers dominate the area, and Java has an instant target audience. Most languages similar to Java have failed because developers will not write code in a language which does not have a reasonably sized user base; this is especially true of commercial software houses.

By definition, Java will be available on every platform that Netscape support which, at the time of writing, includes every major variant of UNIX as well most of the popular desktop platforms. As Netscape capture new markets and new platforms, Java will automatically move there as well.

Sun are betting a lot on Java

Another key element in the future of Java is that Sun are betting significant resources on its success. For example, in November 1995 Sun announced a Java programming competition with prizes totalling $1,000,000 in Sun equipment.

Sun are also known to be an open-systems company. They have publicly stated that they will not charge for the use of the language and are actively seeking a standards body to assume responsibility for the continued development of the language definition. The company hope to make money not from the basic language specification but from selling development tools and development platforms, adding tools such as Java compilers and debuggers to the range of SunPro products.

So, while previous unsuccessful languages have been developed in academic research labs, Java has the credibility to succeed because Sun is a large commercial organization with huge resources. There have been concerns expressed regarding the implications of Sun claiming rights on Java code at a later date but this is very unlikely considering both the licence agreement which is shipped with Java and Sun's previous record in the field.

Commercial compilers and packages

Already this confidence from Sun is starting to pay off. At the time of writing this book several implementations of Java development environments have been announced from commercial vendors. Third-party library packages providing additional functionality are also emerging although currently these are from organizations that do not charge for the use of the code.

The emergence of commercial libraries is almost certain, but it is currently unclear how software houses may profit from Java packages. Conventional language libraries are compiled into application binaries by developers. The library vendors charge the developers either on a one-off basis or on a royalty system linked to the number of applications that are distributed. This model does not work as well with Java since classes can be loaded dynamically by browsers. There is a difficulty of vendors keeping track of those who have used the packages.

One idea that has arisen is that packages could be distributed as native methods compiled into platform-specific binaries which are sold to the end user and must be installed before Java code can make calls to the routines. There are several problems with this, not least of which is that it limits the use of applets using these classes to platforms which the developers support. Some packages which make use of platform-specific functionality will be forced to adopt this model, but it is unclear how this will work with general-purpose code.

These issues will be resolved in some manner and in the early stages of the Java deployment the models used by developers are likely to be varied, both in technique and success, especially as the functionality inherent in Java requires a new model of software distribution. Rumours suggest that Sun are actively considering this issue with a view to defining a number of distribution models which will meet the needs of the majority of commercial developers. It is a significant issue, however, since the model that companies currently use to raise revenues for development projects is, at best, ill-suited to the Internet and is completely at odds with the philosophy of Java. We are quite confident that companies will be unable to resist the lure of Java and the huge potential markets that it represents and will commit to development projects even before there is some unified distribution technique available.

Strategic alliances

Java is an undeniably powerful and flexible system whose release has been timed well. To this end, other companies have signed strategic alliances with Sun to embed some or all of the core Java features into other products.

In the long term we can expect to see Java in systems ranging from consumer-electronics through to telephone switches. In the short to mid-term other software products will embed Java into existing systems. The most significant of these may be the inclusion of Java into MacroMedia's authoring tools. MacroMedia dominate the multimedia authoring arena with products such as *Director* and *Authorware* and the company has recently committed to including Java-centric functionality in a range of products. This will allow developers to take advantage of professionally authored content as well as content authors to take advantage of the Java system.

Remember that while Java is currently a developer's tool, firmly centred in the realm of programmers and programming, the Internet will become increasingly focused on content and the quality of content. Much of the material that would be popular for large-scale online distribution through a medium such as the Internet is too rich for the relatively simplistic support that Java embodies, and Sun are well aware of this fact. By taking the underlying power and flexibility of Java, and incorporating the powerful tools which MacroMedia have developed for content authors, Sun are hoping to extend the Java language to create an environment which can deliver rich multimedia content while removing the current limitations imposed by the existing deployment systems. It should provide a compelling approach to content-houses, since they are no longer constrained to writing systems for specific platforms and operating systems.

Java as a scripting language

We have already mentioned that Java is a programmer's language and requires an appreciation of programming logic and development tools. Clearly, the bulk of Internet users are not sufficiently skilled to develop Java code.

However, a large proportion of Internet users do try to deliver some form of content using HTML, and to a more limited extent simple support using scripting languages such as Perl and TCL. Such users will also want to deliver executable content using Java, but are limited by the lack of developer skills.

To this end, Netscape and Sun are jointly developing a Java-like scripting language. One of the main attributes of a scripting language is that the code is not compiled. The raw text source code is passed to an interpreter and executed on a line-by-line basis. There is no compilation process to check for syntax errors and the user is able to see and modify the source code for use in other projects. Clearly, any scripting language designed for mass consumption must be a good deal simpler than full Java and it is for that reason that we use the term *Java-like*.

We expect the Java-like scripting environment to use a very different language, and we'd be very surprised if it were object-based. The similarity to Java will come from the way that a single code fragment can be downloaded and executed dynamically on any machine which implements the interpreter and, as with the Java run-time system, we expect to see the interpreter embedded primarily in Web browsers.

So, given that a novice user can now write cross-platform executable content, is there any point in using the full Java language? Yes, for a number of reasons. Firstly, a scripting language for mass Web use will have to be very simple, and this will result in a loss of functionality compared with the full Java system. We expect to see a radically reduced set of libraries and a much lower level of primitive support. We also anticipate that the scripting language will be focused into a number of specific support roles – such as basic graphics/animation and interactive forms support (remember that forms and CGI have been a prime instrument in the expansion of the Web). Secondly, the scripting language will be procedural instead of object-oriented. This will remove the benefits of large-scale reuse in that although scripts will be able to access some local libraries, the degree of reuse within a script will be minimal. Additionally, it is very difficult to use procedural scripts for large development projects so scripting will generally be used for small and simple solutions.

Scripting languages also suffer from an inherent performance loss as the run-time system must process each line of the code sequentially. Java also suffers to some extent from this problem because the Java run-time system must interpret the byte-codes for execution, but the scale of latency for scripts will be larger by orders of magnitude.

So is there a future for Java developers? We feel there is. For projects which have a commercial value, developers will not want to make intellectual property freely available. For projects which require access to the full range of Java packages and facilities, full language development will be required. For applications and applets which need to run quickly, Java provides a good compromise between flexibility and speed and, when byte-compilers are available, Java code can be expected to run as quickly as conventional programming languages. Java is well-suited to large development efforts and the use of objects ensures that wide reuse is available in a single project as well as in multiple projects. So we feel that Java will still be a valuable tool and there will be a demand for Java and Java developers. We know of one large telecommunications provider who has decided that, within two years, Java will be the only programming language they will be using, and they have embarked on an aggressive training programme to ensure that they maintain an advantage against the competition. This will not be an unusual case and we fully expect Java to make an increasing penetration into large companies within the next few years. The demand from these companies will cascade into smaller organizations and the demand for Java developers and Java development will increase. We already know of more than 20 universities around the world who have selected Java in preference to C++ to illustrate the use of object technology; this will serve to provide a body of developers who have some limited knowledge of the Java philosophy and technique.

12.7.2 Competition to Java

At the moment, Java is the only language ideally suited to Internet development which has the backing of a major corporation. Although some companies have decided on Java as a language of the future there are bound to be other languages which will emerge as direct competition to Java.

One development effort which has attracted a lot of attention is from Microsoft, who are intending to produce tools aimed at users wishing to develop content for the Microsoft Network (MSN). These tools will initially be targeted only for the MSN, but it is rumoured that Internet versions of the authoring platforms will be delivered later.

While this is not in direct competition to Java (after all, the MS efforts are content-based, whereas Java is just a general-purpose programming language) it is worthy of note, not least because of Microsoft's domination of the PC. Java is born from research laboratories paid for by a high-end workstation manufacturer, and there are some significant cultural differences between the UNIX and PC mentalities.

The essence of this section is to remind the reader that Java is not guaranteed success. Despite a range of alliances with other large corporations and backing from Sun, Java will face some stiff competition to gain acceptance as the language of choice.

12.8 The value of testing

For this final section of the book we will take the opportunity to expound the value of testing code before release, as well as discussing some of the features which we think make polished code.

One of the elements of Java which makes for an interesting and challenging environment is that anyone will be able to download software which will give the user an impression of your company; if there is a commercial incentive linked with the code, the quality of the development will have a direct effect on the profits of your organization. Therefore, it is critically important to be sure that the code will create the impression that was intended and that the user is left in the right frame of mind.

12.8.1 Interface design

One of the most important elements of software design is also the most frequently overlooked. The way that the user interacts with your software is of prime importance.

It is not sufficient simply to bolt together an interface without regard to how it will function or how the user will operate the software. Instead, the whole of the design of the interface (and potentially, therefore, elements of the internal code structure) should be carefully planned, involving a human factors analysis wherever possible.

We cannot overstate the value of a well-designed interface. It is perhaps the most important part of any software system – regardless of the language or the design model.

12.8.2 Cross-platform testing

One of the most important features of Java can also be one of the most important problems for releasing code. The cross-platform support inherent in Java means that one set of compiled code can run on a whole range of machines without any changes. While this is true in theory, the practice is that as Java is ported to an increasing range of platforms by an increasing range of organizations, there are bound to be some differences in the way that the run-time environment is implemented. This means that code which should operate in exactly the same way on all of the platforms may exhibit strange behaviour on certain types of machine.

The best way to address this is to test the code on a wide range of equipment before shipping to the user. Since Netscape will almost certainly be the dominant browser for at least the next 12 months, it might be sufficient to test on just the platforms which are directly supported by Netscape. The amount of testing that you will perform will be directly related to the importance of having your code run correctly universally. For some free code issued by an individual, the amount of testing may be limited to the machine used to develop the applet. For a large organization, looking to support 100 000 users simultaneously, the testing might be exhaustive and include every platform which can support Java and would be extended to testing different levels of hardware under different operating systems.

However, the importance of a test strategy and the allocation of development time to address any problems which might arise is very important. Badly tested code will break and the problems this causes will be linked to the value of the code and the reputation of the company.

12.8.3 Debugging code

One of the tasks that developers often seem to forget is to remove debugging aids from code. These aids may be print statements which display the value of a variable or progress reports which are issued as a method is called and executed. Whatever they are they should be removed before the code is shipped.

Our approach is to include a method which is called by any method which wishes to write a debugging message. When we ship code we simply disable the method. This is a slightly inefficient way of handling the problem (since there will still be calls to the disabled method), but it is an effective solution to ensure that all debugging output is disabled.

12.8.4 Irritating behaviour

Our final piece of advice is to ensure that the finished product doesn't do anything that will irritate the user such as playing long sounds that cannot be interrupted or embarking on complex animations which the user cannot stop. Other examples might include streams of modal dialogs or selfish programming which affects other systems sharing the same resources (this is more the case with applets).

The best way of determining the response your software will get from users is to test it out on those who are not involved with the development. Ideally, you should select testers who will have the same level of technical expertise as the target user group. It is too easy for developers to see software in similar terms and ignore the the fears, insecurity and lack of experience of users.

12.9 Summary

You have now come to the end of the book and, we hope, are keen to develop some large Java applications or applets.

The book has taken you from programming concepts, via control structures and object concepts to some of the most important components of the Java library. It has concluded by examining both applets and applications. We hope that by the time you have finished this book you will be able to write substantial applications and applets given you are able to access the Java class libraries and their associated documentation.

The main aim of this book has been to equip you with a knowledge of all the concepts of Java – something missing in current technical material. We have left out quite a bit of detail because of this aim. However, much of this detail can be currently found in the existing Sun documentation and will no doubt be found in the large amount of reference material that we know to be under development.